ON EARTH AS IT IS IN HEAVEN

SAM SOLEYN

All rights reserved. This book is protected by the copyright laws of the United States of America. This book may not be copied or reprinted for commercial gain or profit. The use of short quotations or occasional page copying for personal or group study is permitted and encouraged. Permission for other usages must be obtained from Sam Soleyn Apostolic Ministry. Unless otherwise identified, Scripture quotations are from the New American Standard Bible®, Copyright © 1960, 1962, 1963, 1968, 1971, 1972, 1973, 1975, 1977, 1995 by The Lockman Foundation Used by permission. All emphasis within Scripture is the author's own.

© **Sam Soleyn Apostolic Ministry, 2022**

SoleynAssistant@Soleyn.com

**Find books and more on
Sam Soleyn Apostolic Ministry App,
available in the Apple App Store and Google Play**

ISBN-13: ISBN: 979-8-9858156-0-3

Acknowledgments

Christ is a corporate Man. Just as the human body functions in its many parts under the direction of the head, so does the Body of Christ. Christ speaks and acts through the many members of His Body. This work entitled *On Earth As It Is in Heaven* reflects this principle by involving many people in different roles during its development. It is my privilege and pleasure to have worked with all of the ones who have contributed their grace to this project. Whereas it is impossible to name each person separately, certain ones have made extraordinary contributions and richly deserve my acknowledgement and recognition. Chief among them is my son Nicholas with whom I began to write this book more than five years ago. His attention to detail and his penchant for research and supporting the many controversial statements made in this work is why the content will stand even the most rigorous scrutiny. The manuscript would have languished unpublished but for the enthusiastic editorial work done by Marsha Vosburg. She took the original manuscript of more than 350 pages and pared it down to its present size. The difficult task of deciding what to include and what to leave out was skillfully navigated by Marsha who knew the material exceedingly well. Her work is indispensable to the book becoming a reality. Marsha enlisted the help of Christine Spring who contributed to the editing and publishing of the book. They worked tirelessly as a team to ensure the final result. Together, they evinced the truth that each part of the Body of Christ is necessary to the functioning of the whole. It is my sincere hope that this book will be a foundational benefit to the Body of Christ.

– Sam Soleyn

Table of Contents

Introduction	9
The Relationship Between Heaven and Earth	9
Part One	15
An Intentional Nexus Between Heaven and Earth	15
God and Man As Spirit	18
Entering the Kingdom of Heaven	19
That Which Is Born of the Spirit Is Spirit	23
Sons of God and Spirit	25
Defining Spirit	27
The Personhood of God	30
Father, Son and Spirit—One Person	31
Father and Son	34
The Personhood of the Spirit	37
Love Gives Form to Spirit	37
The Glory and Purpose of the Sons of God	39
The Word Becomes Flesh	42
Love and Power	44
Man As Spirit	46
A Limitation on Power	48
Unlimited Love	49
Putting the Father on Display: The Body of Christ	50
The Spirit of Christ	51
Summary: No One Comes to the Father Except by Christ	56

Part Two	**59**
The Personhood of God	59
Introduction to the Seven Spirits of God	59
The Seven Spirits	64
The Spirit of Lordship	65
Evidence of Righteous Rule	67
Mature Rule	69
The Widening Circle of Rule	71
Marriage	71
Children Obey Your Parents	75
Employer-Employee Relationship	75
Lordship in the Kingdom	77
Calling or Template of Rule	80
Lordship Over Nature	82
Conclusion Regarding the Spirit of Lordship	85
The Spirit of Wisdom	85
Contrast Between Wisdom and Reason	88
Wisdom Builds the House	91
The Renewing of the Mind	96
Sons of Zion vs. Sons of Greece	100
The Sons of Greece	100
The Sons of Zion	104
The Conflict Between the Sons of Zion and the Sons of Greece	105
The Spirit of Understanding	108
Seeing and Not Seeing and Hearing and Not Hearing	110
Out Resurrection	112
Understanding From the Throne of God	117
An Eternal Point of View	119
The Spirit of Counsel	122
The Counselor as Messenger of God	125
Prophecy As the Counsel of God	127
The Working of the Spirit of Counsel	130
The Spirit of Power	134
Jesus the Almighty One	137
The Boldness and Courage of the Early Church	140

When I Am Weak Then I Am Strong	144
The Grace That Labors	146
The Spirit of Knowledge	152
The Knowledge of God	153
Human Knowledge	156
A Contrast Between the Views of God and Man	158
Christ the Eternal Branch of Knowledge	162
The Fear of the Lord	168
The Fear of the Lord, the Foundation of Rule	172
The Fear of the Lord, and the Rule of Mature Sons	174
The Fear of the Lord, the Beginning of Wisdom	176
Part Three	**179**
God is Love	179
The Characteristics of Love	181
Love Is Patient	183
Love Is Kind	186
Love Does Not Envy, It Does Not Boast, It Is Not Proud	188
Love Does Not Dishonor Others	191
Love Is Not Self-Seeking	194
Love Is Not Easily Angered	195
Love Keeps No Record of Wrongs	198
Love Rejoices in the Truth	202
Love and Tolerance	203
Love Always Protects, Always Trusts, Always Hopes, Always Perseveres	209
Love Always Protects	210
Love Always Trusts	213
Loves Always Hopes	217
Love Always Perseveres	219
Love Never Fails	222
Part Four	**227**
The Economy of the Spirit	227
The Incarnation	228

Incarnation Through Reconciliation	230
Incarnation, Predestination, and Rest	231
The Economy of God's Presence	236
A Table in the Wilderness	239
The Brazen Serpent	246
Contrasting Economies	250
Truth and the Divine Economy	253
The Fullness of Grace	255
The Grace of Salvation	259
The Power of the Grace of Salvation	262
The Principle of the Resurrection	265
The Power of the Resurrection	267
The Grace of Reconciliation	270
The Grace of Conformation	273
The Grace of Maturation	274
Wisdom for the Mature	281
Suffering and Maturity	286
Carrying the Glory of God	290
The Grace of Exact Representation	293

Conclusion	**297**
The Image and Likeness of God	297
The End From the Beginning	297
The Extent of the Fall	298
The Entrapment of the Systems of the Kosmos	299
Suffering That Saves the Soul	299
Biblical Predestination: Conformation to the Firstborn	300
Entering God's Rest	301
Corporate Man in the Image and Likeness of God	303
Let There Be Light	305
The Church of the Firstborn	308
The Government Shall be on His Shoulders	312
Jurisdiction	314

Introduction

The Relationship Between Heaven and Earth

God is ageless. He is eternal. The Hebrew word 'owlam', meaning everlasting, eternal or perpetual, corresponds to the Greek term 'aion', referring to age upon age or endless ages. Scripture says that "God created the heavens and the earth," which reveals two important conclusions.[1] First, that God is eternal. He transcends creation, including the limitations of human perception of creation that give way to the concept of time. Second, everything in creation came out of God. Even His purpose for creation is contained in God's person.

When God created the heavens and the earth, He began a new epoch of time, recorded in the Scriptures beginning at Genesis 1. This creation was intended for specific purposes related to the beginning and end of this epoch.

God's creation expresses aspects of His being in many different ways. The heavens were designed to accommodate aspects of God that would remain invisible from the earth. The earth was designed to contain elements of creation that would be visible and tangible and to house humanity, God's heirs. The heavens could contain spiritual realities whereas the earth, though it can contain spiritual realities, was meant to accommodate physical manifestations of those spiritual realities. Everything on the earth has its reference to the more complete realm of heaven. It was meant to contain types and shadows of the more complete realities in heaven until the appointed times when those spiritual realities would be clothed upon by physical form and would exist in the earth in a form that is like how they existed in heaven. God chose to put in the realm of heaven the standard of His being which includes His Lordship and rule so that all authority would flow from His throne and wherever He ruled, both in heaven and earth. The same standards of authority and forms of administration would be evident, irrespective of which realm these standards existed in.

In the book *My Father! My Father!* we discussed the purpose of God creating people and elaborated on our relationship to God as Father. That perspective is necessary for the broader discussion of this book, but is still one that begins *in media res,* focusing on the unfolding drama of humanity's fall and return to God as His sons. Looking deeper, beyond our relationship to God into what it means to be sons of God, will lead us to inquire about God's very nature and character. This revelation will bring us close to the beginning of the story, who God is, His nature and character, and how His "personhood" defines us as sons and how we must then act and mature according to His nature. The goal is to conform our relationship to God, not just as sons to a Father, but as those created for a specific task that would test the true nature of God Himself.

The form God chose to issue the creation of both heaven and earth was by the decrees of His word—by utterance. God said and it was so. He chose to embody this power and the accompanying authority in a manifestation of Himself that corresponded directly to the manner of creation, and that manifestation of God was called Word. The Word made everything, and without whom was not anything made that was made. The Word also sustains all things that have been created in the heavens and in the earth.

In Scripture, water carries the symbolic representation of the Word of God imbued at the creation. There was water before creation.[2] God "separated the waters from the waters." "God made the expanse and separated the waters which were below the expanse from the waters which were above the expanse; and it was so."[3]

The water in heaven took on a different meaning.

> *For as the rain and the snow come down from heaven, And do not return there without watering the earth And making it bear and sprout, And furnishing seed to the sower and bread to the eater; So will My word be which goes forth from My mouth; It will not return to Me empty, Without accomplishing what I desire, And without succeeding in the matter for which I sent it.* Isaiah 55:10-11 NASB

Water in the heavens came to be Word and when it came out of heaven as Word, it was as rain to water the spirit of man and produce bread so that man might eat of the riches of heaven and be kept in remembrance of his heavenly status as a son of God.

The Word did, indeed, take physical form and come to earth:

> *In the beginning was the Word, and the Word was with God, and the Word was God. He was in the beginning with God. All things came into being through Him, and apart from Him nothing came into being that has come into being. In Him was life, and the life was the Light of men. …And the Word became flesh, and dwelt among us, and we saw His glory, glory as of the only begotten from the Father, full of grace and truth. … John testified saying, "…He who sent me to baptize in water said to me, 'He upon whom you see the Spirit descending and remaining upon Him, this is the One who baptizes in the Holy Spirit.'"* John 1:1-4, 14, 32-33 NASB

Jesus connects the Word to Himself as bread and analogizes to the manna that fed the bodies of the forefathers in the wilderness.[4] He presents Himself as the bread of the presence of God, which was designed to feed all mankind.[5] Jesus makes the Word from the mouth of God, personified by His own presence, like bread. This connection between the heavens and the earth is deliberate. When Jesus fed the multitudes He was not only performing a miracle by multiplying the loaves and fish, He was also revealing a mystery about the relationship between heaven and earth.[6] When He received the food and prayed, it left the natural realm and was accepted into the heavenly realm, taking on a spiritual significance that would alter its material form. The fragments related to something of value that He did not intend to be lost in the process. When the disciples collected up the fragments after feeding the mass of five thousand, there were twelve baskets full. The thing that would have been lost was the heavenly message symbolized in the simplicity of each man holding a basket full of partially eaten bread. The baskets symbolized the carriers of grace and would relate to the disciples. The partially eaten fragments in the baskets represented the Lord, whose words and whose Spirit would be carried by His disciples into all the world, even though Jesus Himself would return to heaven. Not only did the bread, when Jesus received it, become a symbol of the manna that their fathers ate, but the manna itself was a symbol of heavenly bread, bread produced from heaven without the toil of man. The continuation of the Word as bread and Himself as the Word plays a central role in Jesus' actions and teachings. And it holds important keys to help us understand the relationship between the heavens and the earth.

When God installed the Word as the authority of both heaven and earth, the throne became the symbol of that authority. In addition to the throne, other realities of God were installed in the heavens with their corresponding connections to the earth. Around the throne in heaven were four creatures and twenty-four elders. The four creatures represented man as a spirit being with four faces—that of a lion, an eagle, an ox and a man. The intent of God was to show that man, who would be clothed upon in the earth with flesh was, in his complete nature, a spirit capable of four distinct manifestations. One such manifestation would be the prophetic reference to the ability of man who is spirit and, like an eagle, lives in the realms of both heaven and earth and has access to the wisdom of the heavens. The face of a lion signifies that man was put in the earth to rule and have dominion over the entire creation. The face of the ox indicates that man is intractable. There is nothing in creation that can turn him from his eternal purpose. The face of a man implies the form in which all four characteristics of being would appear. The venue was both heaven and earth, for man is, at the core of his being, a spiritual creature who was created to bring the rule of heaven upon the earth as a son of God. He was created in the image and likeness of his creator. The twenty-four elders also surrounding the throne represent the number twelve times two. The number twelve is the number of government and twice twelve would indicate that the government would function in two realms—both heaven and earth. So, we are given the complete picture of the rule of heaven over the earth.

Additionally, before the throne seven lamps were perpetually blazing. They are the seven Spirits of God which are the characteristics of God's nature. These, too, would in time find their corresponding manifestation in the earth in the person of the Lord Jesus Christ. Because this human would be endowed with the characteristics of God, He would make judgments in the earth not by the seeing of the eye or the hearing of the ear, but in the way that things would be designed and would function in heaven.

Prophecy is the revealing, in the earth, of the times and manner in which heaven comes into the earth. As such, stories, parables, allegories, symbols, numbers, and dreams and visions are the language by which the invisible is disclosed and becomes visible, and the mysteries of heaven become observable in the earth.

While God Himself remained distinct from both heaven and earth, He created heaven to hold the revelation of Himself that was spiritual and earth to hold the shadow and type of this reality until such time as that reality moved from heaven into the earth. When that manifestation of the person of God was brought out of heaven into the earth, He left the glory of His accomplishments and the environments of His power and emptied Himself of all that He was in heaven and came into the earth and took on the form of a subordinate, although in nature He is equal with God. When it became necessary for this manifestation to clothe Himself with flesh and come into creation, He chose the designation 'Son' by which to be defined. The Son, of whom Hebrews 1:3 says, '...who being the radiance of His Father's glory and the exact representation of His Father's being', discloses the nature of God by putting on display the characteristics of God so that He is the image and likeness of His Father.

This established an intentional nexus between heaven and earth which served the purpose of God for the epoch He had just begun.

---

[1]Genesis 1:1 NASB. [2]Genesis 1:2 NASB. [3]Genesis 1:7 NASB. [4]John 6:48-51 NASB. [5]John 6:63-64; Matthew 4:4 NASB. [6]Mark 8:19-21; John 6:26 NASB.

PART One

An Intentional Nexus Between Heaven and Earth

Before God created the heavens and the earth, His thoughts remained hidden in Himself for long ages past, for age upon age, because God is beyond the reckoning of time. Heaven and earth were conceived by God with the specific intent of disclosing Himself. He knew that this would require the creation of both realms and the introduction of time. Earth would be governed by time and the heavens would be timeless. Timelessness is a requirement of that which accommodates spiritual things, for spiritual realities are, by themselves, transcendent of time and space. Whenever a matter that is eternal is brought into time, it is clothed upon by the limitations of space and time. However, when the same thing exists apart from the earth or the visible created world, it exists without those limits and is, therefore, better able to accommodate an understanding of God, who is Himself beyond the quantification of any limits. Heaven and earth were both necessary realms for the intention of God to disclose Himself because there was no place else where such intentions could be placed.

When God created heaven, it was with the idea of being boundless and unlimited in the disclosure of those aspects of His being that could exist and be expressed in a spiritual realm. However, neither the heavens nor the earth together can contain the reality of God, for He existed outside of both realms and created them as part of a plan

PART ONE

to put His desire to become known into action. All of what is contained in heaven are the aspects of God that He intends to disclose in the earth. The timelessness of the heavens allows God to repose the aspects of His being fully in those realms until it is time to disclose them in the natural realm. The creation of the visible world was consistent with giving form to such intentions and, therefore, the creation of the earth, in particular, was the last piece of the puzzle that had to be complete before the movement of things placed in the heavens could be manifested in the earth. Once God created the earth in its fullness, everything was then in place that would accommodate the manifestation of Himself that He intended to ultimately be visible in the earth, and nothing was left unfinished.

Before God created the earth, He covenanted with Himself to rescue man, whom He was about to create, from his departure both from God and from the purpose of His creation. God knew that the form of this rescue would be the reality of His manifestation in heaven upon the throne, moving into the earth and being clothed upon with flesh to replace the errant son with the standard that was the reality installed in heaven at the creation of the world. It was, therefore, unavoidable for Christ, the Word, the ruler of heaven who became incarnate, to have to come into the earth and restore the purposes of God for the revealing of Himself as Father and of His divine nature of love in the earth. That is why when Jesus asked whether the final price to be paid on the cross of Calvary could be avoided, there was not, nor could there be a substitute because heaven contained the standard to which the earth had to be corrected. There was no other standard. God had ordained it so by creating and installing the realities in heaven, to be brought out of heaven in the fullness of time, to replace the shadows and types of such things that would be placed in the earth incrementally to hold in the earth the connection to the heavens. God, therefore, covenanted with Himself to rescue man by coming in the form of man to restore the order of heaven and grant man access back to God.

PART ONE

When God said in the beginning, "Let Us create man in Our own image, after Our own likeness," He foresaw the entire process. He foresaw not just the creation of Adam, who would be a spirit clothed in flesh, but He foresaw the last Adam, coming also clothed in flesh, but carrying the endowment of grace from God to reconcile man to God. That reconciliation would be accomplished not through the physical man Jesus, but through the spiritual Christ, Christ being the Spirit endowed by God into the man Jesus. This was for the specific purpose of assembling the spirits of men again to God, so that the unity between God and man, indeed the unity between Father and son that was lost in the garden, might again become the reality in heaven and on earth. So, the man God intended to create in His image and likeness was a spiritual Man, the only one capable of bridging the gap created by the fall of Adam between God and man. This was always what was envisioned in the designation of the spirit Man as a corporate being.

God installed Christ first as ruler of heaven and subsequently as ruler of earth. That is why Jesus prayed that upon His return to heaven God would again glorify Him with the glory He had before He came to the earth, and it is also the reason why He must remain in heaven until all things in heaven and on earth have been brought under His rule. It is the destiny of everything in heaven and on earth to be brought under one headship, namely that of Christ. Before the creation of the world, then, God saw that man would be reconciled to God in Christ. In the fullness of time, God reconciled mankind to Himself in Christ. We are, therefore, members of His body, parts of a spiritual Man. The body is corporate, but the spiritual Man is one—one body, many members. We are meant to be one with Christ in the same manner in which He is one with the Father.

Biblical predestination is that God always intended that when man was rescued, he would be conformed to the standard of Christ, for Christ is the excellence of the Godhead available for assembling man to Himself and, therefore, to God. Assembled to Christ, who is the perfect incarnation of God in the earth as Son, we are individually sons of God because we are part of the corporate Son of God. That is why He could say, and it is an unalterable truth, that no man can come to the Father except through Christ for He is the way the Father is, He is the truth of who the Father is, and He has the life of the Father in Himself. Failing being assembled to the Son, there is no alternative pathway to God. We were foreordained to be conformed to the standard of Christ. This is the only form of predestination that is referenced in the Scriptures. All other discussions of predestination were attempts to conform biblical truths to Greek reasoning.

The intentional connection between heaven and earth was established at creation and the nexus is undeniable. Heaven is the greater realm and earth the lesser realm. The earth is described as the footstool because it is typical for rulers to govern the terrain upon which their feet tread. The manifestation of the rule of heaven was always destined to be over the earth so that the Kingdom would come on the earth as it is in heaven. The reference to the Kingdom is a reference to those particulars of rule that define the orderly nature of God installed in heaven to be incrementally released in the earth as part and parcel of the elevation of man in the earth to the status of a son of God and away from a definition of himself as formulated by his employment of reason over things he sees in creation.

God and Man As Spirit

Understanding God as spirit is necessary to understanding both man as the son of God and man as spirit, which is to describe two expressions of the same concept. God is "the Father of our spirits."[1] He created humankind as spirit beings to represent Him in the earth—made in His likeness and clothed in flesh. God came in this form as the Son to reposition mankind in this representative capacity by restoring the relationship of sonship.[2] The Son's death and the resurrection of His Spirit continued God's purpose for mankind, allowing people to mature as one corporate Son that can translate God's intangible divine nature to the venue of the earth. The result will be that the Kingdom of Heaven will exist on the earth as it exists in heaven, translated into creation through the corporate Son.

This understanding is central to the apostolic doctrine for this season.[3] The corporate Body of Christ should, by now, be far beyond laying the foundations for maturity with the daily application of the elementary teachings.[4] Now is a time of preparation in which the holy nation becomes a kingdom under the headship of Christ, in both form and function. As the corporate Son takes the next step toward the grace of exact representation, the Kingdom of Heaven will become visible in the earth.

---

[1] Hebrews 12:9 NASB. [2] John 1:12-14 NASB; Romans 8:14 NASB. [3] Acts 2:42 NASB.
[4] Hebrews 6:1-2 NASB.

Entering the Kingdom of Heaven

> *The Kingdom of God is not eating and drinking, but righteousness and peace and joy in the Holy Spirit.* Romans 14:17 NASB

People build earthly kingdoms to aid their innate preoccupation with survival and to protect the perceived rights to pursue their individual provision and protection. As an example, the founding fathers of the United States of America declared independence from Britain based on the idea that governments are created to protect certain inalienable rights of the governed (rooted in this instance in nature). The colonists asserted that Britain had undertaken to violate their rights systemically, which being so far contrary to the purpose for government in the first place, was grounds to overthrow and replace the existing government.[1] This philosophy of human governance is predicated on the sovereignty of the individual and is motivated by the imperatives of an orphan culture, one that does not retain any concept of a relationship to God as Father, and it should not be confused as being anything else.

The Kingdom of Heaven empowers a life that pursues a destiny as a son of God. It supports a way of life in the earth that reveals the nature of God.

> *Then the King will say to those on His right, "Come, you who are blessed of My Father, inherit the Kingdom prepared for you from the foundation of the world. For I was hungry, and you gave Me something to eat; I was thirsty and you gave Me something to drink; I was a stranger and you invited Me in; naked and you clothed Me; I was sick and you visited Me; I was in prison and you came to Me." Then the righteous will answer Him, "Lord, when did we see You hungry and feed You, or thirsty and give You something to drink? And when did we see You a stranger and invite You in or naked and clothe You? When did we see You sick or in prison and come to You?" The King will answer and say to them, "Truly I say to you, to the extent that you did it to one of these brothers of Mine, even the least of them, you did it to Me."* Matthew 25:34-40 NASB

The Kingdom of God, or Kingdom of Heaven, does not describe a fixed location. Specifically, the Kingdom of Heaven is not synonymous with the place "heaven" or any particular location, such as the 'heavenly realms.' If the Kingdom referenced a place, humans would only enter it after death. However, Jesus said to a gathering, "Truly, I say to you, there are some of those who are standing here who will not taste death until they see the Kingdom of God after it has come with power," indicating that some people alive in Jesus's time would see the Kingdom before they died.[2] Jesus also discussed the Kingdom as being within us.[3] Though the Kingdom is discussed as something one may "enter into," it is clearly not a place that exists apart from visible creation. Jesus' teachings about the Kingdom were about a pattern of life, not a set of requirements for going to heaven. He taught, "Not everyone who says to Me, 'Lord, Lord,' will enter the Kingdom of Heaven, but he who does the will of My Father who is in heaven will enter."[4] There is no provision for entering the Kingdom of Heaven in any afterlife state unless one has entered the Kingdom of Heaven during the term of his or her lifetime.

Being born again is a prerequisite for entering into the Kingdom while one is still alive. "Truly, truly, I say to you, unless one is born of water and the Spirit, he cannot enter into the Kingdom of God."[5] Jesus said that it was not even possible to see that the Kingdom existed unless one was born again of the Spirit. Clearly, Jesus was not speaking of going to heaven upon one's death, since the transformation He describes does not happen after one has died.[6] Whereas it is generally true that one of the outcomes of this transformation results in a person "entering the Kingdom of Heaven." That is not a statement that focuses upon going to heaven. He was setting forth the requirements for both seeing the existence of the Kingdom as well as entering it while one is still on the earth.

The confusion surrounding being born again comes because of the historic emphasis on going to heaven in the afterlife and the erroneous concept that the Kingdom of Heaven is accessible in that manner.

> *I also say to you that you are Peter and upon this rock I will build My church; and the gates of Hades will not overpower it. I will give you the keys of the Kingdom of Heaven and whatever you bind on earth shall have been bound in heaven, and whatever you loose on earth shall have been loosed in heaven.*
> Matthew 16:18-19 NASB

PART ONE

Some religious traditions are based upon the idea that Jesus, when He recognized that God had chosen Peter to announce the advent of the Kingdom in the earth to Jews and Gentiles, gave Peter the authority to determine who went to heaven and who went to hell. Purveyors of this tradition further assert that Peter created an institution into which he endowed this power. Though erroneous, this tradition has shaped all religious thought on the concept of a Kingdom of Heaven and is the source of all turbidity regarding Jesus's declaration that one must be born again in order to both see and enter the Kingdom of Heaven. But the folly of trying to vest any institution with divine authority or attributes has been discussed previously.[7] The idea that any religious institution manages the ability to grant access to heaven lends itself to a merchandizing possibility—an institution that will perpetuate itself absent the Spirit of God—that has been historically impossible to resist.

However, if one correctly understands that the Kingdom of Heaven is something entered into while on the earth, not in the afterlife, then Jesus' charge to Peter reads much differently. The Kingdom of Heaven itself is a reference to the authority and power that sustains the House of God wherever it is found. The House of God is simultaneously located in heaven and on earth.[8] Jesus was revealing the nature of the Kingdom on the earth and that the authority of Christ would support the revealing of the Kingdom of Heaven on the earth. The result would be harmony between the Kingdom on the earth and how it exists in heaven.

Being born again is not a requirement that focuses upon going to heaven when one dies. Instead, it speaks of a transition that is necessary to live a life of 'righteousness, peace and joy in the Holy Spirit' as evidence that one is a citizen of the Kingdom of Heaven.[9] If one indeed enters the Kingdom of Heaven while yet upon the earth, then when he dies, his body returns to the earth from which it originally was taken, and his spirit is no longer tethered to the earth by this form. "The spirit will return to God who gave it."[10] Then, as spirit, the person resides in the reality of the Kingdom of Heaven that is to be found in heaven. Thus, being located in the Kingdom is a matter of citizenry, not location, into which one is born or more accurately, born of the Spirit.

---

[1]From the Declaration of Independence: We hold these truths to be self-evident, that all men are created equal, that they are endowed by their Creator with certain unalienable Rights, that among these are Life, Liberty and the pursuit of Happiness. —That to secure these rights, Governments are instituted among Men, deriving their just powers from the consent of the governed, —That whenever any Form of Government becomes destructive of these ends, it is the Right of the People to alter or to abolish it, and to institute new Government, laying its foundation on such principles and organizing its powers in such form, as to them shall seem most likely to affect their Safety and Happiness. Prudence, indeed, will dictate that Governments long established should not be changed for light and transient causes; and accordingly, all experience hath shewn, that mankind is more disposed to suffer, while evils are sufferable, than to right themselves by abolishing the forms to which they are accustomed. But when a long train of abuses and usurpations, pursuing invariably the same Object evinces a design to reduce them under absolute Despotism, it is their right, it is their duty, to throw off such Government, and to provide new Guards for their future security. [2] Mark 9:1 NASB, Luke 9:27 NASB. [3] Luke 17:20-21 NASB. [4] Matthew 7:21 NASB; see also Matthew 5:3, 10, 20; Matthew 11:12; Matthew 16:19 [5] John 3:5 NASB. [6]See Soleyn, Baptisms, The Elementary Doctrines Study Series. [7]Soleyn, *My Father! My Father!* [8]Ephesians 3:14-15 NASB; Matthew 6:10 NASB. [9] Romans 14:17NASB *supra*. [10]Ecclesiastes 12:7 NASB.

That Which Is Born of the Spirit Is Spirit

The purpose of being born again is to fundamentally change the nature of one's being from a previous state to a new form. One must already be a life in being in order to be born again, because a second birth is not possible unless there has been a prior birth. The change from one state of being to the other is so total that there is nothing in the prior life with which to compare it. Therefore, the discussion is not about evolving within a present order to some greater extension of that present order, but rather the arising of a completely different form, unidentifiable by its previous existence. This is a metamorphosis so complete that the only appropriate metaphor by which to describe the change is that of a birth.

However, the term "being born again" is widely used in evangelical circles to refer to a process involving a confession of Jesus as the Lord for a consequence that occurs after the person dies. The effect of being born again in this presentation is that it repositions the individual to avoid the horrors of hell and to enjoy the joys of heaven when death inevitably comes. This concept ignores the plain and obvious emphasis of the passage in which it occurs: "Jesus answered, 'Truly, truly, I say to you, unless one is born of water and the Spirit, he cannot enter into the Kingdom of God. That which is born of the flesh is flesh and that which is born of the Spirit is spirit. Do not be amazed that I said to you, 'You must be born again.'"[1]

The new birth releases a being that is spirit in the place where the prior being existed as flesh. An example of this transformation is what occurs when a seed is germinated and eventually produces a plant or tree of such total difference of form and existence as to be unidentifiable in terms of the seed from which it originated. The human spirit is like a seed with an outer casing of flesh. Through a process of repentance, death to the self as defined by flesh, and resurrection as a new life, one is born again and begins the process of life as a spiritual being. A being that is spirit results in the place where the predecessor was flesh. This is the intent of Jesus's statement that one must be born again.

Being born again indicates the beginning of a process of life that emphasizes being a spirit. It is not meant to emphasize the results that may come at the end of life. Instead, it is a beginning that contrasts a previous life that emphasized the needs and desires of a being that is flesh. Accordingly, being born again of Spirit does not mean that one simply changes into a spirit being, but it begins the process of functioning as a spirit being until the body, which serves as a house to the spirit, loses its ability to function in that capacity and dies. At that point, the spirit does not die, but is released from its captivity and encasement in a perishable house. The body dies, but the spirit continues.[2]

The inquiry becomes, "What is a spirit?" and "How is man different once he is released through rebirth from an identity of flesh to one of spirit?" This says nothing to define how one is different once he or she is released from the identity of flesh and born again as spirit; nor has it defined the nature of spirit itself. A lesser concept is always subsumed in the greater expression. By focusing upon the greater expression, the lesser expression is thoroughly understood. These issues are pursued only by exploring the very nature of God as Spirit, from whom man derived his origin as a spirit. God imparted spirit out of His own person into formed earth that He had made, resulting in the enclosure of man's spirit within a vessel of earth. Therefore, understanding the nature of man as spirit is inseparable from a discussion of God as Spirit.

---

[1] John 3:5-7 NASB. [2]Ecclesiastes 12:7 NASB; Luke 23:46 NASB.

Sons of God and Spirit

Mankind was first created as a son of God, not as the son of man. He was spirit clothed in flesh. Clothing spirit with flesh was God's design to put and to keep a son in the earth for a specified period of time.[1] While the human form is meant to exist only for a finite period of time, humans were not designed to be separated from God.

Only in a capacity as spirit beings are humans capable of relating to God as sons. The nature of the Spirit allows the individual to commune with God.[2] It allows for the individual to perfectly represent some aspect of God's character, and it is the only component of the human being that allows humans to exist simultaneously as individuals and as a single corporate body.

When a person is born again as a spirit, it begins the process of nullifying the effects of the fall and restoring the very nature of the individual to God's original intent, removing the old identity inherited from Adam's fallen state in which one sees himself as merely flesh, separate from God as Father and subject to the rule of Satan. His soul's motivation is that of survival and his culture is that of an orphan.

This process begins with repentance in which a person dies to the identity in Adam and includes the symbolic death, burial and resurrection of water baptism performed person to person.[3] Each person then has an advocate in Christ to establish the fact that they are free from condemnation before God.[4] The process culminates with one's resurrection as a new creation, confirmation of one's identity and being baptized with the Holy Spirit.[5] This is the foundation for a person's introduction into the Kingdom of Heaven and for stewarding growth and maturity as a son of God.

Jesus is the prototypical Son of God. He serves as a model of one who was never separated in His Spirit from His Father. His life shows the nature of the relationship between God and mankind that God originally intended, and He made it possible for mankind to be reconciled to God as sons.[6] The Spirit of Christ stewards this new way of life.

The first evidence of change when one is born again of the Spirit and begins to see all things from a spiritual point of view, is the way the person sees his relationship to God.[7] The Spirit testifies with our spirit that we are the children of God. A person born again experiences the restoration of the primacy of his spirit over his soul and begins to awaken to the understanding that an entire spiritual existence co-exists with a natural one. Christ begins to refocus his sight, and he begins to see himself and others differently.

It takes time for his understanding of what he sees to mature. In that respect, a spiritual man who is newly born again is similar to a natural man born as an infant. The natural man grows and becomes accustomed to the physical world and learns to live in it and interprets its secrets and eventually becomes fluid in his functions. So also, a spiritual man understands the reality of God his Father and grows in his ability to receive insight and revelation from God and begins to walk confidently in the earth as a son of God. Eventually, his competence to understand and interpret the ways of God defines his purpose as a son who represents his father.

God originally enclosed a spirit with flesh to keep a son on the earth so that God might be seen within this venue.[8] A son of God, therefore, can only be a spirit being. Discovering man as a son of God and, therefore, a spirit requires an exploration of the genre of spirit in order to discover the true meaning of man as a son of God. The context of understanding spirit inevitably leads back to the understanding of the nature of God Himself. For God is Spirit from which all human spirits derive their origins.

---

[1] 2 Corinthians 5:1-5 NASB. [2]Romans 8:16 NASB. [3]Acts 2:38, 41 NIV; see Repentance from Acts that Lead to Death, Elementary Doctrine Series. [4]1 John 2:1 NASB. [5]See Matthew 3:16-17 NIV; Acts 10:37-38 NIV. [6]John 1:9-14 NASB. [7]Romans 8:14-16 NASB. [8]2 Corinthians 4:11 NASB.

Defining Spirit

Humans are familiar with things of the natural world and almost entirely unfamiliar with the invisible, spiritual world. Instinctively, humans will analogize to natural things in order to comprehend spiritual things. The understanding of spiritual things, and in particular God as Spirit, suffers as a result. This is one of the main difficulties in understanding the personhood of God. Humans struggle with the understanding of God as a Spirit because they are accustomed to defining persons by physical characteristics. Similarly, one's accomplishments, possessions, or habits provide comparative traits that are used to define the person socially. In these examples, ultimately it is one's environment that defines the person or how the person exists in the realm of light, physics and other visible or tangible aspects of hard sciences. Defining a person this way, by reference to other people or things, in no way defines one's "personhood"—who that person actually is.

Physical frameworks cannot define or identify personhood as it relates to spirit. Without discussing physical characteristics, what spiritual framework might define the person? This question lies at the heart of understanding people as spiritual beings and understanding God's nature as the source and origin of all human spirits. The personhood of God is essential to unlocking the insight into us as spirit. Historically, man has arranged divine insights of God, as revealed in Scripture, according to his own physical insights into the common categorizations used to define "personhood" in the natural world. The results are often confusing and extremely difficult to understand.

Descriptions that begin to scratch the surface of understanding God as Spirit are those that themselves transcend quantification and the limitations of a physical framework. For example, Scripture refers to a oneness, and a state of being "all in all" with reference both to God and Christ.

> *That they may all be one; even as You, Father, are in Me and I in You, that they also may be in Us, so that the world may believe that You sent Me. The glory which You have given Me*

PART ONE

> *I have given to them that they may be one, just as We are one.*
> John 17:21-22 NASB

> *When all things are subjected to Him, then the Son Himself also will be subjected to the One who subjected all things to Him, so that God may be all in all.* 1 Corinthians 15:28 NASB

> *And [God] put all things in subjection under [Christ's] feet, and gave Him as head over all things to the church, which is His body, the fullness of Him who fills all in all.* Ephesians 1:22-23 NASB

This "oneness" and the description of God being "all in all" allows us to accurately employ descriptions of the Spirit who is God in terms such as omnipresent, omnipotent, and omniscient. Omni means all. These terms describe God as unquantifiably "All": all-present, all-powerful, and all-knowing. Yet, this description seems to contrast references in Scripture that define God as a person, or more accurately, as three persons: Father, Son and Holy Spirit. Reconciling these descriptions of God moves us a great deal forward in understanding God as Spirit and therefore, the spiritual nature of mankind as well.

If God is All in all (omni), He must also be only a single being. If God as Spirit is omnipresent, for example, then there can only be one God. If, instead, one claims that three separate beings exist as Father, Son, and Spirit, the existence of any more than one entity diminishes the presence of the one. This result is inconsistent with being omnipresent, since a being cannot simultaneously be "omni" and limited by another being. God is one Spirit, yet He is traditionally presented as three in one. These descriptions are not necessarily in conflict with each other. Rather, human understanding is limited in its ability to comprehend the nature of spirit, creating contradictions of the mind.

The historical explanation is that the three are one, because they have the same substance. This explanation, however, betrays the use of human standards, namely substance, to define the nature of that which is by definition insubstantial. Finite man, without the revelation of God, is obligated to view everything from its identifiable substance. Here, the confusion lies not with the personhood of God, but with the ability of man to see and understand God's nature, while man himself is hindered by the limitations of his human form.

The Personhood of God

For My thoughts are not your thoughts, Nor are your ways My ways, declares the LORD. For as the heavens are higher than the earth, so are My ways higher than your ways, and My thoughts than your thoughts. Isaiah 55:8-9 NASB

The realities of spirit are of such a higher order from the reality as perceived by humans that the human interpretation of spiritual things will always be limited to the perception of the natural mind. Humans, then, must wait upon the revealing of spiritual realities in their appointed times to comprehend those realities, and when revealed, the spiritual reality always subsumes the previous human interpretation. Spiritual things must pass through the filter of the senses to be expressed in time and space, and mankind may only understand God when and how He chooses to reveal Himself. Absent the clarity of revelation from God, human knowledge is inadequate to either fully express or understand God's nature as Spirit.

It is certain that God intends to reveal all of who He is to mankind, but He must first prepare a people who are capable of carrying His presence. God incrementally has been filling in the inevitable gaps in human knowledge and understanding about Him. However, God cannot reveal Himself or any matter of significance until He has produced a people in the earth who can receive the revelation and walk in the responsibility associated with that revelation. Otherwise, the revelation has no basis by which to be seen in the earth.

Part of this preparation is the dismantling of institutions of orthodoxy as the contrasting truth is revealed to a generation that has relentlessly pursued God. Institutions that claim knowledge of God derived through the exercise of human reason occupy the high ground claimed by orthodoxy. Orthodoxy often bestrides the path of truth and understanding like a colossus and often obstructs revelation by its incessant demand to be considered as the standard of what is true.

Father, Son and Spirit—One Person

The Father is Spirit and the Son is Spirit because God is Spirit:

> *...being diligent to preserve the unity of the Spirit in the bond of peace. There is one body and one Spirit, just as also you were called in one hope of your calling; one Lord, one faith, one baptism, one God and Father of all who is over all and through all and in all.* Ephesians 4:3-6 NASB

Orthodox Christianity has taught that the reference to Father, Son, and Spirit is a reference to three persons, namely the person of God known as Father, another distinct person known as Son, and a third distinct person known as Spirit, who is qualified with the description of "Holy," and all three are the same substance. This concept was originally put in creedal form from the First Council of Nicia in AD 325, and it has become the bedrock of orthodox confession. These traditions insist that there is only one God yet offer no plausible explanation for viewing God as three separate persons. This simplistic view falls short in understanding or representing God as Spirit.

PART ONE

Beginning with the plain language of these descriptions of God, it should be clear that the terms Spirit, Father and Son represent two different types of descriptions. "Spirit" refers to an essence or personhood, like the terms "flesh" or "soul" in describing a human being. "Spirit" describes God's nature at the most basic level. "Father" and "Son," however, refer to a relationship. Relational terms such as these are more specific descriptions of personhood, relating certain characteristics with reference to another. It is important to understand that God defined Himself as Father and Son prior to creating mankind. How God defines this relationship through actions and reference to Himself defines the spiritual reality of this relationship as it is intended to exist on the earth. The human interpretation is limited, and the experience of that natural relationship does not define Father and Son as God first intended it. For example, for humans a father and son relationship requires two separate persons, but for spirit no such requirement exists. God defines Himself through reference to an existing relationship that is distinct and specific.

Neither expression, Father nor Son, is distinct from Spirit. Jesus attempted to communicate this concept, making statements such as "I am in the Father, and the Father is in Me."[1] Father and Son are in Spirit before being on display distinctly. However, when that distinctiveness is displayed, Father is still Spirit and so is Son. Indeed, God is called "the Father of our spirits" and Jesus is referred to as "the Word," which is spirit and life. Therefore, Father is not distinct from Spirit and neither is Son.

This aspect of the nature of God is first visible in the creation of Adam, but it has been God's nature forever. When God made Adam, Eve was already in him. The two were encased in one flesh. Eve was Adam and Adam was Eve before she was separated out and given separate, visible status. Her identity was a continuation of that which was already in the person of Adam. Adam had within him all the races of mankind, but apart from the separate expressions of himself, which he described as "bone of my bones, and flesh of my flesh" the generations within Adam would never become visible in the earth.[2] They would remain as the potential enclosed within the seed.

Yet, the defining relationship is crucially important—it is the way God chose to show Himself to the world. It is the manner of relationship for which He originally created mankind, and it is therefore, the most fundamental description of the personhood of God to be found in Scripture. God is describing Himself, not for His own benefit, but for mankind's understanding. He is using the distinguishable qualities of father and son, with which every human being is personally familiar.

The whole concept of creating man as a son of God originated with God. Mankind became the recipient of this decision, and creation itself was made pursuant to this concept. Since we know that God intended to put Himself on display through His representative sons in the earth, the question arises as to what about God's nature did He intend that mankind would both observe and eventually display through the relationship described as Father and Son. The answer, of course, is love. From God's viewpoint the highest form of the expression of love is contained within the relationship of father and son. When God elected to put the essential nature of His person on display, His love was expressed in the form of that relationship. Not only is God Spirit, but God is love. God is a Spirit who loves.

> *Beloved, let us love one another, for love is from God; and everyone who loves is born of God and knows God. The one who does not love does not know God, for God is love. By this the love of God was manifested in us, that God has sent His only begotten Son into the world so that we might live through Him. In this is love, not that we loved God, but that he loved us and sent His Son to be the propitiation for our sins. Beloved, if God so loved us, we also ought to love one another. No one*

has seen God at any time; if we love one another, God abides in us and His love is perfected in us. By this we know that we abide in Him and He in us, because He has given us His Spirit.
1 John 4:7-13 NASB

---

[1]See e.g., John 14:10-11, 20 NASB. [2]Genesis 2:23 NASB.

Father and Son

Adam was the first being God created to put His love on display, and his relationship to God was perfect, meaning it was exactly as God had intended it to be. Though Adam lived for a time as the exact representation of God, he was not empowered to display God's omnipotence, omnipresence, and omniscience—aspects that are results of God being Spirit. Strict imperatives governed his existence on the earth. God and Adam lived as Father and son until sin separated them. After mankind's fall in the garden, the relationship changed. Though God remained the Father of our spirits, mankind was unable to relate to God as sons.[1] Creation itself showed God's intent that mankind's role in representing Him would take many generations.[2]

An individual son of God is meant to encapsulate and show a measure of God's personhood, but one that is not equal to God in His entirety. Indeed, equality with God was the original temptation that separated mankind from God.[3] Jesus, however, refused to fall for that temptation.[4] Instead, Jesus, the undisputed and perfect Son of God, inhabited a capacity of strict obedience. "For as through the one man's disobedience, the many were made sinners, even so through the obedience of the One, the many will be made righteous."[5] Jesus as the Son of God, did not start out displaying the quality of omniscience. He was perfect, but yet "He learned obedience from the things which

He suffered."[6] Although He never sinned, He suffered as a means of refining Him to be both perfect and complete.

The concept of completeness relates to the full measure of one's destiny in revealing part of the Father, and it is central to understanding love and maturing from the viewpoint of the son. Stages of sonship, in which one may be perfect in every stage but continually striving for completeness, is similar to the cycles of a tree bearing fruit. In the springtime, the apple blossoms on the tree are the present state of the fruit. They are perfect, but incomplete. Throughout the growing season, the brisk spring winds remove the blossoms and leave in their places small nodules that have neither the beauty of the blossoms nor the purpose of the ripened fruit. These, too, are perfect. It is at the end of the season when the fruit is both perfect and complete. Jesus grew to be the complete expression of the Son through His perfect obedience to the Father during His ministry. He started out as a child and became the Man who was sacrificed on the cross, fulfilling His destiny before ascending to heaven.

If the role of the Son is the same as that of the Father, the Son would be possessed of the same power and authority and be able to do all that the Father could do independently of the Father. However, Jesus never sought equality with God, nor did He exercise any measure of power and authority on His own. It was not until the very end of His life, just prior to His return to heaven, that the Son claimed any authority of His own. Having concluded His earthly assignment, He only claimed power as being given to Him by the Father.[7] Both the process of training and the display through a mature Son are designed to consume the Son's independence. When one has attained this state, the Father Himself is put on display through the Son and, to those observing, the Son is indistinguishable from the Father. The Son may say, "I and the Father are one."[8]

PART ONE

The love of the Son for the Father manifests itself in unwavering obedience. Undergirding this manifestation of love is trust. The complete understanding and trust is that the Father has in mind the outcome before He establishes the requirements, and that all He requires of the Son is for the Son's benefit. The Son may then act with complete obedience, even if the Son is unsure of the future consequences of doing so. Although the Son is aware of what is required and is independently able to either soften the effects of His trials and sufferings or avoid them altogether, His trust of the Father prevents Him from acting in any manner that positions Him in opposition to the Father's intent. Because the Son voluntarily obeys the Father, even though the Father's demands are personally painful and arduous to endure, His agreement with the Father entitles Him to the same considerations attributable to the Father. It is certain that the Father will never reject or abandon the Son, regardless of how bleak the condition of the Son may be—either during the time of training or in the time of representation.

---

[1] See Hebrews 12:9 NASB. [2]A far greater purpose for the creation of man is revealed in the preparations God made for the advent of man into creation. God designed a world that would renew itself for a very long time, indicating that His purposes for the creation of man were meant to unfold over many millennia and would include a vast number of human beings. God established an entire economy to provide for His sons. He created "seed-bearing plants and trees on the land that bear fruit with seed in it, according to their various kinds." (Genesis 1:11). He created "living creatures according to their kinds: livestock, creatures that move along the ground, and wild animals, each according to its kind." (Genesis 1:24). Then, after He created man, He declared that these things were intended for man's provision: I give you every seed-bearing plant on the face of the whole earth and every tree that has fruit with seed in it. They will be yours for food. And to all the beasts of the earth and all the birds of the air and all the creatures that move on the ground—everything that has the breath of life in it—I give every green plant for food. (Genesis 1:30). God created a son in God's own image and in His own likeness. The purpose for the creation of man is contained in this fact. [3]Genesis 3:5 NASB. [4]Matthew 4:2-4 NASB. [5]Romans 5:19 NASB. [6]Hebrews 5:8-9 NASB. [7]Matthew 28:18 NASB. [8]John 10:30 NASB.

The Personhood of the Spirit

Only by spirit and not physically may man participate in a very limited way in the realities of the eternal.[1] The personhood of Spirit is capable of acting in the present on the basis of the eternal. Spirit rules over both the realm of time and the realm of the eternal, and it moves freely between those realms. By contrast, human beings are anchored in time by their bodies. Even though, through prophetic visions and dreams, they might be caught up into the realm of Spirit and into the eternal, they eventually return to earth.

The personhood of Spirit emphasizes attributes of character in the absence of attributes of material substance. Spirit is capable of making grants of Himself in furtherance of attributes of character. It is connected to God relationally as a Son.[2] Similarly, God would cast Himself in another role by endowing another Spirit into flesh. This Spirit would be called the Spirit of Christ. This Spirit's role is of reconciling the former spirit of man back to his place in God by being reassembled to God through the Body of Christ. The Spirit of Christ would be housed in the body of a man named Jesus, who would also be the Son of God.

---

[1] Revelation 4:1 NASB; 2 Corinthians 12:2 NASB. [2] See e.g., Luke 3:38 NASB (." . . Adam, the Son of God.").

Love Gives Form to Spirit

It is the nature of love that motivates God in all of His actions. Love gives form to Spirit, creating the aspects of Father and Son that may be understood separately but are only complete in the context of the relationship. The love of the Son for the Father is seen in the surrender of His being for the Father's use and the vulnerability inherent in that positioning. The reason the Son does not act independently of the Father is that the relationship exists to show the nature of the Father as revealed through the Son. This requires the Son to forego all independence of the Father. This is the fashion in which the Son loves the Father.

How the Father chooses to appear through the Son becomes the Son's daily mandate. His destiny becomes defined by His designated role as predetermined by the Father.[1] It is understandable that the role of representation makes the Son vulnerable to the will of the Father. For Jesus, His vulnerable trust of the Father culminated in the loss of His physical life. Whether this degree of trust is warranted comes from the understanding of love from the Father's point of view using an eternal lens. According to the Father's plan, Jesus' trust and vulnerability was fully accounted for in His resurrection from the dead and His exaltation to the throne of God.

Jesus was required to die on the cross, and all of His humanity is consumed in that event. Yet, upon His resurrection, He comes forth out of death with the power to give life to all who would choose to invest their hope in Him. Not only does He regain His own life, but He has life within Himself, which He may give to the spirits of men because His resurrection elevates Him to the realm of the eternal and seats Him on the throne of His Father, far above the condition of earth or even of death. God chooses the relationship of Father and son as the vehicle for the display of His love because He intended this display to take place in the realms of heaven and earth. The intent was that heaven might appear on earth through a son and that the ways of God, together with the rule of heaven, might illuminate the darkness of earth and fallen man. Wherever heaven appears, the light and glory of God restores order.

---

[1] John 18:37 NASB.

PART ONE

The Glory and Purpose of the Sons of God

It is the glory of the sons of God to provide the order for the restoration of the Kingdom of Heaven in creation. Creation exists to resolve the issue of sin and to remove its taint from heaven and earth.

The enemy who rebelled against God's choice of man as His heirs introduced sin into creation. The nature of the love of God was destined to confront the enemy. In Adam's unsuccessful confrontation, separation from God and the attendant fatherless culture resulted.

The angels that rejected the order of God rebelled against the choice of man as God's heir. Satan and the fallen angels have exerted influence over mankind since the earth's creation. Whereas they have done so from their perch in the second heaven,[1] their own destiny is to be brought to earth at the conclusion of the present age:

> *"For this reason, rejoice, O heavens and you who dwell in them. Woe to the earth and the sea, because the devil has come down to you, having great wrath, knowing that he has only a short time."* Revelation 12:12 NASB

They will be unrestrained in their fury against the sons of God and against the order of His Kingdom.

Christ came into the world to establish and rule as the king over the Kingdom of Heaven.[2] As the head, He continues to exercise dominion and rule over the whole earth from His place upon the throne of God. "The Government shall be upon His shoulders."[3] His body in the earth is the instrument through which He exercises His sovereign authority. All of the activities of rule associated with the Kingdom of Heaven are designed to bring eternal standards to bear on human circumstances. As earlier noted, this process replaces the culture of sin with a heavenly culture of righteousness. The existence of the sons of God employing the authority and rule of Christ establishes the culture of the Kingdom of Heaven upon the earth.

This has the effect of challenging the model of life that has evolved out of the kingdom of darkness. The light and glory of the Kingdom of Heaven projected through the rule of sons has, among its effects, the ability to reclaim mankind for God and to do so by "destroying the works of the devil."[4] God intends not only to judge and destroy Satan's works by revealing the corporate Christ and the glory of His governance, He means to bring to judgment the angels who sinned and, ultimately, to eliminate them from the created world as part of His intent to purge the taint of sin from both the visible and the invisible creation. To understand the purpose of the judging of angels, it is necessary to understand why God created the world.

One of God's great purposes in creating the world and putting mankind into it was to permit the vindication of the righteousness of God in the choice of man as His heirs, His sons.[5] God originally conceived of man as a creature who would be endowed with a spirit out of the person of God and therefore, man would be capable of loving both God and his fellow man in the same manner in which God Himself loves. When a man loves as God loves, the essential nature of God is displayed. "A new command I give you: Love one another. As I have loved you, so you must love one another."[6] The standard of love in this commandment is the same standard for God and man.

> *For to which of the angels did God every say, "You are my Son; today I have become your Father?" Or again, "I will be his Father, and He will be my Son?"... Are not all angels ministering spirits sent to serve those who will inherit salvation?"*
> Hebrews 1:5, 14 NIV

Angels were created to serve both God and man. The angels who rebelled considered that they had been unjustly relegated to serving man whom they regarded as an inferior being.[7] They wanted to be the sons and heirs of God. Because they were not created to carry and portray the love of God, their view of inheritance was related to the exercise of power rather than the restraint of love.[8] Some of the angels, under the leadership of Lucifer, called into question God's righteousness in His choice of man as His heirs. Although God could have obliterated the angels who sinned, He understood the nature of their challenge and chose to pursue them through righteous judgment.

Had He simply annihilated them, the issues of the righteousness of His decision to eliminate His opposition would have been left unanswered. Alternatively, had He given them an answer, He would have lowered Himself to the same plane of created beings and empowered the creation to judge its creator. This would have replaced divine order with chaos and eliminated all standards of righteous judgment. Instead, He elected to provide an answer through the very creatures who were the subject of the dispute. God's answer would be that man would put on display the righteousness of God and, by that, destroy Satan's deception and hold all the angels who sinned to account. Man's righteousness as a mature son of God would put on display the exact nature of God, his Father, and become the standard for judgment of the angels themselves.

The first man, Adam, was provided the choice of relying upon the presence of God or the tree of the Knowledge of Good and Evil as the basis of his decision making, and he chose independence from God. He was aided in this choice by the active participation of Satan. Jesus, the last Adam, was subject to the same temptation to proceed by the wisdom of convenience. Instead, though hungry from forty days of fasting, He chose and feasted upon the bread of God's presence. His decision restored to man the right to live again in the presence of God.

In every epoch, the responsibility of the righteous in the earth is to judge the unfolding of events in their day accurately by eternal standards and to reposition themselves and their mindsets in the unfolding will of God in their times. The glory of the sons of God will be established by the manner of their response to unrestrained evil. The standards established by the righteous acts of the sons of God will become the standard of judgment that ultimately results in the extinction of evil and the expunging of the taint of sin from creation.[9] Simultaneously, the love of God will be put on display through His sons in the midst of this conflict.

---

[1]See e.g., Ephesians 6:12 NASB, 2Co 12:2-4 NASB (supporting the proposition that there are three heavenly realms). [2]Isaiah 9:6-7 NIV. [3]Id. [4]1 John 3:8 NASB. [5]Soleyn, *My Father! My Father!, Ch. 6 p.57 (2012).* [6]John 13:34 NIV. [7]Hebrews 2:6-9 NIV. [8]Galatians 4:7 NIV. [9]Revelation 12:11 NIV.

The Word Becomes Flesh

Prior to the beginning of creation, hidden in God was the love of God, but it had no recipient and, therefore, no outward expression.[1] Prior to the revelation of the relationship of Father and son, He made preparation for it to be shown. He moved as Spirit and power.

God began creation by arranging preexisting elements. "Now the earth was formless and empty; darkness was over the surface of the deep, and the Spirit of God was hovering over the waters."[2] Prior to God's first act of creation recorded in Scripture, some of the things that already existed were "the deep," "the waters," and the land covered by the waters.[3] Prior to God speaking the words that would form the present creation, the deep, the waters and the earth were not arranged in their present form. He commanded the dry land to appear and separated the waters with a firmament. He removed the darkness upon the surface of the deep by commanding light to appear, and He gathered the waters below the firmament into a continuous body of water, permitting the dry land underneath to appear.[4]

All creation arose in response to God's declarations.[5] God's form during this bout of creativity is called the "Word," because of the exercise of power according to the declaration.[6] The Word is an identifier of the Spirit of God that is synonymous with His power. This does not imply that prior to creation there were two persons to God, namely Spirit and power or Spirit and Word. Rather this shows that God's focus at the time becomes the descriptor of how God presents Himself, in this case as the Word.

The aspect of God previously identified as the Word of God makes His advent into the creation that He has constructed. His entrance into the physical creation is as an embodied spirit.

> In the beginning was the Word, and the Word was with God, and the Word was God. He was in the beginning with God. All things came into being through Him, and apart from Him nothing came into being that has come into being. In Him was life and the life was the Light of men... And the Word became flesh, and dwelt among us, and we saw His glory, glory as of the only begotten from the Father, full of grace and truth."
> John 1:1-4, 14 NASB

He wore the familiar form known to us as Jesus, the Son of God. The Word became the Son when God chose to put His love on display through the model of Father and Son. The previous executive authority for the display of the power of God, becomes the Son. He assumes a role that is starkly contrasted with His prior role. He is divested of all power and authority as He takes on the role by which the love of God will be made visible. The Son understands that He has come into creation to give the Father a place in time from which to put on display the nature of the love of God. This puts the entire power of God under the authority governed by the love of God, embodied as the Father.

Curiously, by defining Himself this way, God chose to subject His power to the humiliation of obedience to the Father and inactivity, and He reduced the creative competence of God, by which the universe was framed, both to a form and a function that denies Him independent action. If God truly is omnipotent, omniscient, and omnipresent, this characterization of His display in the earth only makes sense if His purpose is to show something other than His great power.

The message is that even the power that frames the universe is subject to the control, and is in the service, of love. God, by this is showing that He will not exercise power apart from the constraints of love leaving no doubt that within the personhood of God, the preeminent characteristic that defines God is not power, but love. It further establishes that power and love are not equally considered in God's description of Himself. Because He makes His power the servant of His love, He conveys an understanding that within the nature of God is a hierarchy of priorities. The preeminent consideration that always determines what God does is love. Power, then may be considered as what God does, whereas love is who He is.

---

[1]Ephesians 3:9-12 NASB (discussing eternal things being hidden in God until their proper times). [2]*Genesis 1:2 NASB.* [3]*Genesis 1:9-10 NASB* [4]Soleyn, *My Father! My Father! pp. 96-97, Ch 9.* [5]See, e.g., Genesis 1:3, 6, 9, 11, 14, 20, 24, 26, 28, 29 NASB ("God said . . ."). [6]Genesis 1:2-3 NASB; John 1:1-4, 14 NASB; Revelation 19:13 NASB.

Love and Power

By subjecting the power of God to the love of God, God leaves no doubt that even in dealing with His enemy the force that overcomes the enemy is love and not power. In this manner of restraint, the righteousness of God is upheld impeccably because God understands that even though He is the creator of the beings that oppose Him, the challenge to His righteousness in choosing man over the angels could not be resolved by forcefully extinguishing the opposition. The use of force to settle a dispute never determines the truth in controversy. It only establishes who is more powerful. As maker of all things, God has the right to destroy anything He has created. But, when the creation has challenged the creator, as those angels who challenged God did, the issue may only be settled by the triumph of God's nature and not by the employment of His power. The standard for the engagement of His enemy to which God elected to limit Himself, is the complete standard of humility. He does not reserve His power in case things go badly. Instead, power is clothed in the vulnerability of the human form and put in a realm "lower than the angels"[1] to confront an enemy who is motivated in his fury by his outrage at the sense of being dispossessed of what he believes to be rightfully his.

In the representation of the Father, the son is completely exposed to that which opposes the Father. For example:

> *Adam...was vulnerable in the matter of the choices that informed the character of his rule. He could rule as a son, controlled by the nature of his Father resident within him, or he could elect to discard that restraint and rule independently, as he saw fit. When Adam chose the latter, his rule devolved into his personal pursuit for provision and protection.* Soleyn, *My Father! My Father!* Chapter 4, p. 41.

God Himself had to come, clothed in the frailty of human form to withstand the challenge. God's choice to appear in such a form in order to confront the extremes of this opposition speaks of a depth of righteousness with which humans are typically unfamiliar. From Jesus' example, the Son did not unleash the powers of creation with which He is intimately familiar. He was restrained from even calling upon the existing creation for help. As Lord of the angels, Jesus could give them a command and they would instantly come in their legions to His defense. Instead, as the Son, His mandate was to forego all use of power in His own defense and to obey the Father who guides Him, unerringly, on the path of love.

The result was that He was personally humiliated and subsequently slaughtered as a sacrificial lamb. His declaration, "No one has taken [My life] away from Me, but I lay it down on My own initiative. I have authority to lay it down and I have authority to take it up again. This commandment I received from My Father"[2] shows that the power of God voluntarily consented to being governed by the love of God even when the issue was His own survival.

Jesus' resurrection represents the triumph of God's love over all the works of the enemy. The Son, who is power, humbled to the requirements of love, establishes the righteousness of God by showing God's willingness to forego the use of His mighty strength in favor of the humility of His love even if dealing with His enemy. This is an element of the glory that adorns the personhood of God. His justice is exercised without the use of force and leaves no doubt that love ultimately triumphs over the greatest depravity of which a created being is capable. The term redeemer properly describes the Son who puts the nature of His Father on display in this manner.

---

[1]Hebrews 2:9 NASB. [2]John 10:18 NASB.

Man As Spirit

God first made people capable of being sons of God by making them spirit beings clothed in flesh. Ultimately, however, God's intent was to clothe Himself with the Son. The Son, as defined by God's personification, is a spiritual, not physical, form. He created the body of man to house His spirit and it was always meant to be perishable and to keep man on the earth until the purpose for his life was fulfilled.[1] Because mankind was designed to house God's spirit, and because as Spirit God may exist fully in one form, undiminished, He could define Himself as Son and come into creation in the body of a man.

The difficulty of viewing man as a spirit is the same as understanding that God is Spirit. It is not the body of man that is his being, but his spirit. Determining personhood without reference to physical attributes is a formidable undertaking, made so by the familiar pattern of reference to the physical world for describing all things. The spirit of man, like God who is Spirit, is invisible. Therefore, to understand people's being as spirits and as sons of God, one must first understand God as Spirit and as the Son in relationship to the Father.

Here are some of the questions that have barred the way of inquiry into this aspect of the nature of human beings:

- Since man is a spirit being, created to express the nature of God, does that mean that man can do anything that God can do?
- What aspects of God are on display in the spirit of man?
- Is man a type of God?
- Can man create a universe?
- Does man possess potential of doing everything that God can do?

Though displays of God's power occur through human vessels, such displays are not the purpose of representing God in the earth.

What then is the limitation, if any, on the endowment of spirit that came out of God to form man? The answer to this question goes to the purpose for the creation of man. A simple analogy would help to express the intention of God in this matter. If one were to dip a bucket of water into the ocean and take it back to a laboratory and do a complete chemical analysis of the water content within the bucket, the findings would absolutely establish the composition of the water within the ocean. In that sense, there is an exact correlation between the water in the bucket and the ocean. So that, if someone unfamiliar with the ocean were given the findings of that analysis, they would know the exact composition of the ocean. However, the water within the bucket is limited in its ability to portray many aspects of the ocean. For example, the ocean is constantly moving—tides, waves, currents—whereas the bucket is relatively still. If one were to pour the content of the bucket back into the ocean, it would immediately become an indistinguishable part of the ocean again.

So it is with the spirit of man. God confined an endowment of Himself in man. God presented through man the opportunity to experience God, but not in the full range of His personhood. Man has been created to permit contact with the love of God and, only in an extremely limited form, contact with the power of God. Man as a spirit is designed principally to put the love of God on display in the earth. He was not designed to show the unlimited power of God.

---

[1] 1 Corinthians 15:35-49 NIV.

A Limitation on Power

All the limitations of a son apply to those who are led by the Spirit.[1] The power one may exercise in creation is directly connected to the scope of that person's responsibility as a son. God put man to rule over the creation so that His love might be put on display through his rule.

The power of God is available to man when he is required to exercise it for the benefit of those under his rule. However, as a son, his exercise of power is constrained by divine purposes governing both himself as well as those subject to his rule. These purposes are determined by the Father. For example, a person in authority may be moved by compassion to act to alleviate the suffering or discomfort of someone under his authority, or even within his sphere of acquaintances. The conditions of adversity themselves may be permitted by God as the only means to effectuate necessary changes within that person. In the exercise of power, therefore, the one in authority is required to understand the intention of God behind the human circumstance. Otherwise, human good intentions may be in conflict with the will of God. This is often why the attempt to exercise power is ineffectual.

---

[1] Romans 8:14 NASB.

Unlimited Love

In the display of the love of God, a son of God is never restrained. Just as the bucket does not contain the entire ocean and is designed as a limited sampling for accurately determining the ocean's composition, so the spirit of man is not the full expression of God but a limited experience providing an accurate sampling of the love of God.

He is unlimited in love because he was designed to put the love of God on display. When love is the motivation for any action, the goal is always the benefit to the other. By nature, love is directed from the source to the object. The goal of love makes the source vulnerable, but its preoccupation with the well-being of the other counts the risk to the source to be worthwhile. Since love is never self-serving, its motivation is beyond being suspect. Love itself is unmotivated by considerations regarding how the object of love might respond. The purity of this motivation is untainted by any element that is questionable. It is, therefore, holy and against such motivation there is not divine prohibition.

God chose a model through which the boundless love of the Father is expressed by His total commitment to the Son. This commitment includes the faithful disciplining and training of a son, until he becomes the suitable vessel through which the Father Himself expresses the full range of His goodness.

Putting the Father on Display: The Body of Christ

God's purpose in casting Himself in the relationship of Father and Son is to put the nature of His love on display through the exercise of rescuing Adam's progeny. Jesus, the Son, was given by the Father for the salvation of mankind. By His obedience, Jesus participates fully in the salvation of mankind and loves man with the same love of the Father. He is, therefore, properly credited with being the savior. Though their participation in the process is different, the outcome speaks of the same love present in both.

The Father is Spirit and the Son is the same Spirit. The attributes of Spirit make this form of manifestation possible. When the Son took on the form of man, He was modeling human behavior toward God and endorsing God's trustworthiness as Father. Thus, He was the pattern Son. In His life, He was restoring the relationship between God and man to the state in which it was prior to the fall.

Every human spirit is unique in its design to put the nature of God on display. Together, they may show the full range of the love of God. However, God designed people's spirits to be able to fit together to form one overarching and continuous display of the love of God. He assembles these spirits into such a corporate display, and the result of which is a complete spiritual Man known as the Body of Christ.

The Spirit of Christ

God has put an investment of spirit, out of His person, into every human being. For example, some spirits depict aspects of the mercy of God, while others present portions of the order of God and these traits are usually discernible in the character or interests of the individual. The full range of all the aspects of the nature of God is deposited in the earth through the destinies inherent in the particular endowment of grace carried by each spirit. His intent was that by this endowment of spirit, each person would have a destiny in the earth to present a particular aspect of the nature of God Himself. This destiny does not depend upon the length of time in which a person lives in the earth, nor does it require a perfect physical body out of which to express this divine message.

Absent divine connection, these potentials languish and are never put on display. Since Adam, man's choice to reject God has resulted in the obscuring of this purpose for being. Alternative destinies have supplanted this divine purpose, and mankind routinely lives to satisfy the imperatives of their souls. Most people are entirely unfamiliar with this truth. As a consequence of the fall of man and the ascent of his soul over his spirit, these divine leanings are only vaguely visible at best. The general absence of the spirit of discernment from among mankind coupled with the loss of the knowledge of God routinely results in divine attributes in humans becoming routinely unrecognizable and, therefore, ignored. The cooperation of man in revealing the nature of God is the requirement. The reemergence of the spirit of man and the gradual reassertion of control over his soul that follows being born again marks the beginning of a journey, the goal of which is to put the nature of God resident in the human spirit on display. God pursued this continuing purpose Himself, in the form of a man invested with a particular spirit.

Christ came to rescue man and to restore him to a divine destiny.

> *For the love of Christ controls us, having concluded this, that one died for all, therefore all died; and He died for all, so that they who live might no longer live for themselves, but for Him who died and rose again on their behalf. Therefore, from now on we recognize no one according to the flesh, even though we have known Christ according to the flesh, yet now we know Him in this way no longer. Therefore, if anyone is in Christ, he is a new creature; the old things passed away; behold, new things have come. Now all these things are from God, who reconciled us to Himself through Christ and gave us the ministry of reconciliation, namely, that God was in Christ reconciling the world to Himself, not counting their trespasses against them, and He has committed to us the word of reconciliation. Therefore, we are ambassadors for Christ, as God. He made Him who knew no sin to be sin on our behalf, so that we might become the righteousness of God in Him.* 2 Corinthians 5:14-21 NASB.

The spirit that appeared in the earth housed in the form of Jesus, the Son of God, was called "the Christ."[1] It is an anointing to reconcile God and man and contains the complete expression of the love of God for man. The fullness of divine intention regarding man is contained within this spirit. To man, who is the object of this love, this spirit invites him into and receives him as part of the corporate Son. The Spirit of Christ carries God's promise of sonship to every son of Adam, that they may be reconciled to God through Christ.

The Body of Christ, therefore, is a spiritual body comprised of all the spirits reconciled to God through the process of being born again. One of the baptisms referred to in Scripture is the means by which this body is assembled in the earth.[2] An analogy can be made to the human body which is comprised of many parts which are assembled properly to create one functioning whole. The comparison is then made to the Body of Christ which is not a natural body but the assembly of all the spirits who have been reconciled to God. They are assembled into a functional whole and form one spiritual body. The manner of this assembly can only be undertaken by God Himself since He is the one who knows the exact endowment of Himself that He imparted into each spirit. The form of the assembly is referred to as the process of baptism, which inherently indicates a process of death and resurrection.

Resurrection is necessary because it directly relates to a transfiguration from the natural to the spiritual. In nature the type and shadow of this principle, which was discussed earlier, is that of a seed, which contains the ability to duplicate exactly the plant of its origin. Typically, it comprises an outer protective casing and an inner core that contains the life to be released. When the seed is buried in the earth, the conditions of its environment allow the life contained within it to be activated. This is resurrection: The process in which life escapes through the breach in the outer casing and ascends toward the surface to begin its cycle of growth above the place where it was buried. When fully grown and bearing fruit, the plant becomes an exact replica of the one that produced the seed. In a very simple form this analogy captures the principle of death and resurrection. A metamorphosis of form results from this process. The result is so vastly different that it cannot be compared to the original form. (See Soleyn, The Resurrection of the Dead from The Elementary Doctrines Study Series)

PART ONE

> *The personhood of all human beings is their spirit, contained in an outer casing of dust and every spirit, is as a seed issued from the person of God. God formed Adam's body out of the dust and placed a spirit that originated out of God's own person into him. The mind of the human spirit perceives all things from a heavenly point of view. God also gave Adam a soul so that mankind could execute heavenly realities in the venue of time and space. Humans, therefore, have the capacity to represent the invisible God in the visible realm in the manner that a seed predicates the source of its origin.* Soleyn, *The Elementary Doctrines*, P. 88.

The spirit known as the Christ is also called "Son" both because it was able to express the depth of the love of God through the body of Jesus as well as its design, upon the death of Jesus and His resurrection, to be the form in which all who would be considered sons of God could be collected into one spiritual corporate Son. This son would have both the capacity and the destiny to put all of the facets of the love of God completely on display in the earth. The individual spirits would display the divine aspect of God present in each spirit, and the entire corporate form is capable of showing the full spectrum of the glory of God intended to be revealed through the Son.

Obviously, the distinction between the individual displays of God of which each spirit is capable and the corporate form would require an order of functioning that would harmonize the display of this glory. The divine order of this corporate form is referred to in the Scriptures as the Kingdom of God. Kingdom, or "basilica," references a source of authority and power that sustains together with an order of administration that produces a vision of the sovereign.

All that was present and on display in the person of Jesus, the Son of God, is meant to be put on display through His corporate form, known as the Body of Christ. He specifically endowed His corporate form with the glory that was given while He was on the earth.³ This is distinguished from the glory He had before the foundations of the world.⁴ Before He came into the world, His glory was the display of the power of God by which all of creation came into being. The glory He had when He came into the world was the right to represent God as the Son. He has left the glory of His sonship in the earth so His spiritual form, the Christ, could relate to God as the corporate Son. The purpose of this spiritual body is to display throughout the whole earth, the same obedient representation of God as was demonstrated in the life and actions as the individual man, Jesus. The order referred to as the Kingdom of God is supported by the authority that Jesus was given from the Father so that all of the representation of God, present in the Spirit of Christ and displayed originally through Jesus, might be shown through the corporate Son.⁵

The order of the Kingdom was on display through Jesus as an individual. The need for this order is greatly accentuated because it is meant to govern many individuals of diverse spiritual gifts and callings. The harmony of this order was perfectly apparent in one man. The necessity of it is indispensable when it is required to govern an entire people. When the Kingdom works perfectly, it will show through a diverse people, harmoniously functioning as one, the full extent of the glory of God that was originally put on display in the earth in the person of Jesus.

The goal of the corporate Christ remains to finish the work originally initiated by Jesus. This work is the exact representation of the love of God in the earth as it is in heaven. In His time on earth, and for the three and a half years of His ministry, Jesus perfectly demonstrated the full extent of the love of God. Nothing was missing from His demonstration. Yet, the purposes of God have continued in the centuries since Jesus returned to heaven. God intended that a people would begin to be gathered from among the nations of mankind to be formed together into one spiritual Body, the purpose of which was to

PART ONE

demonstrate how under the rule of Christ all of the divisions among mankind that had resulted from Adam giving heed to Satan would be eliminated altogether. Man would be restored to God's original design and intent and would function as a nation of people among the nations of the earth, showing by their way of life that they had overcome all of the attempts of the enemy to nullify the purposes of God for the creation of man.

---

[1]This Greek term is descriptive of the Hebrew word "Messiah" or "anointed one." This is one of the most complex terms found in any language. It straddles the realms of the eternal and the temporal, like Jacob's ladder. [2]1 Corinthians 12:12-14 NASB. [3]John 17:22 NIV. [4]John 17:5 NASB. [5]Matthew 28:18 NASB.

Summary: No One Comes to the Father Except by Christ

The Body of Christ in the earth connects creation to God and to heaven. Under the rule of Christ, the head of this Body, the way of life for this population of humankind can mirror the order of God and of heaven itself perfectly in the earth. They can exist apart from the consequences of the fall and display the harmony and peace that eludes the nations of the world. This display is the evidence that their order, like their nature, was not informed by the precepts and practices of earth but comes from the throne of God. Going to heaven is a consequence of how their lives are lived, but the goal while on this earth is the representation of the love of God—making His invisible character visible to the earth through the Son.

The Spirit of Christ works with the authority to restore to the earth the standards of divine rule. Everyone born again of the spirit is assembled to the Spirit of Christ and is made a son of God by becoming a partaker of the grace of sonship, fully embodied within the Spirit of Christ. The Spirit of Christ is the sole and absolute access to God. Therefore, it would be impossible even to contemplate an independent relationship to God as a son apart from the corporate Son.[1]

Jesus claimed that a relationship to God as Father is exclusively attained by assembly to the Spirit who dwelt with Him. Jesus remarked, "I am the way, and the truth, and the life; no one comes to the Father but through Me."[2] He is not merely claiming access to heaven. His claim is much more profound than being a door to a destination. He spoke of the Spirit known as the Christ. He is the resurrection. In Him is the relationship to the Father that may be enacted in the present and is established forever.

---

[1] John 11:25-26 NASB. [2] John 14:6-7 NASB.

PART

The Personhood of God

Grace is the substance of God Himself. It is the economy He supplies to the son as an inheritance to change his identity and to fully enable him to fully function in his destiny. Because God is invisible, who He is cannot be detected through the five human senses. However, He may be experienced through His seven characteristics. These characteristics enable everything He desires to transmit from the heavens to be accomplished and evidenced in the earth. There is no effective counter measure the enemy may deploy to prevent God from accomplishing what He intends.

The task of understanding God as spirit, and by extension, human beings as spiritual beings, requires the discussion of the characteristics of God's person by which He reveals Himself and His nature. In this sevenfold display God shows the distinctiveness of His person and makes Himself knowable and available. Our own transformation into His image and likeness is to become a spirit that lives and functions in these characteristics.

Introduction to the Seven Spirits of God

There are two instances in John's vision in which he identifies the seven Spirits of God. This identification is curious since as we have begun to define God as spirit, and importantly as one Spirit, we have struggled both with this concept of one that is also many and with an identification of God's personhood as defined by Spirit. First, John identifies seven lamps as the "seven Spirits of God."

> *Out from the throne come flashes of lightning and sounds and peals of thunder. And there were seven lamps of fire burning before the throne, which are the seven Spirits of God; and before the throne there was something like a sea of glass, like crystal; and in the center and around the throne, four living creatures full of eyes in front and behind.* Revelation 4:5-6 NASB

Next, John identifies the seven Spirits of God as the seven horns and seven eyes upon the Lamb that was slain, Christ:

> *And I saw between the throne (with the four living creatures) and the elders a Lamb standing, as if slain, having seven horns and seven eyes, which are the seven Spirits of God, sent out into all the earth. ...And they sang a new song, saying, "Worthy are You to take the book and to break its seals; for You were slain, and purchased for God with your blood men from every tribe and tongue and people and nation," ...saying with a loud voice, "Worthy is the Lamb that was slain to receive power and riches and wisdom and might and honor and glory and blessing." And every created thing which is in heaven and on the earth and under the earth and on the sea and all things in them, I heard saying, "To Him who sits on the throne, and to the Lamb, be blessing and honor and glory and dominion forever and ever."* Revelation 5:6, 9, 12-13 NASB

Therefore, the seven Spirits of God describe something about Christ that unifies both He and God in Spirit.

PART TWO

Further delving suggests that indeed the seven Spirits are an anointing on Jesus Christ and connected intimately with revealing God's character to the earth.

> *Thus says the LORD of hosts, "If you will walk in My ways and if you will perform My service, then you will also govern My house and also have charge of My courts, and I will grant you free access among these who are standing here. Now listen, Joshua the high priest, you and your friends who are sitting in front of you—indeed they are men who are a symbol, for behold, I am going to bring in My servant the Branch. For behold, the stone that I have set before Joshua; on one stone are seven eyes. Behold I will engrave an inscription on it"* declares the LORD of hosts, *"and I will remove the iniquity of that land in one day."* Zechariah 3:7-9 NASB

The branch and the stone both refer to the Lord Jesus Christ. The prophet Isaiah wrote about Christ, "Then a shoot will spring from the stem of Jesse, and a branch from his roots will bear fruit."[1] Similarly, Christ is also called "the chief cornerstone"[2] and of which God said, "Behold, I am laying in Zion a stone, a tested stone, a costly cornerstone for the foundation, firmly placed. He who believes in it will not be disturbed."[3] This stone, Christ, as foretold in Zechariah[4] also has seven eyes, just like the Lamb in John's vision. Isaiah identifies each of the seven Spirits:

> *Then a shoot will spring from the stem of Jesse, and a branch from his roots will bear fruit. The Spirit of the LORD will rest on Him. The spirit of wisdom and understanding, the spirit of counsel and strength, the spirit of knowledge and the fear of the LORD.* Isaiah 11:1-2 NASB

The seven Spirits of God, then, are the Spirit of the Lord, or Lordship; the spirit of Wisdom; the spirit of Understanding; the spirit of Counsel;

the spirit of Strength; the spirit of Knowledge; and the Fear of the Lord. These are part of the essence out of God (Spirit) that are like eyes on the Lamb of God, the Branch, when He came into the earth.

Isaiah further identifies the attendant results of the seven Spirits of God being upon Christ:

> *And He will delight in the fear of the LORD, and He will not judge by what His eyes see, Nor make a decision by what His ears hear; But with righteousness He will judge the poor, and decide with fairness for the afflicted of the earth; and He will strike the earth with the rod of His mouth, and with the breath of His lips He will slay the wicked*. Isaiah 11:3-4 NASB

Ultimately, when the seven Spirits of God are displayed in the earth they show "His ways" through righteous rule. Thus says the LORD of hosts, "If you will walk in My ways and if you will perform My service, then you will also govern My house and also have charge of My courts, and I will grant you free access among these who are standing here."[5] If there is further question as to the effect of the seven Spirits of God being righteous rule, the same lamp stand as described by John is also described by Zechariah as a sign of righteous rule: "He said to me, 'What do you see?' and I said, 'I see, and behold, a lampstand all of gold with its bowl on the top of it, and its seven lamps on it with seven spouts belonging to each of the lamps which are on the top of it; also two olive trees by it, one on the right side of the bowl and the other on its left side.' ...Then he said to me, 'This is the word of the LORD to Zerubbabel saying, 'Not by might nor by power, but by My Spirit, says the LORD of hosts'"[6] Zerubbabel was the ruler during this period and the word to Zechariah was to rule by the Spirit, emphasized by the symbolic appearance of the lampstand, representing the seven Spirits of God.

PART TWO

The manner through which God chooses to be seen comes as a result of the seven Spirits of God, brought to us and demonstrated through the anointing of Jesus Christ, the Lamb, the Branch, and the Chief Cornerstone. Their purpose is to transform the people of God also into "living stones" and a royal priesthood to display the light of Christ in the darkness.

> *You also, as living stones, are being built up as a spiritual house for a holy priesthood, to offer up spiritual sacrifices acceptable to God through Jesus Christ. For this is contained in Scripture: "Behold, I lay in Zion a choice stone, a precious cornerstone, and he who believes in Him will not be disappointed." This precious value, then, is for you who believe; but for those who disbelieve, "the stone which the builders rejected, this became the very cornerstone," and "a stone of stumbling and a rock of offense"; for they stumble because they are disobedient to the word, and to this doom they were also appointed. But you are a chosen race, a royal priesthood, a holy nation, a people for God's own possession, so that you may proclaim the excellencies of Him who has called you out of darkness into His marvelous light; for you once were not a people, but now you are the people of God; you had not received mercy, but now you have received mercy.* 1 Peter 2:5-10 NASB.

It is in the discussion of these seven Spirits that the Body of Christ learns to practice and to recognize Christ's rule and in this manner the Kingdom of Heaven is expanded on the earth and visible through how God's people rule.

---

[1]Isaiah 11:1 NASB. [2]See Psalm 118:22 NASB. [3]Isaiah 28:16 NASB; see also Matthew 21:42 NASB. Acts 4:11 NASB; Romans 9:33 NASB (echoing the Isaiah 28:16 writing about Christ). [4]Zechariah 3:9 NASB. [5]Zechariah 3:7 NASB. [6]Zechariah 4:2-3,6 NASB.

PART TWO

The Seven Spirits

By the seven Spirits of God, a son of God is retrofitted to put the nature of his Father on display in the exact representation. The opening lines to Isaiah 11 help decode some of the mystery. The shoot out of the stump of Jesse is a prophetic reference to Jesus, who is the son of David, the son of Jesse. He is attached to the house or line of Jesse for his humanity, but He is a new growth whose life is derived directly from God. In this capacity, Jesus was given into the earth both to present the nature of God and to reconcile man to God. Jesus put on display every aspect of these seven characteristics, and He intended that their implementation would continue through His corporate form. His person, though an invisible Spirit, is meant to be fully demonstrated in the earth through the Body of Christ.

As human history progressed, in the millennia since Adam's separation from God, mankind has mostly lost any awareness of these characteristics of God. Although Jesus fully revived and restored them, the decline of man has yet continued and the characteristics of the Spirit of God that the human spirit is able to emulate have largely remained dormant and ineffective. By reconnection to the Spirit of Christ, one of the clear intentions of God is to revive the rule of the human spirit over his soul and to restore and renew the effective functioning of these seven characteristics. God has always intended to reintroduce and revive the nature of God in man.

In all the stages of growth, a son of God begins to exhibit with increasing consistency the seven characteristics of the Spirit of his Father.[1] These characteristics may be put on display in each individual spirit and are intended for a full representation in the corporate Christ. A mature son will readily display them in his normal way of life.

---

[1] Galatians 4:19 NASB.

PART TWO

The Spirit of Lordship

Rule is a perfect vehicle for the demonstration of love. The condition of the subjects of a ruler is the best indication of the character of the sovereign, and the administration of the sovereign's rule. Any demonstration of love, great or small, is voluntary. It is not motivated by the possibility of a reciprocal act.

Similarly, rule is purely voluntary since one is not under any obligation to perform in as much as he has no overseer. The ruler is the ultimate authority within a system. He is sovereign. The kindness or the corruption of a ruler's motivation is on display in his rule. In whatever manner a sovereign rules, his invisible nature is put on display through the decisions that indicate the character of his rule. Rule is the condition that allows for the greatest display of God's character.

God installed Adam as the ruler of the earth, with the intention that the nature of the Father would be reflected through the rule of the son. In his unfallen state, Adam's nature was a mirror of God's own nature. When Adam was given the right to rule, God's own judgement of all of creation, including Adam, was that everything God had made was "very good." By God's own assessment, Adam's nature reflected the goodness of God which God referred to as "His glory."[1] Adam was capable of putting the invisible qualities of God on display through his rule. That is why God gave him dominion over all the earth. It was the same as if God Himself sat enthroned as ruler over the earth.

Whenever God gives a gift of a son to rule, He intends the benefit of rule to attenuate to the subjects of His rule. Though Adam's rule failed, this result is evident in Jesus' rule. He is called the "Prince of Peace."[2] And, His birth is heralded by a declaration of peace for the benefit of the earth.[3] Whoever submits to the rule of the Kingdom of God has been given the promise of peace.

PART TWO

Adam displayed sufficient rule in his unfallen state to provide a glimpse into the original intent of God for establishing him as the ruler. Although Adam himself rejected the ways of God and adopted an adversarial posture to Him, his understanding of order continued to reference his pre-fall knowledge of the source of origin. He lived for nearly 1000 years after the fall and knew all the original families of mankind. He presided over their emergence from families to tribal forms. Thus, the original human coalitions were established along the more enduring lines of familial order. A legacy was bequeathed to mankind by Adam, the original ruler.

Whereas the rule of heaven by a son of God brings peace, the fatherless culture creates rule dominated by the imperatives of provision and protection and the ruler's own survival. For millennia survival and its imperatives have been the primary goals of both governments and their rulers. To counteract the pure self-serving interests displayed by many of history's supreme rulers, humankind has created entire bodies of political philosophies and implemented various accompanying systems, all designed to counteract the harmful nature of this kind of rule. The results are, typically, checks and balances upon the power of rulers and some form of accountability to try and ensure that the government or ruler adheres to some inviolate rights.[4] These systems and philosophies are attempts to buffer the subject of rule from the anticipated unrighteous rulers, because humankind has long forgotten that the possibility exists for righteous rule.

The power that supports righteous rule is the throne of God. Rulers within the Kingdom of God are representative sons of God under the headship and direction of Christ. These rulers are matured to be held accountable to the standards of God's own nature. The necessity of the restoration of a vision of the rule of heaven has reached a critical point in the earth and it will take the arising of a people who have received and host the spirit of Lordship and who increasingly rediscover the principles of righteous rule inherent in the spirit of

Lordship to begin to model among the nations of the earth the original governance of man. The original form of governance and rule was a mirror of heaven's own rule. Adam represented his Father, God, and the purpose of the rule of Adam was to produce the same harmonies on earth that characterized the rule of God in heaven.

The form of Adam's governance was an indispensable part of his functioning as king. The order of fathers and sons, households, clans and tribes is an order of family. It was an arrangement of humanity that would also accommodate the arrival of subsequent generations. Adam's rule established a physical reflection of what would become a spiritual reality of which Christ would be the progenitor.

---

[1]Exodus 33:18-19 NASB. [2]Isaiah 9:6 NASB. [3]Luke 2:13-14 NASB. [4]See, e.g., Magna Carta of 1215, clause 61.

Evidence of Righteous Rule

Give the king Your judgments, O God, and Your righteousness to the king's son. May he judge Your people with righteousness and your afflicted with justice. Let the mountains bring peace to the people, and the hills, in righteousness. Psalm 72:1-3 NASB

The spirit of Lordship empowers people to display God's nature through the spheres of their rule. Any sphere of rule, whether expansive or modest, brings with it the opportunity to display some aspect of God's character. By the spirit of Lordship, even non-believers have the opportunity to experience the righteous rule of heaven.

The spirit of Lordship results in righteousness, peace and joy for those who benefit from the righteous rule. These results are specific to heavenly mandates and are only possible in the Spirit. Righteousness

PART TWO

concerns adherence to the standard set by the character of God. This standard is synonymous with His holiness and is only accessible through an eternal perspective provided by the Spirit. Righteous rule occurs when every act or undertaking contemplates the well-being of the person subject to it.[1] Righteous rule requires putting others before oneself and, in this way, is a demonstration of the love of God informed by the Spirit of God.

The peace imparted by the spirit of Lordship is not circumstantial, but rather something imparted by the presence of the Spirit of the Lord Jesus Christ.[2] This peace is internal having to do with the mindset of the Spirit.[3] Accordingly, this peace exists in the midst of chaos, hardship and tribulations.[4] It only comes through impartation, in this case, through ruling according to the spirit of Lordship given to us through the Lord Jesus Christ.[5] It therefore surpasses all comprehension of the secular world.[6]

> *But as for Me, I have installed My King upon Zion, My holy mountain. I will surely tell of the decree of the LORD; He said to Me, "You are My Son, today I have begotten You."* Psalm 2:6-7 NASB

The authority and standard for rule is sonship, which is the exact representation of the Father in the manner of the Son's rule. When one rules in his or her sphere as a son, God enters the domain of the ruler. This manner of rule shows the way of life that comes from the Spirit as opposed to acts of benevolence of which even an unredeemed person is capable. Those influenced by the form of rule that comes from the spirit of Lordship experience the enduring nature of God's goodness appearing in a human vessel which may be the foundation of that person's faith needed to grow in maturity.

---

[1]Romans 14:15-16 NASB. [2]See John 14:27 NASB. [3]See Romans 8:6 NASB. [4]See John 16:33 NASB. [5]See Acts 10:36 NASB. [6]See Philippians 4:7 NASB.

PART TWO

Mature Rule

The greater the sphere of rule, the greater the responsibility to the son. Responsibility and maturity are directly correlated in the Kingdom of Heaven since the mature son represents his or her own interest less and less while moving toward the grace of exact representation. Though it is the Father that assigns each person's spheres of rule, one's goal should be to rule well, so that the sphere of one's rule may be increased. The full representation of God that ultimately defines a person's destiny typically is reserved for the person's full maturity as a son of God.

Maturity is defined by specific aspects of knowledge, understanding and functionality in increasing levels of complexity and responsibility. Regarding their maturity, Paul wrote to the Corinthians, "I resolved to know nothing while I was with you except Jesus Christ and Him crucified."[1] He explained, "Brothers, I could not address you as spiritual but as worldly—mere infants in Christ. I gave you milk, not solid food, for you were not yet ready for it. Indeed, you are still not ready."[2] Paul equates knowing nothing but Christ and Him crucified as "milk" for infants. He also equates their state of being infantile with them also being "worldly" or "carnal." Carnality means being motivated by the desires of the flesh and not the Spirit, making one unable to make common and ordinary distinctions consistent with the life of a mature believer. From Paul's assessment of the Corinthians, simply knowing Christ and Him crucified does not mean that a believer is mature. He made it clear that, without more knowledge and understanding, one is carnal and immature. This highlights the need for maturity as a prerequisite for receiving and understanding the wisdom that comes from God, which is in turn required to rule in a manner reflective of God's character.

Rule progresses in ever widening circles according to one's maturity. The smallest circle in this progression is the self. Learning to rule one's soul by one's spirit is the first stage of rule and the beginning point for developing the characteristic of the spirit of Lordship. A person born again starts his life in the spirit as in infant regardless of their physical age. Through distinct stages the believer matures in the direction of being consistently able to represent the interests of God the Father.[3]

Every entrenched position of the human soul will, in time, be assailed as firmly and as resolutely as God determines is necessary to bring about a transition from the rule of the soul to the rule of the spirit. It regards repositioning so that the person is again able to hear God and to act upon God's instructions. Once this process is underway and well before it is complete, God begins to affirm the progress that is being made toward maturity by adding broader dimensions of rule to the person.

---

[1] 1 Corinthians 2:2 NIV. [2] 1 Corinthians 3:1-2 NIV. [3] From Soleyn, *The Elementary Doctrines*, Introduction: A son of God in Scripture has not only specific meaning regarding one's positioning in the will of God, it also has multiple distinct usages that denote one's level of maturity. To be a son of God, one begins with the born-again experience, by which one is repositioned in Christ and enabled to be led by the Spirit. Everyone who is born again has been given "the power to become sons of God." John 1:12 KJV. Beyond this inceptive rebirth, there are various distinct usages of terms meaning "son" in Scripture that acknowledge the progression from a newborn to a mature son who represents his or her Father. See Galatians 3:26-28 NIV (" You are all sons of God through faith in Christ Jesus, . . . There is neither Jew nor Greek, slave nor free, male nor female, for you are all one in Christ Jesus."). A newborn believer is referred to by the term "nepios," which refers to a son newly born into the family. However, when that son grows up and is competent to represent the interests of his father as a fully mature son, the designation "huios" is used appropriately to distinguish the fully mature son from the newborn infant. Romans 8:14 NIV (In his letter to the Romans, Paul wrote that "those who are led by the Spirit of God are sons of God." (Referring to a son in the huios stage, which is one who is a mature son, fit to represent the Father)); see Strong's G5207, huios. Between the newborn and the fully mature are other distinct specific stages of sonship, each referencing a growing level of maturity through which the believer progresses.

PART TWO

The Widening Circle of Rule

As the spiritual development of a son of God increases, he or she can expect to experience broader spheres of rule along with greater authority to act. This greater expression typically leads to a clearer view of the individual's purpose for the endowment of spiritual gifts. God adds other external dimensions of rule commensurate with the maturing of the specific son. This widening circle of rule tends to stretch toward rule over others, such as in jobs, families, and social or relational contexts. The direction of change, along with recurring patterns of interests and activities, also begins to reveal the nature of one's calling. Greater rule and greater responsibility also bring less freedom to operate out of one's soul, with the benefit of giving greater expression to one's gifts and calling.

The concept of widening rule should occur naturally throughout one's life. Rule exists in the relationships each person experiences throughout time. These are natural relationships that exist in everyone's lives. For the believer, however, Scripture describes these relationships based on a concept of rule that reflects the person of God.

Marriage

In every relationship in which the love of the Father and Son is meant to be displayed through rule, there is one who should submit to another and one who is required to rule righteously. Such is the general set piece for rule that sets forth the character of God through the exercise of authority. In the husband-and-wife relationship, wives are required to submit to their husbands, and the instructions for the rule of the husband over the wife is meant to model the rule of Christ over the church. Only together do these roles accurately portray some aspect of the Kingdom of Heaven.

> *Wives, be subject to your own husbands, as to the Lord. For the husband is the head of the wife, as Christ also is the head of the church, He Himself being the Savior of the body. But as the church is subject to Christ, so also the wives ought to be to their husbands in everything.* Ephesians 5:21-24 NASB

The husband's authoritative role is defined as loving the wife:

> *Husbands, love your wives, just as Christ also loved the church and gave Himself up for her, so that He might sanctify her, having cleansed her by the washing of water with the word, that He might present to Himself the church in all her glory, having no spot or wrinkle or any such thing; but that she would be holy and blameless. So husbands ought also to love their own wives as their own bodies. He who loves his own wife loves himself; for no one ever hated his own flesh, but nourishes and cherishes it, just as Christ also does the church....* Ephesians 5:25-29 NASB

These roles have no connection to or basis in social constructs of competition, fairness or superiority and inferiority. The submission of a wife to a husband is designed to instruct the husband how to behave toward Christ since in the husband's role as part of the bride, he is required to submit to Christ in the same way that his wife is required to submit to him. Both husband and wife are sons of God. God assigns these roles based upon the housing in which their spirits are placed. If a person's spirit is placed in the human form of a woman who becomes the bride to a husband, then a certain role is designated to this spirit. Similarly, if that spirit is placed in the human form of a man who becomes a husband, a different requirement of rule is assigned. In both cases, whether the flesh in which a spirit appears is male or female, the intent of God in assigning these roles is that of representation rather than that of comparative positioning.

Within the configuration of marriage, involving a husband and a wife, the eternal picture of Christ and the church is presented as bringing the values of the rule of Christ and the submission of the church within the reach of those marriages that might benefit from observing this model. In that regard, marriage is holy because the rule of the husband is deliberately designed to depict the reality of Christ as husband who puts the interests of his wife ahead of his own life and elicits the response from a wife worthy of such boundless love, namely her complete trust of his motives.

In neither the role of the husband or the wife is attention given to preserving personal goals at the expense of the designated representation. Each role is given full expression by the requirements of divine representation. The husband trusts that his determination to fashion his rule after the example of Christ is designed to honor the character of Christ by putting it on display through the sacrifice of his own interest. His belief is that, because Christ is real, the outcomes of his rule will enjoy the support of the presence of Christ.

Similarly, the wife who submits to her husband makes herself vulnerable. Her representation of the bride of Christ submitting to Christ affords her husband contact with that reality that is capable of transforming him into becoming part of the obedient bride. Absent her example, he has no real chance of learning to submit to Christ and is thus excluded from availing himself of all the benefits that come from being positioned accurately in Christ.

The goal of representation is fundamentally different from that of the preservation of one's personal rights as defined legally or socially. The model for marriage is by no means a model of equality. Equality suggests competition in which the goal is to avoid the creation of advantaged or disadvantaged participation in the relationship. In the model of rule depicting Christ and the church, the notion of equality is replaced by the recognition of unique positioning. Equality serves the mindset of the orphan in that it seeks to preserve the imperatives of provision and protection with some degree of certainty of the outcome. The uniqueness of the roles associated with exact representation anticipates both the individual and corporate display of Christ and the church within the model of rule presented through the relationship of a husband and wife. It therefore depends entirely upon the support of Christ for its effectiveness. It is a model unsuitable for anyone except those whose deliberate intent is to put the nature of the love of God on display within the marital form.

The reality is that the marriage model itself becomes holy because it is deliberately set apart to house the purposes of God. Therefore, marriage among believers is incomparable to all other forms of union between two people. Marriage in society is ordinarily entered into in the hope of discovering a greater level of happiness and companionship. This union also has benefits for the society as a whole. Such benefits might include stability for the lives of children and predictability for the continuation of society. But, marriage as defined by any governing body for any reason is not intended to house the presence of God with an eye toward displaying the relationship between Christ and the church. In the Kingdom, however, husbands and wives enter into marriage with the specific intent of displaying the glory of the relationship between Christ and the church and the results of happiness and well-being attend in greater and more lasting ways than just marriage as a form.

That marriage should be a context in which a wife recognizes the authority of the husband and submits to it and that the husband lays down his life for his wife is not a model that is advisable for anyone other than those who have been properly taught and prepared for such a concept of marriage.

Children Obey Your Parents

Similarly, the child-parent relationship in Scripture is one of obedience and righteous rule. "Children obey your parents in the Lord, for this is right. Honor your father and mother (which is the first commandment with a promise), so that it may be well with you, and that you may live long on the earth."[1] The instruction to submit is paired with an instruction on ruling righteously. "Fathers, do not provoke your children to anger, but bring them up in the discipline and instruction of the Lord."[2] Paul explains the purpose of such rule: Children are raised in the "discipline and instruction of the Lord" when fathers rule righteously and when that righteous rule is reciprocated by obedience in the children. This mirrors the Father who loves and the Son who trusts.

Here the model is the presentation of God the Father and His children, operating within the model of a family. Again, the picture is that of human relationships depicting eternal realities. Children are the ones ruled over, while fathers exercise a heavenly mandate to rule righteously. The instruction to those over whom rule is extended is to obey, while those whose duty it is to rule are required in their rule to show the nature of God which is to disciple and provide the instruction of the Lord. Children raised under the rule of fathers who deliberately expose them to the character of God through the manner of the father's rule will very likely transition easily to a personal faith in God the Father as adults.

---

[1] Ephesians 6:1-3 NASB. [2] Ephesians 6:4 NASB.

Employer-Employee Relationship

Paul provides a third set piece for examining rule in relationships:

PART TWO

> *Slaves, be obedient to those who are your masters according to the flesh, with fear and trembling, in the sincerity of your heart, as to Christ; not by way of eyeservice, as men-pleasers, but as slaves of Christ, doing the will of God from the heart. With good will render service as to the Lord, and not to men, knowing that whatever good thing each one does, this he will receive back from the Lord, whether slave or free. And masters, do the same things to them, and give up threatening, knowing that both their Master and yours is in heaven, and there is not partiality in Him."* Ephesians 6:5-9 NASB

Though not directly applicable in modern society, this applies well to instances of voluntary servitude in the employer-employee relationship. Based on these instructions, employees who are believers are required to serve their employers as they would serve Christ, and godly employers are required to model the character of the one who is Lord over all and rule righteously, without partiality for favoritism.

Many believers find themselves in one of these two positions. For the employee, the instruction is to serve as one who is "a servant of Christ doing the will of God from [his] heart."[1] And, to the employer, the model of oversight recognizes that the employer himself has a "master in heaven and there is no favoritism with Him."[2] In this model, the employee's service is not merely for pay, but demonstrates the role of a servant of God who is motivated by love. Even if the employee is treated harshly or with disrespect in the workplace, and even if he seeks redress, all his actions should display an attitude consistent with that of a representative of Christ.

From the employer's viewpoint, rule is meant to be undertaken in a fashion that deliberately sets forth the nature of God, the Master on display. The employer should rule for the benefit of those subject to the rule. Considerations of this sort would not only include thoughtful care for the employees' well-being, but also the establishment of an environment of peaceful and harmonious interchange between employees. Success or productivity in the business is secondary to these considerations and should not be pursued in a manner devoid of the Spirit of God.

The vision or rule in each of these three examples from Scripture is one that puts the authoritative nature of God the Father on display as husband, father and employer, and showcases a complete picture of rule when those under authority similarly display the nature of the sons through submission, obedience, and service to righteous rule.

---

[1]Ephesians 6:7 NASB. [2]Ephesians 6:9 NASB.

Lordship in the Kingdom

These contexts for rule neither require nor suggest reciprocal rule or submission. Love expressed from a position of authority only reflects the character of Christ when it is undertaken without the promise or expectation of reciprocity or benefit to the one in authority. Indeed, the one in authority is asked to adopt the mindset of sacrificing himself or herself for the benefit of those under authority. This makes rule inherently an expression of the spirit of Lordship.

Lordship characterizes rule in the context of the Kingdom of God. All authority to rule in this manner stems from the purpose of representing God the Father in the manner of one's rule. Outside the authority of the Kingdom, rule cannot effectively mimic heavenly principles. Whether the goals are personal success or the maintaining of a religious institution, Lordship does not serve purposes that exist outside of or contrary to the display of the Kingdom on the earth. Therefore, this type of rule cannot be forcibly imported into relationships not predicated on the representation of God nor should anyone try to impose secular social concepts on righteous rule.

Lordship does not place the one in authority into a position of mutual submission. It would be absurd and chaotic if parents were supposed to submit reciprocally to their children. Similarly, there is no suggestion that in the same way that an employee ought to submit to an employer with the expectation that the employer is required to reciprocate by submitting to the employee. If this were true, any righteous rule on the employer's part would be negated by obligation rather than showing a motivation to rule for the benefit of others rooted in love. In the same way, there is no hint of reciprocal submission between husbands and wives. Those under righteous rule receive its benefit without the burden of a quid pro quo, and the one under authority often has the opportunity to express the love of a son by reflecting the character of the one in authority, thereby bringing glory to the one who rules righteously and to Christ whose character is displayed in both the ruler and the one under authority.[1]

 However, there has been a long history of the abuse of wives by husbands and children by fathers, and the church structure has typically proved impotent to address this form of abuse meaningfully. Lacking the ability to affect change, wives are commonly told to submit regardless of the abuse heaped upon her by her husband, because there is this requirement of Scripture.

There are two bases for this (mis)-instruction. The first is that within the form of the state church, one becomes a member simply by being born within the territorial limits of that secular nation. By being baptized into membership and confirmed in adolescence, the individual is considered to have met all the requirements of church membership. From there, the state church has depended upon the existing culture, together with its decrees and teachings, to shape the convictions and, therefore, the social behavior of its members. The reality, however, is that over time society has changed. Most people only attend church when they are christened, confirmed, married, and buried. It is common for people to refer to themselves as members of historic denominations without even minimal participation in formal church activities. Their moral convictions are almost entirely informed by the prevailing societal views whether or not such views contradict the official standing of their church denominations. To require wives to submit to husbands whose behaviors and decisions are entirely unrestrained by an actual relationship to God is highly irresponsible and represents an attempt to maintain the illusion of the influence of Christ where no such restraint actually exists. It is at best farcical, and at its worst has often been lethal.

A second common source of this advice, showing a complete lack of the spirit of Lordship, comes in the context of evangelical and charismatic church memberships where rule is centralized in a single leading figure, and the goal is to have as wide an influence in society as possible. The emphasis is on the numbers of people who regularly attend church meetings. It is common in these settings to advertise for church attendance, and part of the appeal is to remove all possible requirements upon those who might attend. These gatherings are meant primarily to showcase the preacher's oratorial skills as well as the marketing abilities of the executive staff. No one is expected to give an account of his behavior. Even when regular church attendees commit the worst of criminal offenses, the standard response from the leader and church staff is to distance themselves as completely from the persons and their activities as to leave no doubt that they bear no responsibility to culpability in the matters.

The churches will teach that God hates divorce but will offer no governmental form capable for either maturing husbands to model the character of Christ in their rule or to provide wives with the basic right of appeal from the brutish rule of their offending husbands. The result is that the churches' claim to speak accurately to the unrighteous rule of the husband is spurious, since the husband is supported in his rule by the insistence that the wife continues to submit to the unbiblical exercise of authority.

Rule in the Kingdom, defined by the spirit of Lordship, only functions properly within the order of a family. In God's family, authority and training are based upon relationships and the stewardship of the believer's life from childhood to full maturity. One should anticipate that the less mature will be trained by those whose lives have already become mature expressions of the attitude and character of God the Father.[2] This is central to the culture of this family.

Once a son of God has begun to see through the eyes of the spirit, he or she may begin to represent the family of God in widening circles of rule. This describes an eternal, as opposed to purely physical, perspective. From this vantage point, every role of every person's relationships are opportunities designed to put hidden heavenly truths on public display. As opposed to simply a message, reduced to a certain creedal formulation, or the practice of benevolent acts, the Gospel is a way of life to be lived consistently among the rest of human society. It is the difference between things that one does upon certain occasions and the way that one is in all of the incidences of his or her life.

---

[1]Hebrews 3:3-4 NASB. [2]1 John 2:12-14 NASB.

Calling or Template of Rule

Greater measures of rule that manifest certain gifts or particular themes always attend the believer's growth in maturity. These specific ways in which the Holy Spirit enables the believer to function in rule are consistent from one sphere of rule to another. For example, if the individual exhibits an inclination for certain gifts such as discernment, mercy, the desire to bring order, or the recognition of where each person fits in a larger picture of the Body of Christ, the community will begin to recognize the nature of that person's gifts and calling from consistent and repeated patterns. Once the gifts have begun to define the person, they should become a matter of historical note for those familiar with the person's life.

One's calling is the purpose for which they were put on earth. It defines the specific Spiritual endowments from God, resident within a person's spirit. The manner in which an individual will represent God in the earth defines one's calling from stage to stage as he or she matures. For example, Jesus' calling to reconcile men to God:

> *Now all these things are from God, who reconciled us to Himself through Christ and gave us the ministry of reconciliation, namely, that God was in Christ reconciling the world to Himself, not counting their trespasses against them, and He has committed to us the word of reconciliation.* 2 Corinthians 5:18-19 NASB

The spirit resident within Him was the Spirit of Christ. He was supported in this calling through the full range of spiritual gifts.

Other examples in Scripture demonstrate the principle that one's spiritual gifts are specific endowments that serve the person's calling. The apostle Paul was called "to bear [the Lord's] name before the Gentiles and kings and the sons of Israel" and "suffer for [His] name's sake."[1] He was supported in this calling by the primary gift of apostleship as well as all other gifts as needed to support him in the different circumstances in which he found himself as he was pursuing his calling.

The spiritual son of God is raised in stages that involve opportunities to handle greater authority, consistent with new stages of development.

PART TWO

The goal is to become a mature son who puts that aspect of the nature of God that resides in the human spirit on competent display. God undertakes all the training and preparation that precedes the presentation of a mature son with this in mind.

---

¹Act 9:15-16 NASB.

Lordship Over Nature

> *And behold, there arose a great storm on the sea, so that the boat was being covered with the waves; but Jesus Himself was asleep. And they came to Him and woke Him saying, "Save us, Lord; we are perishing!" He said to them, "Why are you afraid, you men of little faith?" Then He got up and rebuked the winds and the sea, and it became perfectly calm. The men were amazed and said, "What kind of a man is this, that even the winds and the sea obey Him?"* Matthew 8:24-27 NASB

This story presents a stark contrast between Jesus and his disciples with respect to nature. Jesus and his disciples were subject to the exact same circumstances, yet He remained asleep while they were in a panic. In a fallen state, mankind has become used to being subject to and dependent upon nature in the constant struggle to survive. This is the perception of the eyes of the soul, which can only react to nature. The world perceives threats whenever natural forces present danger to the physical body, and in the same manner the soul may perceive nature as benevolent or matronly because nature provides sustenance for the physical body. This state of being leads people to both fear and worship nature.

Jesus, however, perceived nature as part of creation and subject to the Spirit of God. The Spirit does not react to, fear, or rely on the creation.

Rather, creation is subject to the rule of the Spirit. Accordingly, a son of God, whose way of life is rooted in the economy of the Spirit will rule over creation rather than fear or worship it. In the story above, Jesus was content to let the storm run its course, because He understood that nature could not alter His purpose in the earth by drowning the ship on which He slept. However, to ease His disciples' panicked state and to demonstrate the command of the Spirit over nature, He commanded the storm, and it obeyed. Jesus' example lays the foundation for the doctrine of Faith and the life that is dependent upon the economy of the Spirit rather than nature.

With the fall, Adam's role in nature changed from one that commanded nature to respond to one that reacted and struggled to survive in his environment. God never rescinded the authority He gave Adam to rule over nature, but He did identify the consequences of Adam's disobedience and rejection of Him:

> *Cursed is the ground because of you; In toil you will eat of it all the days of your life. Both thorns and thistles it shall grow for you; and you will eat the plants of the field; by the sweat of your face you will eat bread, till you return to the ground, because from it you were taken; for you are dust, and to dust you shall return.* Genesis 3:17-19 NASB

As the centuries wore on, mankind lost altogether the expectation of ruling over nature and instead grew in his sophistication of invention and use of technology to understand the world around them and to survive. This change represents a movement from ruling by decrees over nature to ruling by force. Forcing nature to conform to one's will for the ruler's own benefit is a false version of rule, stemming directly from Adam's fall and abdication of the authority God gave to him.

Jesus restored the reality of mankind as rulers in nature. In the desert, He confronted Satan's claim to rule over the earth. He countered

PART TWO

the enemy's lie with the truth that all creation, Satan's included, serves the Lord. Jesus walked in the commission to rule in the earth. He arrested the slide of mankind's departure from this designated place as ruler by demonstrating rule over nature.

In His capacity as the head over the spiritual body known as Christ, He put on display the spirit of Lordship to which each son of God is reintegrated when placed again in the Body of Christ. Regarding the restoration of the right to rule over nature, one can expect to be provided with evidence of that restoration by examples of nature responding to the Spirit's commands. One must learn the propriety associated with accurate and mature rule. The Spirit of God sees and understands the delicate balance of nature and informs the human spirit as to the timing and command of nature. God established the patterns of nature which are generally designed to benefit humans overall. Jesus neither sought to restrain nature continuously, nor did He constantly command nature to serve Him. In the example in which He calmed the storm, Jesus was not compelled by the ferocity or threat posed by the storm itself, rather the incident provided the opportunity for Him to demonstrate command over nature, serving as a lesson in faith, the economy of the Spirit and Lordship over nature. He gave extraordinary commands to nature only when divine interests were facilitated by such commands.

The Lord Jesus Christ could exercise rule over the elements because He remained in the position to which He had been appointed by God and had not conceded to the enemy's attempts to draw Him into rebellion and disobedience. As the Son, representing God on the earth, He carried the seven Spirits of God, and the spirit of Lordship includes being lord over creation. As in all forms of rule, rule over nature should neither distort its natural cycles nor exploit it for the purposes of those struggling to find provision and protection. The spirit of Lordship is characterized by rule designed for the betterment and well-being of those subject to rule.

Conclusion Regarding the Spirit of Lordship

Imparting the spirit of Lordship to His body, Christ restored both the vision and the practical implementation of righteous rule, representing the Father like ambassadors to the earth. The restoration of that Spirit re-inaugurated the rule of the Kingdom of Heaven upon the earth. Until now, the structure of this rule was veiled in various archetypes. Moses, David and others are types of the individual rule of Jesus. The nation of Israel under the rule of David and Solomon, and later when it reemerged from the captivity in Babylon, Nehemiah and Zerubbabel, present depictions of the corporate governance of the Kingdom of God. In light of the restoration of the spirit of Lordship, the Kingdom of God has emerged from among the nations of mankind. The spirit of Lordship will present a government showing the good order of heaven, characterized by righteousness and peace and will be visible in the countenance of its citizenry.

The Spirit of Wisdom

> *Wisdom has built her house. She has hewn out her seven pillars; She has prepared her food, she has mixed her wine; She has also set her table; She has sent out her maidens, she calls from the tops of the heights of the city: "Whoever is naïve, let him turn in there!" To him who lacks understanding she says, "Come, eat of my food and drink of the wine I have mixed. Forsake your folly and live and proceed in the way of understanding."* Proverbs 9:1-6 NASB

> *By wisdom a house is built, and by understanding it is established; and by knowledge the rooms are filled with all precious and pleasant riches. A wise man is strong, and a man of knowledge increases power. For by wise guidance, you will*

> *wage war, and in abundance of counselors there is victory.*
> *Wisdom is too exalted for a fool; He does not open his mouth*
> *in the gate.* Proverbs 24:3-7 NASB

Wisdom arises from the complete understanding of God's purposes from epoch to epoch. From a human standpoint, experiencing and observing creation from the inside, human history often seems disjointed, haphazard, unconnected, and unintentional, but Scripture clearly says that God knows the end from the beginning. Within God exists the beginning and the end of all things.[1] Not only does He know the entire course of human history, but its events come from within Him, serving His purposes throughout the epochs.

> *It is He who made the earth by His power, Who established*
> *the world by His wisdom; and by His understanding He has*
> *stretched out the heavens.* Jeremiah 10:12; 51:15 NASB

The structure of creation came out of Him. Wisdom is the result of understanding this concept, which one can only fathom through the Spirit of God's impartation.

The Spirit is not confined to any particular epoch of time. God describes this characteristic of omnipresence by introducing Himself to Moses as "I AM."[2] Jesus also described Himself to John on the island of Patmos, as "the Alpha and the Omega...who is and who was and who is to come, the Almighty."[3] The wisdom of God is an attribute of the Spirit whose reality invades every aspect of the temporal so thoroughly as not only to *know* the beginning and the end of any matter, but to *be* the beginning and the end of the matter. He is present in everything.

For those pursuing their destiny in Christ, hindsight will often reveal the wisdom with which the Spirit guides their steps. As an example from Scripture, the young Joseph, having been sold by his brothers into slavery in Egypt eventually found himself in the king's prison.

PART TWO

Through a series of events beginning with visions of a grand destiny, he eventually finds himself the prisoner of the envy of others in complete captivity in an Egyptian dungeon. He could objectively say that his life was an unrelenting series of dreadful circumstances, each succeeding phase being more horrifying than before. As he approached his thirtieth year, perhaps half his life had been spent in dreadful circumstances. Although, he himself lived a relatively blameless life. Yet, he became the ruler of Egypt, helping to save and perpetuate the family that carried the promise of Christ.

Every mature son of God must at some point become personally familiar with his own version of Joseph's story. One can easily acknowledge God's wisdom when experiencing the end result of His benevolence and kindness. It is much more difficult to walk in the wisdom of the Spirit, who knows the end of the matter, while in the grip of arduous circumstances, when one cannot see his circumstances from an eternal point of view. However, these are the situations that allow God's wisdom to shine through the believer's life. When, by faith, one lives a life informed by the spirit of Wisdom, the end result is that God's love is visible not only to the believer, but to any who observe his way of life.

God's point of view is eternal. Whereas, the way man sees everything is from a temporal point of view. God's point of view is incomparable and incompatible with the human perspective, but it is the source from which the wisdom of God springs forth. One must see through the eyes of the human spirit and judge matters from an eternal perspective to access the wisdom of God. It is not possible for man to share in the wisdom of God without being joined to the Spirit of God. The availability of the spirit of Wisdom is exclusively within the person of Christ and is first pure, then peaceable, gentle, reasonable, full of mercy and good fruits, unwavering, without hypocrisy.[4]

---

[1]Revelation 1:8, 21:6, 22:13 NASB. [2]See Exodus 3:14 NASB. [3]Revelation 1:8; See also 21:6; 22:13 NASB. [4]James 3:15, 17 NASB.

PART TWO

Contrast Between Wisdom and Reason

Even though determining the course of future events is beyond human wisdom, the value of knowing where the future will lead has occupied people at every level of society through the span of history. The bane of humankind is the loss of control. Fear, bordering on paranoia, is often the underlying motivation for this relentless search for control. Whoever manages to predict future trends and to position themselves or the entities they lead advantageously vis-à-vis future trends are considered to be the exceptional leaders and the wisest people of their times.

Temporal orientation and human reasoning are inextricably linked. Humans either take information that precedes that which they are trying to understand and deduce a logical conclusion based on observation and analysis, or they begin with the current subsequent information—the effect in a cause-and-effect relationship—and attempt to induce a preceding (in time and generality) greater truth. In every case, human reasoning is the filler where truth and certainty are absent. If we were to place the process of reasoning and time on the same line, absolute truths would all be points of origin. The Spirit of God knows all things, making the spiritual perspective a singular view of beginning to end. Mankind's soul and consciousness are trapped within the temporal resulting in guessing at everything that is not experienced directly, that is everything that comes before or after an instantaneous moment in time.

All rationalizations seek to predict the human soul's range of possible responses based upon patterns of prior behavior and progress along a linear path. The greatest focus in this process is on those variable factors that have the potential of influencing the ultimate conclusion. The goal of asserting or retaining control motivates the process from beginning to end. The preoccupation of the human soul is the search for relevance within a single lifetime. The result ignores the overarching events of human history that lay on the path of God's intent to produce a predetermined outcome. From the linear perspective, the absence of an overarching direction establishes the potential of the extraordinary as the ultimate obsession.

Within this view, it is possible for everyone to shape circumstances to express their unique convictions. Nothing is predetermined and everything is subject to the possible control and influence of those powerful and strong enough to shape the future as they will. Although, it remains inexorably true that "the paths of glory lead but to the grave," (Thomas Gray, "Elegy written in a Country Churchyard") the illusion of shaping history by one's life remains a dominant motivation among mankind.

The spirit of Wisdom imparts the incomparable advantage of an eternal point of view, which exists and is informed by the state of knowing the end from the beginning. Instead of trying to assert control over all the important variables, the spirit of Wisdom operates by parsing those things that carry eternal value from the things that are merely incidental. An eternal point of view casts all humans as players within a predetermined plan, which has been moving forward inexorably through time, and the end of which is known from the beginning. The destinies of individuals are designed to unfold within the ambit of this preexisting direction. The value of an individual's life does not eventually shape or alter this plan. The only exception to this was when God chose to enter the realm of man in the person of Jesus to correct the deviation from the plan and to restore the ability of people to continue to function within God's divinely established original intent.

The foundations of wisdom are established upon the recognition that God has already preempted the trajectory of all human existence, and humans were created with specific roles to play that would fulfill this preexisting divine imperative. Individual destinies are designed to contain and to present portions of this divine imperative. The biblical concept of predestination is that "we are His workmanship, created in Christ Jesus for good works, which God prepared beforehand so that we would walk in them."[1]

Jesus was thoroughly aware of this fact and considered that His life on earth was foreordained to divine specifications. Even in His most anguished moment, He yet possessed the awareness of this truth. In the battle between His soul and His spirit waged in the dead of night in the inner recesses of His being as He knelt in prayer in the garden of Gethsemane, for Him it came down to one definitive declaration, ."..yet not as I will, but as You will."[2] This was the ultimate acknowledgement that even He possessed only the choice between the illusion of control and submitting ultimately to the eternal plan.

Entrance into divine wisdom begins with the acknowledgement of this preemption. The choice of man, therefore, is not whether he is able to influence divinely set foundations, but simply whether he will find his peace in his discovery of the eternal imperative and finding it, submit fully to it. The quality of the submission of the human soul to the sovereignty of God defines the extent to which he loves God. It also defines his practice of the fear of the Lord. Obedience that is credited as faith springs from the fear of the Lord although ultimately it is the expression of the manner in which one loves God.

The spirit of Wisdom restores the understanding of an eternal point of view, not only that one exists, but defines the nature of it as well. The certainty of an eternal point of view is rooted in the reality that from the vantage point of the throne of God, all that will ever unfold in the realm of humanity has been foreordained, and with the exception of the individual's right to participate, everything else has been predetermined.

---

[1]Ephesians 2:10 NASB. [2]Matthew 26:39 NASB.

PART TWO

Wisdom Builds the House

> *Therefore, holy brethren, partakers of a heavenly calling, consider Jesus, the Apostle and High Priest of our confession. He was faithful to Him who appointed Him, as Moses also was in all His house. For He has been counted worthy of more glory than Moses, by just so much as the builder of the house has more honor than the house. For every house is built by someone, but the builder of all things is God. Now Moses was faithful in all his house as a servant, for a testimony of those things which were to be spoken later; but Christ was faithful as a Son over His house—whose house we are, if we hold fast our confidence and the boast of our hope firm until the end.* Hebrews 3:1-6 NASB

The House of God must be understood from an eternal point of view in order for the building of it, in the present, to be consistent with the original intent of God. Viewed from an eternal point of view, the House of God is His family. It is comprised of His sons throughout the generations of mankind. Inevitably, the existence of a son establishes the household of his father in the location in which the son has been put. Earth, therefore, was created to host the family of God. Not only did God intend to have a son in the earth, but the mandate to be "fruitful and multiply and replenish the earth" indicated that God anticipated the long-term tenure of His family in the earth.

Between Adam and Jesus, the first and last sons, are sixty-two generations. The House of God can only be described, then, as a multigenerational family. Although it is common to think of building the House of God as a matter of recruiting converts to denominational alliances, the eternal point of view of the House of God is quite different. It is the unrelenting progression through the generations of those who are connected by spirit to God Himself and being assembled to the Spirit of Christ.

PART TWO

The exact order of the House of God existed in the mind of God before the foundations of the world. The earth itself was created to host the advent in time of the House of God. Throughout history, when man lost the knowledge of God's original intent, his behavior predictably turned to the worship of nature. Yet, from an eternal point of view all of the natural world, indeed the entire universe, was established to host the family of God.

Nothing could be of greater importance to God than the relentless unfolding of His eternal plan for His family. Although all mankind was created with the destiny of being included in the family of God, not all will choose to be assembled into Christ. But for those who choose to be, they will participate in the unfolding of this divine imperative during their time upon the earth. Beyond their lives on the earth, their existence will continue until the final consummation of all that was originally in the mind of God for His family. The duty of the assembled sons is to faithfully execute the requirements of their destiny as servants of God. In the corporate Body, or House of God, each part fits its predesigned destiny and can only function after it has been properly assembled into its predetermined place.

The House of God is not an institutional house, but an organic one. Its functions are not by positions but by relationships. Particular grants of authority are given on the basis of one's calling. Receiving Christ as He appears in another requires that one submit to the authority of Christ in the other. The purpose of God in building a house is not merely to show that He can build one. His family exists on the earth to put the complete nature of His love on display.

The arrangement of the parts is in furtherance of their function so that the totality of divine order might be displayed in a governmental form that might become instructional to the nations as a pattern for national life. It is the reason that those employed in laying out the order of the House of God must be faithful to establish the administration according to its existing form in heaven. Only then can the result present the heavenly mandate.

Moses was instructed to build the tabernacle according to the pattern that he saw on the mountain because the pattern was a type and shadow of what was in heaven. The Levitical priests served at a sanctuary that was a copy and shadow of what is in heaven. This is why Moses received the warning: "See to it that you make everything according to the pattern shown you on the mountain. But in fact, the ministry Jesus has received is as superior to theirs as the covenant of which He is mediator is superior to the old one, since the new covenant is established on the better promises."[1]

Whoever is born of the Spirit has the capability of seeing the reality of heavenly things. However, he must wait until the revelation of the reality is given. To everyone else, there is no reality beyond the visible. So, in order to prepare mankind to be able to receive heavenly realities when they come, types and shadows of the realities are given as placeholders until the reality comes.

All religious beliefs and practices stem from a view of the types and shadows as the realities themselves. The types and shadows are endowed with a mystical quality that elevates them to a transcendent place and relates to them as an undisclosed mystery. The practitioners of religion position themselves as keepers and decoders of these symbols, thereby making themselves indispensable to whatever understandings they manage to convince others are referenced by these symbols. They are, in fact, functioning priests whose task it is to connect people to the advantages that flow to them as a consequence of their devotion to the mystery.

The appeal of both the religious form and the attending priests is based upon how widespread the acceptance of these concepts among human societies and within human culture is. As such, they form a considerable opposition to the reality in as much as they succeed in defining human culture by reference to these symbols and the referenced mysteries that they portend. They also become fruitful ground for manipulation of large segments of the population by manipulating them through both fear and familiarity. If we build according to the convenience of man, it cannot serve the purposes of God. Religion, therefore, is perhaps the most valuable tool for the service of the enemy of both God and man.

The realities that presently exist in heaven are destined to come to earth in their appointed time. When they appear upon the earth, they take on the forms and functions on earth as they have been previously in heaven. At that time, the shadow merges into the reality, and the heavenly becomes the earthly.

From the foundations of the earth, the Lamb was slain. From the days of Cain and Abel to John the Baptist, the symbol of the lamb dominated the practice of fallen man's access to God. The lamb was the most significant religious symbol linking God and man until the day when the reality came to replace the type and shadow. On that day the reality of heaven made its appearance on the earth. A Spirit known as Christ had come from heaven and was contained in the body of a man named Jesus. God would reconcile man to Himself in Christ and the man, Jesus, would allow God the use of His body up to and including the cross which was the place where He would meekly submit, as a lamb, to being offered as a sacrifice to God.

With that in mind, John the Baptist would declare, "Behold the Lamb of God who takes away the sins of the world." In his capacity as a fully qualified Levitical priest, whose father was himself qualified to offer the sacrifices in the temple thus making John a priest in line to offer sacrifices, John's first and only known act as a Levitical priest was to examine the sacrifice to be offered and to declare its suitability for that purpose. Jesus, having been judged to be the Lamb of God, "without spot, wrinkle or blemish" as required by the law, then requested of the priest to wash the sacrifice so that it was ritualistically made ready to be sacrificed. Upon the completion of John's acknowledgement and preparation by washing, God Himself confirmed that John had declared on earth what was true in heaven: "This is my beloved Son in whom I am well pleased."[2] Jesus was anointed from heaven in the presence of all when the Holy Spirit took the form of a dove and alighted on Him.

It is common for the Spirit of God to be depicted symbolically as oil. In this case Jesus was not anointed with the symbol of the Spirit, but with the Spirit Himself, because the type and shadow was being replaced with the reality. Jesus was the Lamb who had been depicted previously in numerous references.

The apostle John was invited into heaven to witness what resulted from Jesus' crucifixion from heaven's viewpoint.[3] He saw the throne of God before which the Lamb appeared as the one qualified to reveal what had been written for long ages past but was sealed up in a scroll under seven seals. Before He took the scroll and began to reveal that which God had purposed to bring about on the earth from ages past, a new song was sung in heaven.[4]

When the reality of heaven is brought to the earth it is meant to be exactly on earth as it is in heaven. Until then, the type and shadow keeps human culture familiar with the possibility of particular heavenly things coming into the earth. What was prophesied to come as a result of the death and resurrection of the Lamb, is as certain to occur as the reality of the Lamb Himself coming was. An entire nation of people will be gathered out of all the nations to be formed into a royal priesthood to represent the full showing of the love of God. This reality has already been shown in heaven and John was invited to come up and to witness it. As surely as the Lamb existed in heaven and was slain before the foundations of the earth in the eternal view of things, eventually that same reality migrated into earth and was true on the earth exactly as it was in heaven. So also, a holy nation previously seen in heaven will appear on the earth and be earth's reality just as has been seen in heaven.

This house will be built in the earth according to the pattern that has already been unsealed in heaven. All of heaven's authority and power is dedicated to seeing this reality come upon the earth. Men are co-laborers with God when they consent to being used for the furtherance of that which God intends. When man attempts to offer his own creations to God, his worship is disregarded in the same way that Cain's sacrifice was rejected. It is not that God does not value the piety of man. It is that his piety cannot by itself produce the will of God upon the earth.

Piety by itself is of no value to God. The advancement of what He intended to do is the only thing that benefits man ultimately, therefore, the offering of one's piety as a substitute for the will of God relegates the person to the status of an immature child. God may have mercy upon a child in his ignorance, but He will not entrust His eternal purposes into the care of the carnal and the immature.[5]

---

[1]Hebrews 8:5-6 NIV. [2]Matthew 3:17 NASB. [3]See Revelation 4, 5 NASB. [4]Revelation 5:9-10 NASB. [5]1 Corinthians 3, 1 Corinthians 2:1-16 NASB.

The Renewing of the Mind

Therefore, I urge you, brothers and sisters, in view of God's mercy, to offer your bodies as a living sacrifice, holy and pleasing to God—this is your true and proper worship. Do not conform to the pattern of this world but be transformed by the renewing of your mind. Then you will be able to test and approve what God's will is—His good, pleasing and perfect will. Romans 12:1-2 NIV

Since Adam's fall in the garden and the resultant opening of the eyes of the human soul, the general state of humankind is summed up as "seeing, they may see and not perceive, and while hearing, they may hear and not understand."[1] Adam's choice to rely on his own wisdom and to disconnect from the mind of God interposed human wisdom and understanding to compete with a spiritual perspective. A spiritual perspective requires a connection with the Spirit of God without the interference from the human soul, and it accepts the restraint of a limited heavenly view because of the underlying understanding that the Spirit knows all things. The soul is unrestrained by a heavenly wisdom and earthbound in all of its perspectives. Through Adam, people's vision for their existence as that of spirit being was lost and replaced by a perspective that we are all purely natural beings. Adam and all his descendants default to an understanding of the natural world as the source for wisdom.

Lacking the innate ability to relate to God Spirit to spirit, as Father and sons, humankind's default position with respect to God who is the Father of our spirits by His original intent, is that of an orphan, unable to recognize God as Father or access that relationship. Humankind's orphan culture exists in a state of understanding and function that responds to the physical environment and adapts to the requirements for survival. The result has been that the wisdom of man comes from observations, history, nature, and patterns therein. This culture evolved around provision and protection as the central imperatives of one's existence. Although people have become adept at survival without God's help, they make very little progress toward reconciling with God as sons, which is the prerequisite for accessing the spirit of Wisdom. To retake the wisdom of God, the mind of man's spirit must be freed from the control of the mind of the soul.

For the son of God, when the human spirit's mind fellowships with the Spirit of God the soul begins to revert to its original subordinate condition. When one operates out of the mind of the spirit, he is said to be "spiritually minded" and when he operates out of the mind of his soul he is considered to be "carnally minded."

> *...Because the carnal mind [is] enmity against God: for it is not subject to the law of God, neither indeed can be. So then they that are in the flesh cannot please God.* Romans 8:7-8 KJV

> *The Spirit Himself testifies with our spirit that we are God's children.* Romans 8:16 NIV

The Spirit of God connects to the spirit of man and imparts the wisdom that resides in God to the mind of the human spirit. Every person has this capacity for a connection to the mind of God—Spirit to spirit. However, mankind's default nature imposes the soul's mind between this connection. The result is supplanting truth with reason based on carnal, sensual, and devilish influences. The fix for this condition is the reclaiming of the spirit's dominion over the soul, in which condition the soul may translate wisdom and understanding from the spirit into the natural environment. This chance comes through a process stewarded by the Spirit of God that mirrors one's growth as a son of God.

The flow of the wisdom from the Spirit of God brings about a renewing of the mind. The wisdom of God changes one's nature so that he is able to accept the wisdom that comes from the way in which God arranges His work among mankind by the understanding that He knows the end from the beginning. This wisdom allows the individual to participate in what God is doing in the earth according to God's timing. When a person is led by the Spirit, he can discern the distinction between God's wisdom and the ways of fallen man and consistently choose to align himself with the wisdom of God in all things.

PART TWO

The renewing of the mind requires a change in culture. Human culture defines one's interpretive paradigms. The restoration of mankind's original nature in which the human soul is subject to the spirit's reality is the only way to unseat the dominant influence of culture as the interpretive paradigm determining the soul's view of reality.[2] Religious traditions form a substantial basis for much of traditional human cultures. Uprooting religious traditions in favor of a living connection with the Spirit of God is, perhaps, the most difficult challenge confronting the sons of God, because religious traditions pretend to be the word of God by interpreting the Scriptures according to these traditions. For example, despite having the Messiah in their midst, the Jewish traditions of antiquity required that they reject Jesus.

Jesus' claim to be the Son of God was at the center of the objections to Him among both the common people and religious leaders. The veil of tradition lies heavily upon the hearts of men and serves the role of keeping them firmly entrenched in the view that is generally acceptable both to them and to their societies. The soul delights in tradition because its requirements may be mastered and obeyed without any loss of the soul's control through uncertainty. One can mechanically or ritualistically fulfill the requirements of culture and tradition and use his accomplishments to ignore personal criticisms.

Sonship is the living out of a relational paradigm in which the Father represents Himself through the son, and the son forgoes his independent ambition to embrace his identity as defined by His Father. In this model, each generation contributes to the plan formed before the foundations of the world, and therefore, participates in the inevitable outcome. When the mind of the spirit rules, the vision of reality is informed by the Spirit of God, and man may act upon God's wisdom and choose to participate in the eternal plan. The renewing of the mind is the transition from the dominance of the mind of the soul to the preeminence of the mind of the spirit. This transition is a fundamental requirement in order for man to be able to understand

and recognize the will of God in every matter. This is a direct requirement for the spirit of Wisdom in an individual.[3]

---

[1]Mark 4:12 NASB; see also Isaiah 6:9 NIV. [2]Mark 7:4-8 NIV; See Galatians 1:14-15 NIV (departure from the traditions that predisposed Paul). [3]Luke 7:35 NIV.

Sons of Zion vs. Sons of Greece

I will bend Judah as I bend my bow and fill it with Ephraim. I will rouse your sons, Zion, against your sons, Greece, and make you like a warrior's sword. Zechariah 9:13 NIV

The Sons of Greece

The wisdom of the soul, formed out of human reason, has come to be the basis of most decision making. This is true in every human endeavor, including religion. Human wisdom is firmly entrenched within ecclesiastical circles. This is evident in the predictability of institutional responses to problems within the congregation or leadership. Church leaders predictably will favor the institution over the people and protect those who act in defense of the institution, even at the expense of truth. Church leaders resort to legal standards as the basis of their decisions. Legalism over truth for the sake of the current institution affected even Jesus' efforts. Those that voted to crucify Jesus rather than to examine the veracity of the claims surrounding His activities reasoned, in part, "It is expedient for you that one man die for the people, and that the whole nation not perish."[1] This was articulated by the high priest Caiaphas.

Caiaphas provides an interesting view on wisdom and understanding of the spirit in contrast to that of the soul's logical reason. Earlier in the same year Jesus was crucified, Caiaphas prophesied correctly regarding Jesus' death and its purpose.

> *But one of them, Caiaphas, who was high priest that year, said to them, "You know nothing at all, nor do you take into account that it is expedient for you that one man die for the people, and that the whole nation not perish." Now he did not say this on his own initiative, but being high priest that year, he prophesied that Jesus was going to die for the nation, and not for the nation only, but in order that He might also gather together into one the children of God who are scattered abroad.* John 11:49-52 NASB

Lacking the wisdom of God, Caiaphas could not see how Jesus' death, one who opposed the ruling establishment, could serve God's purposes without also serving the establishment's interests. To him, knowing Jesus was meant to die for the benefit of God's children could only be interpreted as nullifying and disproving Jesus' claims. Whereas, God's wisdom would have revealed what Peter spoke on the day of Pentecost:

> *Men of Israel, listen to these words: Jesus the Nazarene, a man attested to you by God with miracles and wonders and signs which God performed through Him in your midst, just as you yourselves know—this Man, delivered over by the predetermined plan and foreknowledge of God, you nailed to a cross by the hands of godless men and put Him to death. But God raised Him up again, putting an end to the agony of death, since it was impossible for Him to be held in its power...Therefore let all the house of Israel know for certain that God has made Him both Lord and Christ—this Jesus whom you crucified.* Acts 2:22-24, 36 NASB

God's purpose endured, but the wisdom of men represented by Caiaphas's own interpretation of his factual prophecy could not see the truth until they were touched by the Holy Spirit acting through the apostles. The pinnacle of human wisdom has as its origin the great

PART TWO

Greek philosophers whose greatest legacy to Western Civilization is their distinctly intellectual culture. Greece represents the conscious development of logical processes as the basis for understanding the world around us and for exploring "metaphysical" concepts like truth and morality. Greek culture is the bedrock of western education.

While the human soul's capacity for rational thought is a powerful tool to breach the natural world and introduce spiritual realities, when that capacity is filled only with human wisdom, the person loses the ability to predicate rational thought on transcendent realities. This makes any search for truth circular—being limited to the present, observable universe—and therefore futile. The inadequacy of reason to apprehend Truth should be apparent. Yet, lacking any soul-based alternative these processes have been enthroned as an adequate means to deem truth as that which can be readily explained or understood by the human mind and present observable reality. Reason as the means of determining truth is a fundamental assumption of western culture. The pretensions of reason go far beyond its actual capabilities, as its ardent proponents are indiscriminate in the application of reason in their attempts to apprehend and examine that which inherently lies beyond the reach of reason, namely the nature of God. As a result, this aspect of the human soul, when unrestrained by the Spirit, loses its intended function of bridging the spiritual and natural realities, and becomes that which defines the whole of reality itself, without consideration of the lost ability to comprehend the spiritual, non-temporal reality.

It is the pleasure of God to make Himself known through His delegates. Accessing the transcendent order of God, though unavailable through reason, is readily available through revelation. Revelation is that which the Spirit of God communicates to the human spirit both directly and through messengers. Revelation does not come to the carnal mind, but to the mind of the spirit. The spiritual mind belongs to the spirit of man and houses the ability to fellowship with the eternal Spirit of God.² This fellowship includes both the communication itself and the understanding or interpretation of the communication, such that, like Caiaphas, one may hear the message, but without a spiritual mind he or she cannot understand or act upon it. Any conception of God that is reached through the rational process lacks value that comes from God's desire to reveal Himself.

The ideas about God that emerge from the Greek legacy are based "on the flesh," meaning they are limited to the natural world and the visible creation. Such ideas are "hostile toward God; for [the mind set on the flesh] does not subject itself to the law of God, for it is not even able to do so."³ In the encounter in the garden between Satan and Adam and Eve, the enemy sowed enmity between them and God. God responded by recognizing that His ways would always be in conflict with the ways of man as influenced by the enemy. Although Greece was not the source of enmity between God and man, it was the situs in which this enmity was given both form and deliberate study and became the preeminent gift of Greek civilization, given first to the Roman Empire, and then ultimately to the entire world. In the day when the wisdom of God is given to renew the minds of men and bring them out of the deep culture of religion and false concepts of God, the struggle will be between the sons of God and the heirs of Greek culture.

The significance of this is the importance attributed to reason as the basis of wisdom. Those who seek to understand God through the process of reason are called the sons of Greece, and those who understand God by revelation are the sons of Zion.

---

[1]John 11:50 NASB. [2]See Romans 8:14 NASB. [3]Romans 8:7 NASB.

PART TWO

The Sons of Zion

The sons of Zion are those who throughout human history, have maintained a continuing contact with God. God has always had a people in the earth, even in the darkest days of human depravity. Noah walked with God when the thoughts and intent of the hearts of men were "evil continually"—so much so that "God repented of making man":

> *And God saw that the wickedness of man was great in the earth, and that every imagination of the thoughts of his heart was only evil continually. And it repented the Lord that he had made man on the earth, and it grieved him at his heart. And the Lord said, I will destroy man whom I have created from the face of the earth; both man and beast, and the creeping thing, and the fowls of the air; for it repenteth me that I have made them. But Noah found grace in the eyes of the Lord.* Genesis 6:5-8 KJV

God wiped out all of humanity with the exception of Noah and his family and effectively restarted His plan with Noah.

Similarly, Abraham was one of the few righteous men in his day and God deposited the promise for the redemption of man into his lineage. This continuity depended upon certain individuals, prior to Christ, because mankind had lost its connection to God as Father and as Spirit. Humanity in general was struggling to maintain God in its knowledge, which had to be preserved through culture. These ancient personages were the human lineage through whom a spiritual people, known as the sons of God, continued on the earth despite the lost connection to God via the human spirit. These sons of God were mostly characterized by their faithfulness to a transcendent order put in place as a showdown of the heavenly order by their primogenitor Adam. There is a partial record of these men of faith in Hebrews 11.[1]

While these individuals helped preserve the culture of a spiritual people through types and shadows and with God's help in giving the law, Jesus was the complete archetypal Son of God. He brought forward the case of Israel's refusal to accept the reminders of God, which were brought to them through these sons of righteousness.[2] Through Him, any person can reconcile to God, Spirit to spirit, restoring God's wisdom to these sons of Zion.

Conflict between the sons of reason (Greece) and the sons of revelation (Zion) is inevitable because each exists juxtaposed to a dramatically different view of reality. Zion represents a distinct cultural alternative to every other permutation of human culture. The sons of God believe that it is possible to live in the earth while being governed in every way by wisdom from heaven. They do not see that life on the earth must be separated from the rule of Christ. The earth itself is considered a territory within the domain of the Kingdom of Heaven, and subject to the rule of Jesus as King.[3] The sons of Zion view themselves as, first and foremost, citizens of the Kingdom of Heaven, comprising both the invisible and visible world and subjects of Christ the King. The bedrock of their wisdom is the understanding that God knows the end of every matter from the beginning and controls the flow of all events so thoroughly that the son of Zion has no need to predict the future in order to live in security and stability upon the earth. Instead, his mandate is to discern the eternal purposes of God that are unfolding upon the earth during his lifetime and to accurately align himself with these mandates.

---

[1]Hebrews 11:1-5, 7-9, 11-13 NASB. [2]Matthew 23:35-38 NIV. [3]Matthew 28:18 NASB.

The Conflict Between the Sons of Zion and the Sons of Greece

The sons of Zion and the sons of Greece represent parallel trends among humanity. Increasingly, human societies believe in the need for uniform rules governing the fundamental systems of global society. The emergence of these systems and the need for regulation requires that, globally, governments ignore religious imperatives in favor of uniform applicability to the point at which secular global government will decide what imperatives should govern every individual's existence in the system. The result will be that spiritual imperatives that do not center on mere survival will be nonconforming and disruptive, at a minimum, and may eventually be deemed harmful to global society.

The mandate of the sons of God remains unaltered and is primarily occupied with showing the nature of God. Within the theological framework of large segments of religious people, the theology regarding the Kingdom of Heaven has deferred its existence on the earth to a future time, but the sons of Zion live and operate within the framework of belief that the Kingdom of Heaven presently exists on the earth and is the basis of their authority and function.

The sons of Zion have always looked to heaven for their purpose and administration. This will resolve itself by the emergence of the sons of Zion, formed into a holy nation, living upon the earth empowered by the Kingdom of Heaven and displaying the wisdom that comes from the Spirit of God. God will work through the sons of Zion to show His divine nature and invite mankind to come to Him for their identity and purpose in the earth.

The sons of Greece will include, among their numbers, a large contingent of religious people. These will provide a spiritual flavor to a secularized view of God, complete with an administration designed to assure human survival and supply through the efforts of man. A kind of spirituality fashioned around a notion of love for humanity and the logic of common survival will be viewed as an altruism that supports the initiatives to produce a framework of cooperation that ensures the survival of humankind in general. A notion of God will evolve out of central values, relating to provision and protection. The books that are considered scripture by the various world religions will be quoted in support of the brotherhood of man as a transcendent and divine concept.

The heart of the conflict between these two types of human beings is nothing short of the summary of the lives of the two sons of God, Adam and Jesus. The deception that Adam embraced in the garden, when he rejected his Father and turned to his survival as his priority, left the legacy of a form of wisdom that glorifies human survival. With dwindling resources and competing philosophies all the populations of the earth that have derived from Adam will reach the zenith of the wisdom of this culture by agreeing to deify the brotherhood of man, out of the necessity of survival.

Jesus, by contrast, never rejected the Father, but submitted His life, including His death on the cross to the representation of the glory of the nature of God. The sons of God, who have been made so by submitting to the truth of the person of Christ, continue to represent God on the earth. All the principles that were put on display in the person of Jesus will be conclusively demonstrated through the collection of the sons of God into the corporate form of a holy nation. They will become the alternative to the coalition of nations into one global government. The wisdom from heaven will seem backward, restrictive, parochial, and traditional. It will be considered the enemy of progress and anti-human-societal-development. This wisdom will be rejected throughout the nations and those who advocate and practice the representation of God will be hated among all the nations:

> *Nation will rise against nation, and kingdom against kingdom. There will be famines and earthquakes in various places. All these are the beginning of birth pains. Then you will be handed over to be persecuted and put to death, and you will be hated by all nations because of me.* Matthew 24:7-9 NIV

PART TWO

Because of the great shift toward this new concept of transcendence, those who hold firmly to the testimony of Christ will suddenly find themselves in the position of being regarded as parochial and unchanged. Change will be viewed as progress, while holding firmly to the truth will be viewed as human regression. The wisdom of God will be unfavorably compared to the wisdom of the world.

The world is incapable of understanding the wisdom of God and will soon become altogether intolerant of it.[1] In the restoration of the spirit of Wisdom, God is restoring to His sons an eternal point of view, against which to see and understand the currents in the world and to choose to position themselves under the mandates of heaven. While the wisdom of the world continues to betray the hope of its adherents, the spirit of Wisdom, sustained by the continuous flow of revelation from the throne of God, will cause the children of God to understand their times and to retain their confidence in the midst of growing alarm. The peace and good order of the House of God is what will cause it both to be hated by the unregenerate and sought after by the honest of heart.

---

[1] 1 Corinthians 1:17-2:16 NASB.

The Spirit of Understanding

The spirit of Understanding and the spirit of Wisdom are closely related. Wisdom is the result, conclusion or decided course of action based upon faith in an eternal perspective that God knows the end from the beginning. The spirit of Understanding is the grant of that eternal perspective, moving beyond simply trusting the Spirit's perspective to accessing some of the details of it. The spirit of Wisdom is administrative, showing how one should act to be consistent with God's purpose. Understanding is when the Spirit is given to know why that action is consistent with God's purpose, which provides a glimpse into the eternal perspective itself.

From the temporal experience, understanding is akin to hindsight in which one can see and understand the value of the path taken. The Spirit of God grants understanding to support the wisdom of His directives.

> *For this reason also, since the day we heard of it, we have not ceased to pray for you and to ask that you may be filled with the knowledge of His will in all spiritual wisdom and understanding so that you will walk in a manner worthy of the Lord, to please Him in all respects, bearing fruit in every good work and increasing in the knowledge of God.* Colossians 1:9-10 NASB

The spirit of Understanding can be translated to the natural reality through communion with the Holy Spirit.

> *The Holy Spirit rightly spoke through Isaiah the prophet to your fathers saying, "Go to this people and say, 'You will keep on hearing, but will not understand; and you will keep on seeing, but will not perceive; for the heart of this people has become dull and with their ears they scarcely hear, and they have closed their eyes; otherwise they might see with their eyes and hear with their ears. And understand with their heart and return, and I would heal them.'"* Isaiah 6:9-13 NIV; Acts 28:25-28 NASB

This speaks of a state of being unable to access the Word of God, which comes through the process of reconciling the spirit of mankind with the Spirit of God. Without this restoration one cannot accurately interpret God's word because he has no basis to understand God's character or purpose.

PART TWO

Seeing and Not Seeing and Hearing and Not Hearing

Both Jesus and the prophet Isaiah, in their times, addressed the people's lack of spiritual understanding. This condition of the soul is best described as seeing and hearing only what one chooses to see and to hear. For the soul, this means all understanding comes from what it can explain based upon present knowledge, circumstances and capacity for logical interpretation. Concerning truth, this perspective lacks the capacity for understanding despite potentially having access to the message itself. This is a form of self-imposed blindness and deafness, resulting not from ignorance, but from a position that does not seek the truth beyond one's personal capacity to understand. In this condition, it is impossible for people to receive heavenly insights and revelation, because it is beyond their ability to understand the imperatives of heaven coming forth upon the earth in their day.

The people of their times rejected both Jesus and Isaiah in part as a result of this blindness. The difference was that, unlike Isaiah, who was a messenger, Jesus was the message itself. Israel's rulers at the time sought to preserve their places of privilege, couching their arguments against Jesus as being for the good of the nation.[1] As discussed earlier, Caiaphas, the high priest, accurately prophesied Jesus' death earlier that year. Based upon his incipient motivation, he believed that Jesus' death would serve the nation. Though Jesus' true purpose in dying included offering salvation to the Jewish nations, the goal was much greater. Caiaphas and the other rulers simply did not understand the prophecy that Jesus' death was "not for the nation only, but in order that He might also gather together into one the children of God who are scattered abroad."[2] This was consistent with the prayer of Jesus just before His arrest. He said, "I do not ask on behalf of these alone, but for those also who believe in Me through their word; that they may all be one; even as You, Father, are in Me and I in You, that they also may be in Us, so that the world may believe that You sent Me."[3]

The apostle John also spoke prophetically about this scattered people brought together as the Kingdom of Heaven on earth. As the Lamb was being celebrated for His accomplishments on the earth, John recorded the new song that was sung in heaven honoring the Lamb's accomplishments.[4] Peter describes this scattered people being brought together as "living stones [who] are being built into a spiritual house to be a holy priesthood."[5] This spiritual house is built upon Jesus, the "cornerstone" whom the builders (Caiaphas and Israel's leaders) rejected.

Paul would use this as an example of those who lack wisdom and understanding:

> *Yet we do speak wisdom among those who are mature; a wisdom, however, not of this age not of the rulers of this age, who are passing away; but we speak God's wisdom in a mystery, the hidden wisdom which God predestined before the ages to our glory; the wisdom which none of the rulers of this age has understood; for if they had understood it they would not have crucified the Lord of glory; but just as it is written, "Things which eye has not seen and ear has not heard and which have not entered the heart of man, all that God has prepared for those who love Him." For to us God revealed them through the Spirit; for the Spirit searches all things, even the depths of God. For who among men knows the thoughts of a man except the spirit of the man which is in him: Even so the thoughts of God no one knows except the Spirit of God. Now we have received, not the spirit of the world, but the Spirit who is from God, so that we may know the things freely given to us by God.*
> 1 Corinthians 2:6-12 NASB

This passage demonstrates the difference between wisdom and understanding as pursued by the secular nations and that which is freely given to God's people.

¹John 11:48-50 NASB. ²John 11:52 NASB. ³John 17:20-21 NASB. ⁴Revelation 5:9-10 NASB. ⁵I Peter 2:5 NASB.

Out Resurrection

> *Yes, for His sake I have been caused to forfeit all things.... In order that I might come to know Him in an experiential way, and to come to know experientially the power of His resurrection and a joint-participation in His sufferings, being brought to the place where my life will radiate a likeness to His death, if by any means I might arrive at the goal, namely, the out-resurrection from among those who are dead.* Philippians 3:7-11 Wuest.

The spirit of Understanding, like the spirit of Wisdom, requires a heavenly vantage point. Whereas the spirit of Wisdom begins with the reality that God knows the end of every matter from the beginning, the spirit of Understanding begins with the fellowship of the Holy Spirit which elevates the human spirit to a position of being "seated in heavenly realms." Jesus describes this as being seated with Him "on His Father's throne."[1]

> *I keep asking that the God of our Lord Jesus Christ, the glorious Father, may give you the spirit of wisdom and revelation, so that you may know Him better. I pray that the eyes of your heart may be enlightened in order that you may know the hope to which He has called you, the riches of His glorious inheritance in His holy people, and His incomparably great power for us to believe.* Ephesians 1:17-21 NIV

To carry the spirit of Wisdom and the spirit of Understanding is to access those aspects of God's personhood and know Him better. With this access, one spans both the natural and spiritual realms, affecting the natural world but being positioned and rooted in the heavenly realm.

Paul understood this positioning as one to which believers should strive to achieve in order to access a heavenly point of view:

> *More than that, I count all things to be loss in view of the surpassing value of knowing Christ Jesus my Lord, for whom I have suffered the loss of all things, and count them but rubbish so that I may gain Christ, and may be found in Him, not having a righteousness of my own derived from the Law, but that which is through faith in Christ, the righteousness which comes from God on the basis of faith, that I may know Him and the power of His resurrection and the fellowship of His sufferings, being conformed to His death; in order that I may attain to the resurrection from the dead.* Philippians 3:8-11 NASB

Paul employs a unique version of 'resurrection' as that to which he wishes to attain. He uses the term *"exanastasis"*[2] instead of the typical *"anastasis."*[3] This usage is best translated as "out-resurrection"[4] and refers to experiential access to the spiritual state achieved by Christ's resurrection, while still existing in our natural bodies. To attain this *exanastasis* is to view all things from a heavenly point of view.

We know that Paul had an experience that confirmed the existence of such a state to him. He wrote:

> *Boasting is necessary, though it is not profitable; but I will go on to visions and revelations of the Lord. I know a man in Christ who fourteen years ago—whether in the body I do not know, or out of the body I do not know, God knows—such a man was caught up to the third heaven. And I know how such a man—whether in the body or apart from the body I do not know, God knows—was caught up into Paradise and heard*

inexpressible words which a man is not permitted to speak. 2 Corinthians 12:2-4 NASB

Paul wrote to relate the reality of the heavenly realm to his audiences. He uses a comparison of himself as both a natural man and a spiritual man. He discusses the vast superiority of his experience in being seated in the heavenly realms and having the eyes of his understanding opened to the reality from that vantage point.

To Paul, the entirety of his accomplishments as a natural man carried no significance when compared to the spiritual man. "On behalf of such a man I will boast; but on my own behalf I will not boast, except in regard to my weaknesses."[5] This represented, for Paul, a fundamental shift in both his nature and his administrations. Previously this proud young Rabbi with the knowledge and consent of the highest Jewish authorities presided over the murder of Stephen, the earliest of the martyrs, and went on to spearhead a virulent persecution of the early believers. Paul was known for his tough-mindedness and his stalwart opposition of the Christian faith. In short, he trusted entirely in the natural man to accomplish his objectives. That he should so thoroughly abandon faith in his own abilities is, by itself, a testimony of the superior abilities of God that he had come to discover. His conclusion was that even his fundamental nature had been reformatted by the understanding that came to him through the experience of being caught up to the throne of God. He could claim no virtue in his natural self except to identify his weakness prior to the *exanastasis* experience.

Whereas Caiaphas was unconcerned and oblivious to the existence of a higher order of reality inasmuch as his focus was upon preserving his position, Paul had not the slightest interest in maintaining an earthly position or point of view. He focused on the obtaining of the position of viewing all things from the throne of God, seeing no other existence as worthwhile. Paul adds the dimension of access to this realm by asserting that his status as a properly assembled part of the spiritual Body of Christ came complete with an invitation to sit down with Christ upon the throne of God. He urged everyone who aspired to maturity to take such a view of things.

Similarly, the apostle John's *exanastasis,* recorded in the book of Revelation, highlights the view of reality from the throne of God as compared to an earthly platform, further demonstrating the value that Paul came to place in an eternal point of view and the worthlessness of human imperatives in understanding the spiritual realm represented by Caiaphas's misguided attempts to fulfill his own prophecy. John's experience with the heavenly realm came by an invitation from the throne of God.[6] By this time, the church had been scattered primarily among Gentile nations nearly forty years earlier. Through the work of Paul and others the tendency to view Christ solely through Jewish traditions had largely given way to seeing and understanding Him from a heavenly point of view.[7]

John was invited to the throne of God as a witness to observe change occurring in the earth from the perspective of God's throne. Heaven itself shifted at the complete fulfillment of ancient prophetic words that defined Jesus' purpose in the earth.[8]

> *And they sang a new song, saying, "Worthy are You to take the book and to break its seals; for You were slain, and purchased for God with Your blood men from every tribe and tongue and people and nation." "You have made them to be a kingdom and priests to our God; and they will reign upon the earth."*
> Revelation 5:9-10 NASB

Heaven heard a sound that was never heard before, a "new song," representing a shift in its focus and creating a new mandate for the earth to which the full faith and credit of the throne of God would be irrevocably dedicated. This sound in heaven was the mandate of a royal priesthood and a holy nation constructed by the design of the Spirit of God out of persons from "every tribe and language and people and nation." John, spanning the natural and spiritual world, received the echo to this sound, releasing it into the earth.

With the scattering of the believers from Jerusalem and work that Paul had done throughout his lifetime among the Gentiles the stage was set for a new understanding of the Body of Christ in the earth. The old constraints that had naturally grown up as a result of the backgrounds of most of the leading figures of the early church had completely fallen away. The church itself had grown to a new level that could now accommodate the intent of God from the beginning. It was not supposed to evolve as a subset of any preexisting religious form. It was meant to accommodate the fullness of the spiritual reality that had previously existed in natural form.

The central message from heaven has always been centered upon the relationship of a father and a son. The first iteration of this message was of God the Father and Adam the son and it was lived out in the context of the natural world and humanity. The second showing of the same message was spiritual. God as the Father and Jesus Christ as the last Son who would redeem the first son, not only from his rebellion but also to reset him in the higher order of a spiritual son. The original showing of this principle came through the natural lineage from Adam but focused precisely through the seed of Abraham for the express purpose of producing the last Son who would redeem not only Abraham's line, but all of Adam's progeny.

In order to fulfill the greater purpose of building the spiritual house out of all mankind, the connection to a natural race had to be abandoned once the purpose for that natural race was fulfilled. Jesus came through the line of Abraham to redeem all of His brothers descended from Adam; namely, the entire human race. This would lead to an assembling in the earth of a holy race, born again of

Spirit and therefore properly assembled as one spiritual Man; not of Adam's lineage any longer, but issued from the very womb of God.[9] A new spiritual race whose purpose is to show to other nations of mankind how the order of heaven functioning among peoples of diverse origins and a vast sphere of experiences might be brought together functionally as one people with the intent of practically showing the vast array of splendors to be found in the person of God Himself.

This understanding, given to John, explains why he valued as paramount the admonition "little children, love one another for whoever loves is born of God and knows God" to be given to the church for the centuries beyond his life as light to guide their way. John's understanding was focused and extended so that his last years were spent positioning the believers to accurately align themselves with the original intent of God that he was allowed to observe when he was invited to witness the formal commissioning of the release of this mandate from the throne of God into the realm of man.

---

[1]Revelation 3:21 NIV. [2]Strong's G1815. [3]Strong's G386. [4]See Wuest *supra*. [5]2 Corinthians 12:5 NASB. [6]Revelation 4:1-2 NASB. [7] e.g. 2 Corinthians 5:16 NASB. [8]Galatians 3:16 NASB; see also Genesis 22:17-18 NASB. [9]2 Corinthians 5:17 NASB; Hebrews 2:11 NASB.

Understanding From the Throne of God

The spirit of Understanding interprets things differently from reason. Whereas reason is linear and the beginning and end of its application is earthly, the spirit of Understanding functions from a heavenly viewpoint. This added dimension introduces factors that are not normally considered when earthborn logic is employed. Base human understanding lacks the entire basis of reality that comes from the throne of God. The knowledge and understanding that originates from a heavenly viewpoint are the basis from which one may begin to understand and evaluate all matters that come from God. This is what separates that which is true from popular human conclusions. Difficulty in understanding what God is saying is usually caused by the absence of this perspective and the muddied waters created by purely human efforts.

Being uninformed by a heavenly perspective one may only act consistent with personal desired outcomes. Like naïve children courting unknown dangers, the human perspective is unaffected by the existence of a much broader spiritual understanding that is freed from the linear nature of time.

One cannot predict the ripple effects of actions that only seek personal fulfillment. A person's walk with God often is perceived as having mixed results because of this truth. Though one has faith that God knows the end from the beginning, often understanding of the path taken only comes with hindsight. While in the midst of difficult times that are necessary from God's perspective, it may be impossible to see the necessity of the path He chooses. Rather than steady predictable steps that reenforce popular perspectives, God pursues His purpose in every individual and His ways may not be presently known or understood.

When John stood before the throne of God, the images and events he observed may have seemed inconsistent from an earthly perspective:

> *I saw in the right hand of Him who sat on the throne a book written inside and on the back, sealed up with seven seals. And I saw a strong angel proclaiming with a loud voice, "Who is worthy to open the book and to break its seals?" And no one in heaven or on the earth or under the earth was able to open the book or to look into it. Then I began to weep greatly because no one was found worthy to open the book or to look into it; and one of the elders said to me, "Stop weeping; behold, the Lion*

> *that is from the tribe of Judah, the Root of David, has overcome so as to open the book and its seven seals." And I saw between the throne (with the four living creatures) and the elders a Lamb standing, as if slain, having seven horns and seven eyes, which are the seven Spirits of God, sent out into all the earth. And He came and took the book out of the right hand of Him who sat on the throne."* Revelation 5:1-7 NASB

Hearing that the Lion of the tribe of Judah would break the seals, the human mind would reasonably expect to see a magnificent lion stepping forward to take the book, or at least some imposing figure to reflect a lion's majesty. Instead, when the Lion is revealed, John sees "a Lamb, looking as if it had been slain." From God's throne the Lion and the Lamb that was slain are perfectly consistent because they represent the complete picture of Christ.

Christ is the Lion of Judah in that He is the overcomer and King over a holy nation. He is also the Lamb of peace, whose victory came through vulnerability and sacrifice, trusting God the Father's nature, rather than through power and overwhelming strength. The strength by which this mightiest of lions overcame was the meekness and humility that characterizes the love of God. It was, therefore, appropriate that the Lamb should be seen when the Lion was announced. To those who see but do not see and hear but do not understand, the announcement of the Lion and the showing of the Lamb is either a mystery or a contradiction. Such concepts are revealed only by the Spirit of God.

An Eternal Point of View

Apostles John and Paul were messengers who ascended to the throne of God and were given insights into the human affairs from heaven's point of view. They were both "in the Spirit" when this occurred.[1] Apostolic figures carry a gift to the Body of Christ as messengers who ascend and descend[2] Most commonly the Body's primary impediment to having an eternal point of view comes from a lack of information. Apostolic messengers impart the spirit of Understanding through spiritual insights into the House of God that help the people of God view events during their time from a heavenly point of view.

Although it is commonly asserted that we are seated in heavenly realms in Christ Jesus, there is typically no common explanation or practice surrounding this foundational truth, since while this may be asserted, reason implies that we are still very much located on the earth. Few understand that we are spirit beings who, upon being born again, are assembled as members of the spiritual Body of Christ that exists simultaneously on the earth and in heaven. We tend to identify only with the part of the Body of Christ that interfaces with the earth, and we understand that to be who we are on a daily basis. That limited point of view ignores one's connection by Christ who is the head and cannot understand the aspect of the corporate Son of God.[3]

This self-imposed restriction denies access into an eternal point of view and severely limits one's ability to understand the will of God and function out of an accurate alignment with an eternal point of view. This impediment is reenforced by various limited topical or circumstantial views of the Gospel, which denominations and influential speakers push to heighten their membership, influence, or monetary value. Those who refuse to believe that we are spirit beings will always assert that an individual cannot know the mind of God or access the same viewpoint that God has of all things. At some point, this limitation finds place when one chooses to ignore God's decision to create all humans as endowments of spirit out of His own person and then to cause them to be born again of the Spirit of God and assembled corporately into the spiritual Man known as Christ.

Such ignorance of basic truths removes the expectation of having an eternal point of view, resulting in a permanent state of spiritual immaturity. These constraints are easily dismissed when God reveals the truth in a person's life and the person simply elects to believe.

The state of unbelief is anchored in the process of reason upon which the human soul relies. Since the fall of man, the soul of man has been dominant, but in its state of separation from God, it has been cut off from an eternal point of view, and therefore it's understanding of reality has been informed by the world around it. The instinctive tendency is to reach back into the familiar influences of culture and personal experiences for its understanding. The results are typically reinforced by others who commonly share the same base of information and experience. The undisciplined soul will naturally default to reason, thereby denying a view of things from the throne of God.

God provides some specific means for overcoming reliance upon one's soul. One of them is a spiritual father. The primary responsibility of a spiritual father is to "keep watch over [one's soul] as those who will give an account" to God for the condition of those under their care.[4] Such a father must be seasoned in his own understanding of the heavenly point of view and is a model of the character of God the Father.[5] The disciplining of the soul to submit to the spirit is the key element of the type of growth that leads to maturity.

A related provision for subduing the soul is the role of one's spiritual family. Spiritual families are the relational context in which the culture of the Kingdom of Heaven is meant to flourish. The change of culture is part of what results from replacing the soul's point of view with that of the spirit. The spirit is connected to the Holy Spirit and the person is, thereby, given access into the understanding of heavenly perspectives. The spiritual family is established around this culture and reenforces the transition from the natural to the eternal point of view. Seeing from the throne of God enables a different vision of life on the earth.

Without provisions from God to make this transition a believer will vacillate constantly between behaviors that evidence the rule of the soul and the rule of the spirit. He or she will be unable to consistently distinguish between the will of God and the choice of the human soul. When Jesus, the "shoot" from the "stem of Jesse" in whom the seven Spirits of God reside, evaluates anything, it is done exclusively from a heavenly point a view.[6] Those who, like Jesus, function from the plane of the eternal are attuned to the righteousness of God and the justice of heaven as the basis of their decision making.

The spirit of Understanding has been provided to enable the believer to mature to a heavenly understanding of all things. As will all of the other characteristics that comprise the seven Spirits of God, it is necessary to restore man to the condition in which he once existed prior to the fall. The spirit of Understanding explains the reason why God says and does everything.

---

[1]Revelation 4:2 NASB. [2]John 1:51 NASB; Ephesians 4:9-10 NASB; See also "aggelos," Strong's G32, "a messenger, envoy, one who is sent, an angel, a messenger from God"; "apostolos" Strong's G652, "a delegate, messenger, one sent forth with orders." [3]Ephesians 1:20, 2:6 NASB. [4]Hebrews 13:17 NASB. [5]1 John 2:13 NIV. [6]Isaiah 11:1 NASB.

The Spirit of Counsel

The Spirit issues forth heaven's resources to support the authority of the Kingdom of Heaven. For those under the headship of Christ, the King, the economy of the Spirit flows into their way of life that is consistent with their submission to His authority over their lives. All of creation is designed to respond to this. However, the Spirit does not exert authority over the lives of those who are not submitted to Him. As such, the economy of the Spirit is not directly accessible to nonbelievers or those who refuse to submit to Christ's headship. Instead, the benefits of the spiritual economy only come to those who are under the authority of the Kingdom of God through messengers who are sons of God. In this way, those who receive the messengers, even if they are unbelievers, may experience the grace that attends the sons of God through his or her righteous actions. This provides a way for the rest of the earth to see and experience God's goodness through His representatives in the earth.

One of the key means of this experience is through the spirit of Counsel. The spirit of Counsel attends the Body of Christ as a means of translating the existing authority and extending the benefit of the precreation covenant to those who might benefit from it, even if they are not currently under Christ's authority. In these capacities He administers the covenant of reconciliation.

> *God, desiring even more to show to the heirs of the promise the unchangeableness of His purpose, interposed with an oath, so that by two unchangeable things in which it is impossible for God to lie, we who have taken refuge would have strong encouragement to take hold of the hope set before us. This hope we have as an anchor of the soul, a hope both sure and steadfast and one which enters within the veil where Jesus has entered as a forerunner for us, having become a high priest forever according to the order of Melchizedek.* Hebrews 6:17-20 NASB

With the vesting of the covenant came a change in the administrative priesthood of God, from the Levitical order to a return to the ancient order of Melchizedek. The order of Levi administrated the law given to Moses and the Israelites. The order of Melchizedek administrates the precreation covenant.[1] The order of Melchizedek is explained as a royal priesthood that is a greater and more exalted priesthood than the order of Levi which came afterward.[2] Melchizedek is more a title than the actual name of a person, meaning "by the translation of [the] name, king of righteousness, and then also king of Salem, which is king of peace."[3] As king, he certainly could claim the title of royalty and as a priest of God most high he was an administrator of a covenant of God. This order conveys the status of royal priest upon administrators of this covenant. The first of these administrators was Adam. When God placed him in creation, He did so as the son of God with dominion and a mandate to rule over all creation.[4] He was the first royal priest to rule in the fashion of the Kingdom of Heaven. His administration was meant to produce the conditions of righteousness, peace and joy—the result of divine order—on earth. Jesus, the second Adam, was sent to restore this original order and to reconnect the earth to its heavenly mandate.

Jesus was given the same mandate as Adam. He was clothed with the authority to rule, with the intent of restoring the relationship of God and man. He carried titles that identified the various roles associated with His rule. The first of these titles is "Wonderful Counselor":

> *For a child will be born to us, a son will be given to us; and the government will rest on His shoulders; and His name will be called Wonderful Counselor, Mighty God, Eternal Father, Prince of Peace.* Isaiah 9:6 NASB

As Wonderful Counselor, He would be God's designated agent on the earth to declare in their season the terms and conditions of the covenant that predated the foundations of the earth. He would resurrect and recommission the original ancient order of royal priests after the fashion of Melchizedek.

> *But you are chosen people, a royal priesthood, a holy nation, God's special possession, that you may declare the praises of*

> *Him who called you out of darkness into His wonderful light.*
> 1 Peter 2:9 NIV

> *[and]has made us to be a kingdom and priests to serve his God and Father—to him be glory and power for ever and ever! Amen.* Revelation 1:6 NIV, See also Revelation 5:10

It is within this same mandate that the spirit of Counsel continues to operate in the corporate Body. Christ delegates His authority to rule, extending the benefits of the precreation covenant to those who receive Him. Every son of God has the potential to act as counselor even to those who are not under the headship of Christ. In that case, the one receiving counsel may overtly benefit in varying degrees up to and including the forgiveness of sins. In this function as messengers of God, they can represent this aspect of God's character while transforming the lives of others.

---

[1]Hebrews 7:17-22 NASB. [2]Hebrews 7:1-7 NASB. [3]Hebrews 7:2 NASB. [4]Genesis 1:28 NASB.

The Counselor as Messenger of God

God's purpose in creating a son and placing him in the earth was to establish a representation of God's nature and character together with His rule in creation, which is a specific venue that allows for this unique relationship between God and mankind. When a son represents his Father, the representation reflects not only the Father's will but his culture as well. Both are made evident in the son's representation. Others may know the Father through the son's rule. Where the Father is righteous and the son's rule affects others, those who accept the son's rule experience the Father's righteousness as well.

Full, accurate and exact representation, however, is the domain of a mature son and is distinguished from the representation of a servant or of an immature son.[1] Though all sons of God have the capacity to represent the Father as mature sons, at any given time, not all believers are sufficiently mature to do so.

The son of God must consider the delegated spheres of authority given to him or her when determining whether to act as counselor to others. The status of "son" and the delegated task as a messenger are not the same. From God's point of view, a son is His beloved.[2] And, the language of affection is used to describe the relationship between God and man.[3] The bonds of love are the basis for the Father's trust of the son as His representative and the basis by which the sons of God are required to trust the Father.

This relationship forms the basis of a culture that is capable of producing sons of God who are mature enough to represent God the Father exactly, so that He may become known through their rule. This began with Adam who was the son of God, and with whom was entrusted all rule over creation. Even in his fallen state he communicated the heart of God to the domain over which he was set, continuing to lay the foundation for a culture that could once again take up the representation of God.

The messenger who acts as a counselor is a mature son within his or her given sphere of rule who represents God in a particular manner. The counselor is a proclaimer of truth in the capacity of a sent one. The word the apostle Paul used to describe this role was *keryx*, translated "preacher" and distinguished from another role which Paul simultaneously filled, of messenger or that of an apostle.[4] In this role the counselor acts on the basis of prophetic insight.

---

[1] Galatians 4:1-2 NASB. [2] See Matthew 3:17 NASB; Mark 9:7 NASB. [3] John 3:16 NASB. [4] Strong's G2783 *keryx*, "a herald or messenger vested with public authority, who

conveyed the official messages of kings, magistrates, princes, military commanders[.]" This form of messenger should be distinguished from that of an apostle, who is one sent forth to carry out specific orders, as opposed to deliver a particular message.

Prophecy As the Counsel of God

The spirit of Counsel involves declaring what God is saying in the earth with an understanding of the substance of what is declared as well. To identify one who is positioned accurately as a counselor in a matter, the individual should exhibit a substantive understanding of the prophetic declaration, commonly experienced as "preaching," as well as the credible authority to declare such things. The twin components of disclosing the substance of what God is saying accurately and possessing the requisite authority to do so are often missing from those who claim to preach. The absence of these things results, for the most part, in empty or vain declarations.

The authority to declare what God is saying comes by specific gifts of grace through the Holy Spirit. This negates those who claim the substance of what they preach because that is designed to fall in line with popular notions associated with standard doctrines of various denominations or ad populum arguments. One cannot create substance out of the sympathies of the masses, particularly those predisposed to agreeing with the stated point of view. Because institutional religions have mostly ignored extra-institutional revelation and recognize only the authority granted within the institutions themselves, rarely does preaching in these venues actually communicate what God is saying from heaven.[1]

It is often believed that the "Great Commission" inherently provided all who would choose to do so the necessary authority to preach from Scripture in the world, and that there are no other considerations, influences, or limits to its mandate.² Anyone who has undertaken a study of religious doctrines feels at liberty to preach wherever he or she so chooses.

After Jesus had commissioned the twelve to go and preach the Good News throughout the earth, He instructed them to go to Jerusalem first, and there to wait for the necessary empowerment that would come through the Holy Spirit.³ Having obeyed His command, they were assembled in Jerusalem in an upper room ten days after He had instructed them to do so, and He Himself had returned to heaven. Suddenly "an [echoing] sound" came from heaven like a rushing mighty wind. They were filled with the knowledge of what they were to say, and they were placed within the audience to whom they were to make these declarations. Those listening were amazed both at the substance of what they were hearing and by the obvious qualifications of the ones declaring these things to do so. They heard the revelation of the Scriptures that explained the events of the previous two months, which events centered around Jesus' arrest, trial and crucifixion, together with the astonishing testimony of His resurrection and ascension. All of Jerusalem was aware of these assertions and the city was alive with the discussion of these matters.

Whereas the Great Commission generally speaks to the direction to which the Body of Christ is called, many other considerations shape the effective pursuit of the goal. God perfectly planned the moment and arranged the circumstances by which Peter and the other apostles stepped forward to provide answers and to shape the discussion surrounding these issues. They became, in effect, heralds who were competent to explain to people on earth the prophetic significance of the events of which they had heard or to which they were actual witnesses. Positioned in this manner they were echoing the sound that came from heaven. As the apostles demonstrated, considerations for preaching also include empowerment from the Holy Spirit and waiting on the Lord's timing.

PART TWO

The content of the apostles' message and the timing both originated from heaven. As fully qualified messengers, they were positioned in the appropriate place and in the perfect timing to speak the counsel of God to the Jewish people. On that occasion, the spirit of Counsel accurately and effectively engaged not only Israel, but the many nations represented there that day. As a consequence, the word of the Lord not only spread throughout Jerusalem and Israel, but also began to make its way into many other nations as well.

A significant component of the spirit of Counsel involves the spirit of prophecy. This further requires a certain maturity of the counselor as in the exercise of prophetic declarations one is particularly vulnerable to being rejected. Often the verification of what is said requires certain events of pieces of understanding, and unless it strikes a resonant chord within the spirits of the listeners, what is said is likely to be rejected because of the unpleasantness of either what is disclosed or of what is foretold.

Before one takes on the role of a preacher pursuant to the Great Commission, it is important that one understands one's calling and the requisite grace that attends that calling. The counselor must understand what the sound from heaven is at the time so that he may reflect that sound in the substance of the message. One must also have an eternal point of view so that the message is not received in the spirit and presented in the flesh. Finally, it is important to understand the Lord's timing and the administrations that cause the message to be effective in transforming the lives and circumstances of those to whom the messenger is sent.

The spirit of Counsel is one of the seven characteristics of the Spirit of God and everyone who receives the Spirit of God has access to all of the seven characteristics. As is the case of all of the seven Spirits of God, the measures of endowment of each one depends to a great extent on the level of maturity to which the son of God has acceded.

The counsel of the Lord, properly presented, brings light into darkness and brings hope where distress normally reigns. It is designed to result in the forgiveness of sins, reconciliation to God, growth and maturity, and a competent representation of the interest of Christ in the earth. All these things and more were fully embodied in Christ and the early apostles.

---

[1]See Soleyn, *The Elementary Doctrines*, The Laying on of Hands. [2]Matthew 28:19-20 NASB. [3]Mark 16:16 NASB; Matthew 28:18 NASB.

The Working of the Spirit of Counsel

The spirit of Counsel is wisdom provided to another that is attuned to the mandates of heaven and informed by the understanding of the heavenly interpretation of the matters involved. The focus of the spirit of Counsel is to overlay the harshest of problems arising from natural circumstances with a spiritual reality. Experientially, the spirit of Counsel operates by interposing heavenly principles in earthly situations. From the viewpoint of heaven the most complete understanding of events and the consequences of one's actions and therefore the most complete resolutions to problems that need remedy exist. The spirit of Counsel eschews any bifurcation of reality into heavenly and earthly components. Instead, the focus is on conduct that represents the order of heaven and the economy of the Spirit to affect the outcome that best fits a heavenly point of view.

Historically, the church has chosen to ignore the spiritual reality outside of theological discussion, instead preferring natural phenomena, scientific and sociological bases for providing counsel. If the discussion centers on transcendent themes, then the discussion employs biblical and philosophical perceptions, but those in places of authority are usually reticent to deviate from accepted social solutions to the most difficult of human problems. Over time, even believers have become completely satisfied with separating their lives into these two distinct categories—their internal spiritual pursuits, like trying to be a good person or see things a certain way, and their handling of external problems, like familial or job-related issues, financial problems, and seemingly illogical tragedies.

Individuals are rarely given coherent or overarching counsel distinctly from a heavenly point of view. The majority of church goers do not have confidence that an eternal point of view is either a practical or sufficient basis upon which to rely for their direction. Much of what is considered Christian or biblical counseling employs the framework established by secular psychologists but adds substance based upon prevailing Christian culture. There is little that distinctly or uniquely represents an eternal point of view.

Perhaps the greatest example of the spirit of Counsel recorded in Scriptures is the counsel Jesus offered His disciples in what is considered to be the Sermon on the Mount (Matthew 5,6, & 7).

The heart of the counsel is on how one should pray:

> *This then is how you should pray:* "*Our Father in heaven, hallowed be your name, your kingdom come, your will be done, on earth as it is in heaven. Give us today our daily bread. And forgive us our debts, as we also have forgiven our debtors. And lead us not into temptation but deliver us from the evil one.*"
> Matthew 6:9-13 NIV

Both in form and in substance, this example reveals the perspective of heaven.

The Word who became flesh and was identified as the one and only Son who came from the Father, was full of grace and truth. God

Himself acknowledged the position of the Son in relationship to the Father as His representative when He declared, "This is My Son, whom I love; with Him I am well pleased." [1]

> *In the past God spoke to our ancestors through the prophets at many times and in various ways, but in these last days He has spoken to us by His Son, whom He appointed heir of all things, and through whom also He made the universe. The Son is the radiance of God's glory and the exact representation of His being, sustaining all things by His powerful word. After He had provided purification for sins, He sat down at the right hand of the Majesty in heaven.* Hebrews 1:1-3 NIV

The spirit of Counsel comes from a fully accredited son who knows His Father, and when he speaks to man, concerning his problems and the issues with which he is faced, he clearly understands the will of God within that context and knows how to administrate the transition from the dilemma of the soul to the liberty and freedom of the spirit. He knows how to encourage the persons to whom he is giving counsel regarding how to align themselves with the mandates of heaven for their situation. The counsel of God will always look foolish to the rational mind, because at times it would appear to take rights and privileges from those who possess them and, in the process, make them quite vulnerable.

The only factor that guarantees the proper outcome from what often seems to be the foolishness of godly counsel is that the outcome depends upon the reality of the living God. Whoever is properly aligned to the counsel of heaven has placed himself and his needs firmly in the hands of the almighty God. This contrasts starkly with the more common experience of pursuing one's rights while asking God to guarantee the outcome.

PART TWO

Examples from the Sermon on the Mount would counsel that one would forgive others their trespasses rather than use them as leverage to gain desirable outcomes. Or, that one should concentrate on investing in the treasures of mercy and kindness, which may often affect one's pecuniary interests. Or, that one should seek, as their priority, to place oneself under the authority and rule of the Kingdom of Heaven ahead of the pursuit of such basic matters of food, clothing, and shelter. The counsel offered in regard to approaching God Himself through prayer would solicit His will being done on earth as it is in heaven. And, while asking for our supply of food, we would be as concerned about not being led into temptation.

On the whole, the spirit of Counsel reflects a very different value than what is normal and customary for humans. Whereas it is normal to be obsessed with preserving our rights and protecting our persons, the value displayed through counsel of the Spirit reflects God's perspective and, therefore, His values. An eternal point of view routinely favors relationships over perishable material and the counsel that flows from the throne of God reflects this preference. In resolving relational differences, the counsel that Jesus offers is illustrated in His statement, "If your brother or sister sins, go and point out their fault, just between the two of you. If they listen to you, you have won them over. But if they will not listen, take one or two others along, so that 'every matter may be established by the testimony of two or three witnesses.'"[2] This procedure, though it may result in the ultimate sanction of the exclusion of fellowship is designed at every step to gain the brother.

Aligning one's self in the earth to the mandates of heaven and preferring relationships over material substance are key elements that illustrate the distinction between counsel based in logic that is likely to appeal to the human soul but places no reliance on God. These insights into the spirit of Counsel, though by no means exhaustive of the genre, are meant to highlight essential distinctions between the common perception of good counsel and the spirit of Counsel. As the believer grows in maturity and the sphere of his rule expands, the spirit of Counsel is an indispensable equipping from God that enables the rule of righteousness within one's assigned domain.

---

[1]Matthew 3:17 NIV. [2]Matthew 18:15-16 NIV.

The Spirit of Power

> *[You] will receive power when the Holy Spirit has come upon you; and you shall be My witnesses both in Jerusalem and in all Judea and Samaria and even to the remotest part of the earth.* Acts 1:8 NASB

In the context of the seven Spirits of God as they were present in the Lord Jesus Christ, the spirit of Power must be distinguished from God's divine creative competence by which He made all things. Instead, the spirit of Power references the manner in which the Son of God has been retrofitted with the requisite character of belief, together with the ability to remain "steadfast, immovable, [and] always abounding in the work of the Lord."[1] The focus of this characteristic of the Spirit of God, as presented through the person of the Lord Jesus Christ, is designed to show the boldness and confidence of a son of God in his Father.

> *And with great power the apostles were giving testimony to the resurrection of the Lord Jesus and abundant grace was upon them all.* Acts 4:33 NASB

Accordingly, Scripture speaks of power, in this context, in terms of those giving witness or testimony regarding Christ. This is the result of the power conveyed upon the sons of God through the Holy Spirit.

As the pattern son, Jesus' entire ministry gave testimony regarding His relationship to God the Father:

> *Therefore Jesus answered and was saying to them, "Truly, truly, I say to you, the Son can do nothing of Himself unless it is something He sees the Father doing; for whatever the Father does, these things the Son also does in like manner. For the Father loves the Son and shows Him all things that He Himself is doing; and the Father will show Him greater works than these, so that you will marvel. For just as the Father raises the dead and gives them life, even so the Son also gives life to whom He wishes. For not even the Father judges anyone, but He has given all judgment to the Son, so that all will honor the Son even as they honor the Father. He who does not honor the Son does not honor the Father who sent Him."* John 5:19-23 NASB

The context of this quotation was that Jesus had healed a man who had been sick for thirty-eight years. In doing so, He both defied the law because He healed that man on the Sabbath and He circumvented the existing order of power by which the sick were healed—in the pool called Bethesda.[2] Jesus' testimony in this act of power was of the love of God in showing Him all things, in establishing the power to "give life" in the Son and in placing the Son in a position to be honored just as God would be honored. This act and Jesus' teaching established the pattern for the workings of the spirit of Power as an act of testimony regarding the relationship between God the Father and the Son.

During Jesus' time, the religious authorities fully embraced the idea that the extent of all their knowledge and experience represented the compendium of understanding concerning the Almighty God. Jesus openly defied both their knowledge of Scripture and their experience as the religious leaders of the nation by acting and speaking in ways that challenged the existing understanding of

God. He would quote and reinterpret sacred texts and hallowed traditions in ways that distinctly opposed the accepted beliefs. An excellent example of this is His teaching on the mountain:

> *For I say to you that unless your righteousness surpasses that of the scribes and Pharisees, you will not enter the kingdom of heaven. You have heard that the ancients were told, "You shall not commit murder" and "Whoever commits murder shall be liable to the court." But I say to you that everyone who is angry with his brother shall be guilty before the court; and whoever says to his brother, "You good-for-nothing" shall be guilty before the supreme court; and whoever says, "You fool" shall be guilty enough to go into the fiery hell.*
>
> *You have heard that it was said, "You shall not commit adultery"; but I say to you that everyone who looks at a woman with lust for her has already committed adultery with her in his heart.*
>
> *You have heard that it was said, "You shall love your neighbor and hate your enemy." But I say to you, love your enemies and pray for those who persecute you, so that you may be sons of your Father who is in heaven; for He causes His sun to rise on the evil and the good, and sends rain on the righteous and unrighteous.* Matthew 5:20-22, 27-28, 43-45 NASB

The change in the interpretation of these matters is from an objective standard meant to induce a certain, definable and enforceable level of conduct to matters that regard one's heart. The established standard of practice for obeying the commandment was that one actually engaged the act itself before one could be judged as guilty. The standard Jesus puts forth is one defined by God the Father. Rather than being a standard for a society it is a standard for sons of God. At the time of this teaching, Jesus' sermon was unthinkable in the way that

He positioned His standard in such an unmistakably superior standing to either the written Scriptures or the traditions of the elders that guided the practice of these commandments and ordinances in daily Jewish life. Thus, "When Jesus had finished these words, the crowds were amazed at His teaching; for He was teaching them as one having authority, and not as their scribes."[3]

A son of God, placed among men, enjoys the distinction of knowing God and therefore understanding, by revelation, what God means to impart by what has been previously spoken. In the mighty strength of God, Jesus withstood all of the forces of tradition and ignorance in His day. Whereas the letter of Scripture remains complete and is therefore unalterable, its interpretation is infused with the appropriate life imparting qualities that it is meant to convey by a son who unlocks the hidden truths within the word through the spirit of Wisdom and Understanding. This manner of unveiling the word of God is at the root of one's testimony as a son of God. One's work in this area will always oppose the conventional "wisdom" of mankind and the strongholds built around them. Combatting these forces by the words of one's testimony is the evidence of the mighty strength of God and the anointing of the spirit of Power upon His sons.

---

[1] 1 Corinthians 15:58 NASB. [2]John 5:2 NASB. [3]Matthew 7:28-29 NASB.

Jesus the Almighty One

[H]ere after you will see the Son of man sitting at the right hand of power and coming on the clouds of heaven. Matthew 26:64 NASB

The mighty God who in ages past demonstrated power yet incomprehensible to the human mind consented to embody His chosen expression for His love. Because God is love, it was always inevitable that He would eventually express His love; and because His love is perfect, His expression of it would also define the nature of love perfectly. That expression involved a creation designed to give expression to the nature of God Himself.[1]

> *Beloved, let us love one another, for love is from God; and everyone who loves is born of God and knows God. The one who does not love does not know God, for God is love. By this the love of God was manifested in us, that God has sent His only begotten Son into the world so that we might live through Him. In this is love, not that we loved God, but that He loved us and sent His Son to be the propitiation for our sins.* 1 John 4:7-10 NASB

The Word is clothed in flesh in this form, full of "grace and truth."[2] The Word represents God's power.[3] Power was made subject to the constraints of love, and God's might was clothed in the humility of flesh.

The highest form of love for and from God is expressed in the desire of the one created to be like God out of whom He came forth. God placed all His power in this form when the Word became flesh. He perfectly demonstrated the manner in which the power of God is made subject to His love and how it works in harmony in the vessel of a human being to put the Father on display in creation. This both demonstrates His love and validates His choice of mankind as His heirs.

However, as the Son of man, He is not known for the competencies by which the universe was formed. Rather, His power lies in His standing before God as the pattern of the restored son. Jesus' determination to exactly represent His Father is tested in every conceivable fashion, and His life was fraught with peril from the moment His advent was announced by the heavenly hosts. This power is evident throughout His life. He was bold at an early age when He began studying the Scriptures. He was steadfast when He was tested in the wilderness, and His will was adamantine when confronted with torture and death.[4]

He clothed Himself with the mind of God and acted with astonishing brilliance and audaciousness even when His physical condition was weakened or broken. Quite often, the greatest breakthroughs to the pure representation of God are not realized because the imperatives of the human flesh and one's physical circumstances demand satisfaction. Often, matters are taken into one's own hands to supply the needs as required by circumstances. By taking up the power of one's own strength, a breakthrough to relying upon the mighty strength of God is averted, and one remains entrapped in a reality framed by human needs. By contrast, Jesus spent only forty days in the wilderness, and when rigorously examined by the enemy, He displayed, with unshadowed brilliance, the extent of His readiness to clothe Himself with the identity of His Father and to resolutely and accurately align Himself with His Father.

After being tempted in the wilderness, "Jesus returned to Galilee in the power of the Spirit" where He began the three-and-a-half-year period of putting His Father's love on display. This period would culminate with His crucifixion, resurrection, and ascension to heaven. During this time, He continued to confront the full weight of all that had been accomplished through the enemy's deception of mankind throughout the millennia since man's fall in the garden of Eden.

With the spirit of Power upon Him, Jesus confronted various forms of authority ranging from representatives of the religious order of His day to the officials of the Roman Empire. His boldness and courage were always on display, and His trust of the Father never lagged. Whether He was rebuking the religious authorities for their hypocrisy and misrepresentation of God, or instructing the highest levels of Roman government that the empire itself had no authority over

Him, His fortitude in holding to the accurate representation of His Father and never moving out of His place of accurate alignment with God characterized His unflagging devotion to His eternal purpose and certifies Him as the pattern Son, worthy of the title "Mighty God." Jesus established that the mighty of the earth are those whose strength is their total reliance on the word that proceeds from the mouth of God.

---

[1]See Soleyn, *supra* Chapter 5. [2]John 1:14 NASB. [3]See John 1:3 NASB. [4]See Luke 2:46 NASB; Matthew 4:1-11 NASB; Matthew 26:63-64 NASB.

The Boldness and Courage of the Early Church

> *Now as they observed the confidence of Peter and John and understood that they were uneducated and untrained men, they were amazed, and began to recognize them as having been with Jesus.* Acts 4:13 NASB

From its inception, authorities opposed the early church, first persecuting its leaders to try and stop the movement but eventually persecuting any whom they called Christian. The root of this persecution began as an issue of authority.

Jesus had been crucified by the Romans at the urging of the Jewish leadership. The intent of the leaders was to undermine and reject Jesus' claim to be the promised king from the line of David and avoid submitting to His authority. They enlisted the Romans help by distancing themselves from Jesus while charging that He was a secular seditionist whose claims were equally false to the Jews and to the Romans. They sought to elevate His claim as King, in the Romans' eyes, to a challenge to the sovereignty of Caesar, essentially a crime of treason. At the crucifixion of Jesus, the Romans attached a copy of the charge to the cross.

PART TWO

Jesus never pitted Himself against a government or ruling body. His teaching and actions offended the Jewish traditions because He brought change to the established traditions regarding God and men, but He never sought to overthrow or undermine the ruling government. To do so would have meant to seek equality with human governments and the power that establish them. Jesus already had "all authority...in heaven and on earth" given to Him from the throne of heaven.[1] Jesus' kingdom is the Kingdom of Heaven.

> *These are in accordance with the working of the strength of His might which He brought about in Christ, when He raised Him from the dead and seated Him at His right hand in the heavenly places, far above all rule and authority and power and dominion, and every name that is named, not only in this age but also in the one to come.* Ephesians 1:19-21 NASB

Citizens of His kingdom are drawn "from every tribe and tongue and people and nation."[2] "You have made them to be a kingdom and priests to our God; and they will reign upon the earth." Christ's kingdom exists outside any human governmental order and can never be put under or made subject to any earthly grant of authority. Therefore, Jesus said to Pilate, who claimed to have the power to release or kill Jesus, "You would have no authority over Me, unless it had been given you from above; for this reason he who delivered Me to you has the greater sin."[3]

This authority and the mighty power of God that accompanies the son's work in the earth is the exact thing governments have railed against by persecuting its citizens. On the day of Pentecost, the early church began in a display that realized the worst fears of the ruling bodies. Peter led Jesus' followers in declaring that Jesus had been raised from the dead and ascended to heaven, and of these facts, they were eyewitnesses. They asserted that these were the two conditions, prophetically established by David, by which it would be known who the Messiah-King was. Their teachings were preceded by extraordinary signs from heaven, including the sudden ability to speak and be heard in multiple languages. Thousands flocked to them and believed their message.

Matters became exponentially worse when Peter and John healed a paralytic at the gate of the temple compound in the presence of all Israel. The dilemma that Jesus' presence and teaching created came roaring back in the form of a movement of people quickly becoming uncontrollable. The Jewish authorities discussed measures for containing this phenomenon and decided to threaten the leaders with severe punishment and even death.

These leaders were required to exhibit the same boldness and courage as Jesus Himself had demonstrated. They met the test fully. When they were brought before the Jewish leaders to explain their action, again the questions were those of authority:

> *By what power, or in what name, have you done this? Then Peter, filled with the Holy Spirit, said to them, "Rulers and elders of the people, if we are on trial today for a benefit done to a sick man, as to how this man has been made well, let it be known to all of you and to all the people of Israel, that by the name of Jesus Christ the Nazarene, whom you crucified, whom God raised from the dead—by this name this man stands here before you in good health."* Acts 4:7-10 NASB

Peter's response to the circumstances exhibits both the same authority and power Jesus showed when dealing with opposition. This is a noticeable change in the same man who denied Jesus three times during His trial.[4] This display of boldness came to characterize the early church and marks a distribution of the spirit of Power exhibited in Jesus' ministry, now filling the entire church with the necessary power to remain steadfast in the face of extreme opposition.

PART TWO

Peter and John returned to be among the new believers. To their amazement the people began to pray to God to be permitted to participate in preaching this same message throughout Israel:

> *And now, Lord, take note of their threats, and grant that Your bondservants may speak Your word with all confidence, while You extend Your hand to heal, and signs and wonders take place through the name of Your holy servant Jesus. And when they had prayed, the place where they had gathered together was shaken, and they were all filled with the Holy Spirit and began to speak the word of God with boldness.* Acts 4:29-31 NASB

The spirit of Power was released to the people. Their prayer evidenced the willingness of ordinary believers to be put in harm's way just as readily as the apostles themselves. This spirit of boldness quickly permeated the company of those to whom Peter and John returned after they were released.

> *And the congregation of those who believed were of one heart and soul: and not one of them claimed that anything belonging to him was his own, but all things were common property to them. And with great power the apostles were giving testimony to the resurrection of the Lord Jesus, and abundant grace was upon them all.* Acts 4:32-33 NASB

Persecution grew and eventually Paul emerged as the spearhead of the effort by the Jewish authorities to arrest the progress of the message of Christ and eventually to uproot this developing movement in Jewish society. Eventually the persecution of the church would become official Roman policy, and the Christian faith would become outlawed throughout the Roman Empire. This spirit of boldness however would persist and even come to define the believers in the first two centuries after the ascension of Christ.

¹Matthew 28:18 NASB. ²Revelation 5:9-10 NASB. ³John 19:11 NASB. ⁴Matthew 26:70-75 NASB.

When I Am Weak Then I Am Strong

He has said to me, "My grace is sufficient for you, for power is perfected in weakness." Most gladly, therefore, I will rather boast about my weaknesses so that the power of Christ may dwell in me. Therefore, I am well content with weaknesses, with insults, with distresses, with persecutions, with difficulties, for Christ's sake; for when I am weak, then I am strong. 2 Corinthians 12:9-10 NASB

The power that attended the Son of God in the earth is "perfected in weakness." The apostle Paul, more than most, had to learn strength in weakness both because of his great calling but also because of his formidable strength of character and of will that marked his life prior to his conversion. Paul taught from his own experience about the necessary transitions from relying upon the strength of one's own will to a complete reliance upon God:

> *I myself might have confidence even in the flesh. If anyone else has a mind to put confidence in the flesh, I far more: circumcised the eighth day; of the nation of Israel, of the tribe of Benjamin, a Hebrew of Hebrews; as to the Law, a Pharisee; as to zeal, a persecutor of the church; as to the righteousness which is in the Law, found blameless.* Philippians 3:4-6 NASB

His pedigree, intellectual accomplishments, social and religious connections, and his personal discipline were all in evidence in his position among the religious leaders of his day. He demonstrated this strength in the force with which he persecuted the early church,

PART TWO

including the orchestration of Stephen's murder, making him the first believer to become a martyr.

When he became a believer, it was necessary for him to learn a different boldness. He had to exhaust the end of his human determination in order to serve eternal purposes. After his conversion and his initial ministry, he mostly disappears from Scripture for a period of fourteen years. Little is known about him during this time except that he was in Arabia for a period of time,[1] and settled in Tarsus.[2] It was not until he moved from Tarsus to Antioch that God reactivated his purpose.[3]

It takes the kind of strength that Paul possessed to undergo the process that produces strength in the Lord from weakness in the flesh. The Lord knew about the changes that He would need to work in Paul before Paul could take up his ministry, saying to Ananias "for I will show him how much he must suffer for My name's sake."[4] Paul had to suffer to be made into the Lord's "chosen instrument."[5] As with all those who responded to their calling, Paul's innate human strength was also necessary to endure that which God put him through to forge Paul to fit his destiny.[6] Paul clearly transitioned, at some point, to a consuming desire to see everything from the throne of God, and to live his earthly life in exact conformity to a heavenly perspective.[7] He was born with a great destiny and both his innate character and the refining process that came after his conversion made him fit to meet it.[8]

God called Paul to be the instrument for the fulfillment of God's promise to Abraham for mankind's reconciliation among the Gentiles. This was a formidable task, ending in Paul's execution, that required "mighty strength." Paul was the sent son for the dispensation of God's House meant to destroy the devil's works among the Gentiles. As formidable as his human strength was, this task could only be accomplished in the strength of God, represented by the spirit of Power that was also upon Christ.

Paul chose God's strength over his own. He was so convinced that the exclusive means by which this task could be accomplished was through divine grace that he relinquished any vestige of his own strength and took pleasure in his weakness. The strength of the human soul is and always has been the plaything for the enemy's craft. Only by transcending the strength of soul and flesh and seeking the strength of spirit, which requires suffering and weakening of the former, may one accurately align with divine provision and hope to fulfill his or her calling.

---

[1]Galatians 1:17 NASB. [2]Acts 11:25 NASB. [3]Acts 13:1-4 NASB; See also, Soleyn, *The Elementary Doctrines,* The Laying on of Hands. [4]Acts 9:16 NASB. [5]Acts 9:15 NASB. [6]Acts 17:26 NASB. [7]Philippians 3:7-16 NASB. [8]Galatians 1:13-24 NASB.

The Grace That Labors

A mature son of God has undergone a process meant to supplant a reliance upon self and soul with a strength that comes from a complete trust in the Father. The maturation process involves many various topics, including stages of sonship and the elementary doctrines, both of which should be studied in other text. The result, however, is a mature son of God defined as one whom the Father will send as a complete representation of the Father within the expression of that person's unique calling. This stage of maturity, identified in Scripture as the *huios* stage of sonship provides an important endpoint or goal in the process of maturing as a son of God. The following parable helps identify the character of the mature son:

> *There was a landowner who planted a vineyard and put a wall around it and dug a wine press in it, and built a tower, and*

rented it out to vine growers and went on a journey. When the harvest time approached, he sent his slaves to the vine growers to receive his produce. The vine growers took his slaves and beat one and killed another and stoned a third. Again, he sent another group of slaves larger than the first; and they did the same thing to them. But afterward he sent his son [huios] to them saying, "They will respect my son." But when the vine growers saw the son, they said among themselves, "This is the heir; come, let us kill him and seize his inheritance." They took him and threw him out of the vineyard and killed him. Therefore, when the owner of the vineyard comes, what will he do to those vine growers? They said to him, "He will bring those wretches to a wretched end, and will rent out the vineyard to other vine growers who will pay him the proceeds at the proper seasons." Jesus said to them, "Did you never read in the Scriptures, The stone which the builders rejected, this became the chief corner stone; this came about from the Lord, and it is marvelous in our eyes?" Therefore, I say to you, the Kingdom of God will be taken away from you and given to a people, producing the fruit of it. And he who falls on this stone will be broken to pieces; but on whomever it falls, it will scatter him like dust." Matthew 21:33-44 NASB

The Son in the parable references Christ, the Son who was sent. This Son's representation of the Father is so complete that He may be knowingly sent into harm's way or even to His death. Such harm is itself an indictment against those who would reject Him, because the Son and the Father are one. The mature son carries a measure of the House of God when God sends him, establishing the standards of righteousness by his representation of the Father. This example helps to illustrate the fully mature, Christ-like, son. A beloved son in whom the Father is well pleased is one who has learned to obey the Father, having been disabused of his own sufficiency through the sufferings he has endured in his flesh. Through the stages of maturity, there is a simultaneous emptying of reliance upon oneself and filling with reliance upon the Father. As the sources of one's strength are broken, a replacement of reliance upon God takes place.

Evidence of this emptying and refilling are the characteristics of boldness and confidence in the face of extreme opposition to a person's representation of the Father. It is not the boldness and confidence of self-assurance. It is attended by patience and peace, instead of arrogance and urgency. Confidence does not have to be proven by the exertion of human effort. It is as a mantle that one wears comfortably. The truth does not have to be proven; it proves itself.

A mature son of God is "full of grace and truth." The power of God, then, flows through the person who has been accurately aligned to the reality of heaven and has grown in the maturity of his response to opposition. Such a person is bold and confident in the Lord and exhibits an unshakable certainty in the truth and its outcome. Vindication is not the son's goal, though he lives with the certainty that whether vindication comes in his lifetime or not, the truth will establish itself. Such persons are routinely the vessels through whom God speaks and acts with great power. The spirit of Power shapes the individual vessels so that they become effective carriers of the message from God and whatever power is necessary to demonstrate the truth that they speak.

Paul said that he worked harder than any other apostle in the spread of the gospel of the Kingdom. He attributes the success of his work, not to the hours he spent or the effort he exerted, but to the "laboring of grace."

> *But by the grace of God I am what I am, and His grace toward me did not prove vain; but I labored even more than all of them, yet not I, but the grace of God with me.* 1 Corinthians 15:10 NASB

Like Jesus, who was full of grace and truth, Paul also was a carrier of grace. The spirit of Power is an endowment of a character of the Holy Spirit that produces a son who is bold and confident as a representative of his Father so that he may carry the message and demonstrate the truth of it when necessary. The spirit of Power is also the way that God chooses to act in support of the truth. Grace is the convergence of the economy of the Spirit and the Lord's appropriate timing. The result is that all things that further the advance of the Kingdom of God are supported through the resources of heaven, requiring no son of God to rely on human strength to pursue his or her calling. For example, Paul claimed a unique grace as well as the administration of that grace:

> *[I]f indeed you have heard of the stewardship of God's grace which was given to me for you; that by revelation there was made known to me the mystery, as I wrote before in brief. By referring to this, when you read you can understand my insight into the mystery of Christ, which in other generations was not made known to the sons of men, as it has now been revealed to His holy apostles and prophets in the Spirit[.]* Ephesians 3:2-5 NASB

Such advances cannot occur apart from grace because they lack either the requisite resources or knowledge of the Lord's timing. The grace of God appears in carriers whose purpose is to utilize the power inherent in grace to establish the truth that they have been given to impart. Until such carriers of grace appear, the effective publishing of the word of the Lord does not occur. Grace carriers are given unique insights into eternal truths that remain mysteries until disclosed through the revelation given, together with the authority and power to administrate the mysteries among those to whom they are sent.[1]

For the Body of Christ, it is important to receive the carriers of grace for each season. For the Body to function within any given season the people must know and engage the timing of the Lord. There are set times by which God accomplishes distinct aspects of His plans for man.[2] In those times, a new endowment of grace to supply the requisite power and authority from heaven to effect the necessary changes on the earth that God intends is deployed. Absent this grace, the enablement necessary to shift the circumstances of earth to conform to the heavenly mandate would be lacking. However, whenever God releases a new increment of His overall intent in the earth, the sons of God should fully expect that it will be accompanied by sufficient grace for that season. This grace enables the successful launch of the mandate and sustains its progress to completion. When a new mandate is inaugurated, a new grace will always accompany it.

Those whom God selects to carry the grace of the revelation of such mysteries will bring with them both the revelation and the understanding of its administration. Grace to reveal and establish the present mandate is upon them because they will also be mature sons of God who have trained and matured to be the ones sent in grace and in power. This is necessary because the greater mandate and calling, the greater the opposition to God's plan. Great opposition is overcome through the spirit of Power upon the carrier of grace.

Just as a son of God matures over time, the corporate Son, the Body of Christ, continues to progress from epoch to epoch. This progression mirrors the changes of a son through stages of maturity, becoming a more complete representation of the Father in each new epoch. The corporate Son continues to progress toward a complete representation of the Father, in which His entire being will be visible through the harmonious function of the Body in the earth. This holy nation will ultimately complete the work Jesus began by presenting a son in the Spirit of Christ that brings the Kingdom of Heaven to the earth in exact representation.

PART TWO

There continue to be epochs of time in which God's intentions for His sons, foretold through prophetic Scriptures, are given in progressively incremental releases. For example, a functioning holy nation does not yet exist upon the earth, but both Peter and John prophesied that the time would come when God would form His people into a nation of kings and priests. The Old Testament prophets Isaiah and Micah saw the same vision and referred to it as "The Lord's house" and likened it to a city on the hill to which the nations are drawn. Presently, the previously hidden mysteries that form the necessary basis for this holy nation are being revealed on the earth together with the administration by which the revelation is given earthly form.

Confidence and boldness in the face of opposition comes from the mighty strength of God. The mystery of this strength is that in the face of any earthly powers or authorities that seek to disrupt God's work on the earth, the sons of God carry the grace that comes from one who is above all others.

> *These are in accordance with the working of the strength of His might which He brought about in Christ, when He raised Him from the dead and seated Him at His right hand in the heavenly places, far above all rule and authority and power and dominion, and every name that is named, not only in this age but also in the one to come. And He put all things in subjection under His feet, and gave Him as head over all things to the church which is His body, the fullness of Him who fills all in all.* Ephesians 1:19-23 NASB

In Christ, the same spirit of Power that anointed Him is available to every son of God. This is the root of the same boldness that Jesus exhibited throughout a life of suffering, danger, and persecution; that defined the early church and its apostles and that became Paul's mark of strength in weakness allowing him to carry a pivotal grace. The sons of God, as they mature, are called to demonstrate this boldness as part of the character of God that each represents in the earth.

The spirit of Power attends the believer's suffering. The mature believer has experienced the refining fire that is suffering.[3] It is this well of harsh experience that causes the mature believers to forgo reliance upon their own strength and to clothe themselves with the certainty that lies in the power of God. As a result, the economy that advances God's purposes is willingly borne into the earth through the reliance of the sons of God. The same anointing of power is upon the entire Body of Christ. This character of the seven Spirits of God should be remembered as the Body moves inexorably, epoch to epoch, toward the holy nation of prophecy. At times, the Body has been called to weakness so that its many parts learn to rely upon the Spirit, but what will emerge is a people whose entire existence comes from the mighty strength from the throne of heaven.

---

[1]Ephesians 3:8-10 NASB. [2]Galatians 4:4-5 NASB; see Colossians 1:26 NASB. [3]See Soleyn, *The Elementary Doctrines*, Baptisms, The Baptism of Fire.

The Spirit of Knowledge

> *"To you it has been granted to know the mysteries of the Kingdom of heaven"* Matthew 13:11 NASB

The spirit of Knowledge retrofits the human being—body, soul and spirit—to interpret the natural world from an eternal perspective. Without the spirit of Knowledge, knowledge that exists as a result of God's point of view outside the limitations of a linear past, present and future is an inaccessible mystery. As demonstrated in Jesus' parabolic teachings, access to this knowledge is the difference between understanding the word of the Lord and seeing and hearing the same word but without comprehension.[1] It is also the difference between living from the throne of God and people's entire existence being a series of reactions to their environment. The mind of the human spirit, when given access to knowledge from beyond human limitations, can engage the natural world as a meaningful earthly bastion for heaven's purposes. Armed with the spirit of Knowledge, the sons of God serve a greater purpose.

---

[1] Matthew 13:13 NASB.

The Knowledge of God

The knowledge that lies behind every word, phrase, or utterance from God to man is inconceivably vast. Thus, every utterance from God that informs the mind of a person also comes with great restraint on God's part. The knowledge behind the communication could overwhelm the limitations of the human mind that perceives reality as a linear progression of time. Therefore, God communicates the substance of His word and only the anointing of the spirit of Knowledge allows one to see enough of God's perspective to both understand and trust the word.

To access the spirit of Knowledge it is useful to understand certain concepts of God's perspective. The knowledge of God reflects His seat over the everlasting, the eternal, and the endless. For purposes of defining these aspects of timelessness, the term "aeon" with a layered meaning of these concepts is appropriate, because while we are discussing concepts that involve time, such concepts are also those that are everlasting and defy futile compartmentalization.

> *Now to Him who is able to establish you according to my Gospel and the preaching of Jesus Christ, according to the revelation*

PART TWO

> *of the mystery which has been kept secret for long ages past, but now is manifested, and by the Scriptures of the prophets, according to the commandment of the eternal God, has been made known to all the nations, leading to obedience of faith.*
> Romans 16:25-26 NASB

God keeps certain things in Himself which He reveals when their moment in time has come. Such things have always existed but yet from the human perspective are time-specific—such as the mystery of reconciliation for the Gentiles.[1] Similarly, God hid the truth of the mystery of what He intended to accomplish in Christ in Himself for past aeons. But, at the appointed time in the present epoch, Christ came into this present world and fulfilled the eternal purposes of God.

God did things in prior epochs in anticipation of the present order of creation. He kept these things "covered" in primordial darkness until He chose to reveal them to the light and order of their present forms. The earth, the waters, and "the deep" existed from prior epochs. It is only the carelessness of traditional positions that obscure the plain meaning of these passages: "In the beginning God created the heavens and the earth. The earth was formless and void, and darkness was over the surface of the deep, and the Spirit of God was moving over the surface of the waters."[2] It is to be noted that these statements are about what existed prior to the first creative acts of God. The first declaration of God that started the present order of creation was the command, "Let there be light."[3] The command had the effect of lifting the veil and bringing into the light what was already there. All that was in the deep was now subject to the arrangements that God would continue to utter.

The materials that would be shaped into the present order of creation, were now subject to the displays of order that God would speak. The Spirit of God hovered over the waters. They came to be subject to the order God would declare concerning them.[4] The earth itself was lacking in its present form and content.[5] It was called up out of the waters and made subject to commands that filled it with its present content.[6] At the end of six mornings and evenings, all of the present order of creation would stand before the gaze of the Almighty for His inspection. And He would declare that it was "very good." From one epoch to another, the Spirit of God changes the shapes and forms of things that existed previously to accommodate His purposes for the present order. The changing of the order of existence from epoch to epoch is according to the purposes of God and is the proper way to account time as it relates to spiritual matters.

Some believers like to argue about the earth's age. The problem is that in doing so they default to a non-spiritual view of time, relating to the temporal measurements that are completely irrelevant to the spiritual world. Referring to aspects of the present creation in terms of billions or even trillions of years misses the point of a spiritual perspective. The shift from one epoch to another cannot be calculated in terms of human measurements, because it represents the eternal (which is without time) entering into and changing the temporal creation. The only perspective that may understand this concept is that of God's eternal point of view. Our position within creation, limited by past-present-future constraints, can only see, consider, or measure human time, leaving out the entire existence or influence of God. When viewed from an eternal plane, the measurement by years of things that result from the changing of epochs are pointless.

God alone is the eternal Spirit, "Him who fills all in all."[7] All of the epochs have come at the behest of God and exist as increments of the inexorable march forward of His divine and original intentions. He imparts the knowledge of the secrets of all things. His view is the only complete source of knowledge. Whenever God speaks, even the most insignificant thing He may appear to say carries the weight of being a distillation of His omniscience. "Heaven and earth will pass away, but [His] words will not pass away."[8] His words are unalterable and will continue from the point of His utterance to their ultimate fulfillments.

When the human spirit is connected to the Spirit of God, the mind of the human spirit is given access to the knowledge of the secrets of God as God chooses to reveal such things in their time. The spirit of Understanding is required to enable the mind of the human spirit to comprehend what it is being shown. Adam's information appeared to have been limited to the natural order of creation as it reflected the secrets of the invisible world and the knowledge of how the natural order aligned with the invisible. When the knowledge of these things was lost, man descended into a lower order of knowledge. Since he began to comprehend things through his desire to be like God but unconnected to the Spirit, his soul subverted the place or pre-eminence and man declined to a source of knowledge that became increasingly tainted and corrupted.

---

[1]Ephesians 3:8-10 NASB; See also Colossians 1:26-27 NASB. [2]Genesis 1:1-2 NASB. [3] *Id.* 1:3. [4]Genesis 1:6 NASB. [5]Genesis 1:2 NASB. [6]Genesis 1:9-12 NASB. [7]Ephesians 1:23 NASB. [8]Matthew 24:35 NASB.

Human Knowledge

With the fall, man immediately evidenced a changed perspective on reality. He saw himself as a mere created thing and not a spirit, endowed with the likeness of his Father. He immediately hid himself, evincing a mindset change. In Adam's mind, God was no longer his primogenitor. Instead of being the provider and sustainer of the man, Adam perceived God as the one in whose presence his life had become imperiled. This change having been initiated by Satan's deceit resulted in the mind of the soul interpreting the circumstances of man according to demonic input.¹ The enemy persuaded man that God had withheld key information from him and that had man known the true facts about God, he would not trust Him. The central deception was that man could be the equal of God. Satan himself had previously sought to establish this equality.

Equality is the highest standard of righteousness possible within a framework of competition. Job mocked his friends saying, "What a help you are to the weak! How you have saved the arm without strength! What counsel you have given to one without wisdom! What helpful insight you have abundantly provided! To whom have you uttered words? And whose spirit was expressed through you?"² In an environment of competition, or equality, if the balance of equity is tipped even slightly, the result is that one is promoted at the expense of another, one becomes superior to the exact extent that the other becomes inferior, and one rules to the exact extent that the other is made subject. The choice of man to accept the word of his enemy produced a shift from the existing order of representation to one of competition and with that, the relationship between God and Adam changed from Father and son to an adversarial and, therefore, competitive relationship.

A son comes out of his father by the design of the father and is commissioned to present the exact nature of his father within the sphere of his existence. He depends for his support upon the estate of his father. Because he is a son, he is also heir to the estate of his Father.³ The certainty of a father's support provides the primary contrast between a son and an orphan, who must rely entirely upon an economy produced by the sweat of his brow.

The fall of man changed the source from which he derives his knowledge. His soul lacked the ability to reach into the wisdom of the heavens and he began to derive his information from the world around him, from the demands of his flesh and from the counsel of his enemy.[4] Job's words show the susceptibility of the human being to this deception that is competition and fairness. He decried God's fairness saying, "I am pure, without transgression; I am innocent and there is no guilt in me. Behold, He invents pretexts against me; He counts me as His enemy. He puts my feet in the stocks. He watches all my paths."[5]

Adam changed his view of himself from the son of God to God's adversary and lost connection to divine insight and knowledge. He replaced the sourcing of information to that which served his perception of the need to survive. All human culture came to be built upon these new priorities. Over the millennia of man's existence this culture of survival and supply has become formalized in intricate systems, which have evolved in their complexities. They lack the vast vistas of God's eternal perspective and rarely ever consider the existence of a transcendent order. They are strapped securely by the process of reason.

The knowledge of man is reduced to the history of his existence upon the planet and the recurring of cycles of human behavior and natural phenomena. It is always in conflict with the wisdom of God and has reached the point of being irreconcilable to the wisdom of God. The wisdom of God has become incomprehensible to the mind of the soul.

---

[1]See James 3:15 NASB. [2]Job 26:2-4 NASB. [3]See Galatians 4:7 NASB; and Psalm 2:6-8 NASB. [4]James 3:15-17 NASB. [5]Job 33:9-11 NASB (Elihu quoting Job).

A Contrast Between the Views of God and Man

This contrast between the knowledge of God and that of man is drastically displayed in the conversation between the Almighty and Job.

PART TWO

In responding to the challenge from Satan, Job is selected to test God's righteousness in a man. In some ways it represents a continuation of this theme of the ongoing war between God and the adversary. Against this macro picture, certain critical aspects of the point of view of man are contrasted with that of God.

Job, whom God introduced by saying, "[T]here is no one like him on the earth, a blameless and upright man, fearing God and turning away from evil," became the subject of trials that he did not understand.[1] He goes from a life of honor, regard, and privilege to a sudden removal of his wealth, fame and finally even his family. In his condition of deep brokenness, some of his friends offer their analyses on his sudden fall from the pinnacle of his society. Everyone knows that Job's position of favor and standing was as a result of his minute devotion to living a righteous life. Everyone unanimously agrees that he is just and upright in all his ways because of his relationship to God.

As the layers of support are removed, Job progressively begins to wonder about his own actions. He seeks for explanations for his sudden change of fortune, while attempting to hold on to his beliefs. Finally, under the strain of unrelenting and ever-increasing adversities, Job responds to the explanations of three of his friends. He honestly searches for explanations that would justify the crash of his fortune and the deaths of his children, and when there is no obvious answer, he alternates between questioning the righteousness of God, maintaining his innocence of wrongdoing, and trying to make sense out of his present dilemma. Whereas he does not deny the existence of God or even his relationship with Him, he begins to assert the unfairness of his treatment as the basis of his revaluation of the integrity of God.

He ended up asserting his unshakable faith in his own goodness while vacillating between the power and majesty of God on the one hand while questioning God's reliability and faithfulness to those who trust Him. His perspectives finally lead him to the conclusion that he was more righteous than God.[2] In his lack of understanding, Job defaults to a similar perspective that Adam exhibited immediately after the fall. It was one that does not know God and therefore, measures God's character from a position of equality, fairness and competition. This is a place to which everyone who seriously pursues God comes at some point in their journey. Confusion results when one has made as consistent and conscientious an effort as he knows how to make in pursuing the best understanding of what God requires that he has. In spite of his best efforts, trials remain unrelenting, and he cannot understand the purpose of his sufferings.

It is the human response to try to understand God within the context of present experiences. It is exceedingly difficult to understand that one's present trials come from a God who's very being is goodness and love and are unrelated to any issue of fault or failing. The reason is that the mind of the human being can only understand transcendent concepts, like love, through comparative analysis. For most people love is compared to fairness, justice and personally developed concepts of righteousness. Suffering, being viewed as a negative thing because it hurts—that comes not as the consequence of wrongdoing or failure or is something to balance the scales—is almost conceptually inaccessible as an act of love and goodness to most minds.

God's perspective differs substantially. He has undertaken responsibility for every person who chooses to be a son of God. This responsibility is to bring each person to the full and complete expression of his or her destiny in the fullness of time. This is the ultimate act of love from God's perspective because He promises to fulfill each son's inheritance, that is, to be a vessel through which God Himself is known, investing that aspect of His exact being in the son. Accordingly, often suffering is God's manner of expanding the capacity of those who seek Him diligently to receive and to contain the next increments of growth and advancement in their maturity. Whereas it is well understood that one who is faithful in little will be given much, the need to be expanded and trained to handle much is commonly overlooked.[3]

God, on the other hand, knows exactly what is required for man to function in greater endowments of the character of God. God routinely assigns higher and more complex assignments to those who have been proven faithful. The advance of His interests in the earth together with the exactness of His representation, given to his sons, is at the center of being an heir of God. The greatest gifts of God to man are not primarily material goods. He gives Himself, together with the right to represent Him as the mature son.[4] All of what was hidden in Job was brought into the light during his testing. Nothing of his nature remained hidden.

When God spoke to Job, He made the contrast between the divine point of view and that of a human stark. As God opened up the vistas of an ageless perspective, Job's preoccupation with his own present dilemma seemed to pale and recede immediately into insignificance.[5] God concluded the showing of His perspective with this final challenge: "Will the faultfinder contend with the Almighty? Let him who reproves God answer it."[6] Job's conclusion upon being shown the vast arc of God's eternal framework of knowledge was a very succinct and abject response. He agreed with God entirely, "Behold, I am insignificant; what can I reply to You? I lay my hand on my mouth. Once I have spoken, and I will not answer, even twice, and I will add nothing more."[7]

The story of Job's conflict with God and God's response is illustrative of how the uninformed point of view of man, as it relates to the knowledge of God, will often lead men to question God on the basis of their own understanding. God's response serves to elevate the discussion from the natural to the eternal and, in the process, to showcase what Jesus declared, "You are from below, I am from above; you are of this world, I am not of this world."[8] Whereas the eternal point of view understands the temporal, it is the superlative of the temporal.

> *"For My thoughts are not your thoughts. Nor are your ways My ways," declares the Lord. "For as the heavens are higher than the earth, so are My ways higher than your ways and My thoughts than your thoughts."* Isaiah 55:8-9 NASB

---

[1]Job 1:8 NASB. [2]See Job 34:5-6 NASB; Job 35:2-3 NASB. [3]See Luke 16:10 NIV; See also, Luke 19:17 NIV. [4]See Hebrews 1:1-2 NASB. [5]See, e.g. Job 38 NASB. [6]Job 40:2 NASB. [7]Job 40:4-5 NASB. [8]John 8:23 NASB.

Christ the Eternal Branch of Knowledge

> *A shoot will come up from the stump of Jesse; from his roots a Branch will bear fruit. The Spirit of the Lord will rest on Him— the spirit of wisdom and of understanding, the spirit of counsel and of might, the spirit of the knowledge and fear of the Lord— and he will delight in the fear of the Lord.* Isaiah 11:1-3 NIV

This Branch, whose human lineage came from Jesse—a descendant of Judah and father of King David—was the promised King who would restore the House of God.[1] The spirit of Knowledge attended Christ and He spoke about the knowledge of heaven's secrets. This knowledge, though available to mankind, will be limited to those who voluntarily place themselves under the rule of this King and are received as subjects in the Kingdom of Heaven. The need for the restoration of knowledge that comes by and through the spirit of Knowledge was as a result of the fall itself.

The subject of the conflict between God and Satan in the garden centered around the tree of the Knowledge of Good and Evil. "Out of the ground the Lord God caused to grow every tree that is pleasing to the sight and good for food; the tree of life also in the midst of the garden, and the tree of the knowledge of good and evil."[2] This tree was emblematic of the potential of a different source of knowledge that had to be available to man if indeed he were given a choice in the sources of his information. Man could not choose to be obedient if he were denied the choice of being disobedient. The tree symbolized the result that would flow from man's disobedience. His soul would derive its knowledge from a different source than God Himself.

All the trees of the garden provided Adam with an abundance of nourishment for his physical form, but Adam's spirit derived his nourishment from his daily encounter with God's presence. Even after Adam sinned, God came into the garden to commune with man, but Adam hid from God.[3] The human spirit needs sustenance that comes from the word of God. Adam's arrangement for the impartation of knowledge was the earliest example of this foundational concept of Scripture. His spirit was fed by the bread of God's presence. "Man shall not live on bread alone, but on every word that proceeds out of the mouth of God."[4] Both sides to a person's existence, spirit and flesh, require sustenance. For Adam, physical food came from the trees of the garden, but spiritual nourishment came directly from the presence of the Lord.

Knowledge, or rather the source of knowledge, defines existence within the bounds of creation. The conflict of knowledge that the enemy incited in the garden concerned specifically the source of mankind's knowledge about God. When the human spirit feeds on the presence of the Lord, it both understands and can assimilate the nature of God Himself, as Father, into one's being. The result is a human being who is a son of God and is capable of representing God the Father.

Knowledge about God that does not come from God Himself creates a false standard for God, a test that exists only in the human mind to judge whether God is God. The writer of the book of Romans understood the change that occurred, concerning knowledge, in the garden:

> *And even as after putting God to the test for the purpose of approving Him should He meet their specifications, and finding that He did not, they disapproved of holding Him in their full and precise knowledge, God gave them up to a mind that would not meet the test for that which a mind was meant[.]*
> Romans 1:28-32 Wuest Expanded Translation

In an attempt to approve or disprove God, the human mind can only evaluate such questions comparatively. Limited to the bounds of creation, the mind cannot fathom any standard by which to measure God outside itself. When Adam sought knowledge from a different source than God's presence, the human mind sought to measure God with itself as the standard. In his own mind, man became greater than God.

This is a fallacy of logic that was the original deception of humankind, to be like God through human knowledge. God exists beyond the limitations of which the human mind can grasp, because He exists outside time and space—in what we call the eternal realm. The eternal realm has no comparative measure within creation. The human mind can only twist personal knowledge, experience and observations toward a philosophical opinion of what the eternal and God might be like. Doing so is like trying to explain the natural world without the benefit or memory of the senses. The mind so bent cannot hope to fathom God. Therefore, the mind must conclude that God does not "meet its specifications." Without actually experiencing God's presence, the human being cannot continue to hold God in its knowledge. The result is the human mind operating in a manner for which it was never intended.

Christ restored the bread of God's presence to humanity, making it possible for any human to reverse Adam's choice of another source of knowledge that fed the body and soul, but left the spirit of man malnourished. Jesus told those following Him, who were seeking physical sustenance after He fed the five thousand,

> *"Truly, truly, I say to you....it is My Father who gives you the true bread out of heaven. For the bread of God is that which comes down out of heaven and gives life to the world...I am the bread of life; he who comes to Me will not hunger, and he who believes in Me will never thirst."* John 6:32-35 NASB

Through Adam's choice, people ceased to retain God in their knowledge and were given over to a reprobate mindset, but Christ assembles the spirits of mankind to commune with His Spirit, the source of all knowledge and wisdom.

The insertion of the Tree of the Knowledge of Good and Evil into creation, together with the command that man should not derive his nourishment from it, signified first that this was not a source of nourishment that was either compatible with what man received from his direct communication with God, nor was it a source useful to sustain his physical life. If it were valuable as an adjunct to support what man received directly from God—if it nourished the spirit—it would not have been forbidden. Likewise, if it were for the sustaining of his physical body, it would have been permitted as one of the choices for food.

Instead, Scripture describes the Tree of the Knowledge of Good and Evil as exciting to the senses and as an alternative source of knowledge.[5] Its primary appeal was choice. The tree appealed to Adam's and Eve's curiosity and to their souls. Like everything else in the garden, however, God placed it there for a purpose, consistent with why He created people. The tree's appeal made it possible for mankind to choose God or himself. This choice is essential for people to represent God as sons.

Creation is limited in its capacity to testify to God's person. Created things are merely able to testify to particular aspects of God, such as His awesome power to create or some evidence of the existence of divine order. God's presence is the exclusive mode of impartation for knowledge regarding His divine nature. Choosing human knowledge over God's presence caused more than the withdrawal from God's company. It cut off human beings' spirits from their essential sustenance from their source, the Spirit of God.

The spirit of Adam was starved for the supply of the presence of God. He lived for 930 years in a state of separation from God. Everything he experienced and passed on concerning the knowledge of God from the point of his choice onward came only from nature's veiled testimony about God.

God continued to shepherd the hope that comes from His presence. For example, ancient Israel was given this hope while it left Egypt and migrated to the promised land in the form of manna from heaven six days out of seven for forty years. God provided physical bread for the sustaining of natural life. He also required that twelve loaves of bread were put daily upon the table of the Lord.[6] The significance of this is unmistakable, as God summarized the entire purpose for Israel's sojourn in the wilderness:

> *He humbled you and let you be hungry, and fed you with manna which you did not know; nor did your fathers know, that He might make you understand that man does not live by bread alone, but man lives by everything that proceeds out of the mouth of the Lord.* Deuteronomy 8:3 NASB

Jesus, the bread of life, began His ministry with a similar testing in the wilderness. He restored the bread of God's presence when He rejected the enemy's attempt to focus upon nourishment for the physical being:

> *And the tempter came and said to Him, "If You are the Son of God, command that these stones become bread." But He answered and said, "It is written, man shall not live on bread alone, but on every word that proceeds out of the mouth of God."* Matthew 4:3-4 NASB

Whereas Adam deliberately departed from the presence of God, Jesus deliberately chose to return to the presence.

From the shoot that came out of the stump of Jesse, a tree that provided the bread of life as its fruit has been raised up as the alternative. The knowledge of God was restored to mankind through the bread of His presence. The spirit of Knowledge is the ability to commune with God, the Father, which Christ reestablished in Himself.

Jesus is the pattern for a life lived based on this knowledge. He spoke as one familiar not only with the eternal but with the nature of God Himself. His words and His actions showed the familiarity with God that a son has of his father. He brought the culture of heaven to the earth and demonstrated the very nature of God. His resurrection established the ultimate proof that He was the "exact representation of [God's]nature" beyond controversy.[7]

The Spirit of Christ that inhabited the person of Jesus is the source by which mankind may be reassembled to the presence of God. A veiled view of God through the soul is no longer people's only choice.

> *Now the Lord is the Spirit, and where the Spirit of the Lord is, there is liberty. But we all, with unveiled face, beholding as*

> *in a mirror the glory of the Lord, are being transformed into the same image from glory to glory, just as from the Lord, the Spirit.* 2 Corinthians 3:17-18 NASB

Assembled to the Spirit of Christ, the sons of God have access to the presence of the Father. The restoration from the fall is complete in Christ, and the purity of man's knowledge may be restored. Resupplied with this knowledge, the Spirit of God communes with the human spirit, sustaining it from a divine source of nourishment. This is a necessary change that must occur before people can authentically represent God's character in their own lives.

---

[1]Zechariah 6:11-12 NASB; See also Jeremiah 23:5-6, 33:15 NASB. [2]Genesis 2:9 NASB. [3]Genesis 3:8-10 NASB. [4]Matthew 4:4 NASB. [5]Genesis 3:6 NASB. [6]Exodus 25:30 NASB. [7]Hebrews 1:3 NASB.

The Fear of the Lord

> *Therefore, knowing the fear of the Lord, we persuade men, but we are made manifest to God; and I hope that we are made manifest also in your consciences.* 2 Corinthians 5:11 NASB

The Lord Jesus Christ exhibited the characteristic of the Spirit of God known as the Fear of the Lord which concerns the relationship between the Father and Son in the context of governance. King David prophesied concerning this aspect of God's character and it is memorialized in the book of Psalms:

> *Why are the nations in an uproar and the peoples devising a vain thing? The kings of the earth take their stand and the rulers take counsel together against the Lord and against His Anointed, saying, "Let us tear their fetters apart and cast away their cords from us!" He who sits in the heavens laughs, the Lord scoffs at*

PART TWO

> *them. Then He will speak to them in His anger and terrify them in His fury, saying, "But as for Me, I have installed My King upon Zion, My holy mountain."* Psalm 2:1-6 NASB

Regarding governance, God installed Jesus as the anointed King and the form of governance represents restraint upon those subject to it. The execution of governance comes through proclamation or decree:

> *I will surely tell of the decree of the Lord: He said to Me, "You are My Son, Today I have begotten You. Ask of Me and I will surely give the nations as Your inheritance, and the very ends of the earth as Your possession. You shall break them with a rod of iron, You shall shatter them like earthenware." Now therefore, O kings, show discernment; Take warning, O judges of the earth. Worship the Lord with reverence and rejoice with trembling. Do homage to the Son that He not become angry, and you perish in the way, for His wrath may soon be kindled. How blessed are all who take refuge in Him!* Psalm 2:7-12 NASB

The newly appointed King initiates His rule by proclaiming the foundation and character of all aspects of His rule. His first decree—that He will proclaim the decree of the Lord—is all encompassing. This means that He will be governed in all of His rule by the decrees of God. He made Himself a vassal to His Father and fully embraced the role of the Son, "the radiance of [God's] glory and the exact representation of His nature" and one who "upholds all things by the word of His power."[1] In David's prophecy, God immediately recognizes that the newly appointed King has chosen to clothe Himself in the authority of His Father and, by so doing, has rejected a form of rule based upon independence from His Father. This dialogue between God the Father and Jesus the Son is meant to show how rule in the Kingdom of God is constituted. God declares His choice and Jesus decrees that He will live to put the nature of God on display. God responds with this second decree by which He names Jesus as His Son.

PART TWO

Jesus' life and resurrection comprise the events that bring David's prophecy into creation. The primary motivation of Jesus was to obey His Father's decrees.[2] This strict adherence to the accurate and consistent representation of His Father brought Jesus into direct opposition with the religious authorities.[3] Whereas the religious leaders ruled by the law, Jesus' rule routinely appeared to transcend the law.[4] For example, He spoke directly to the authority of the law as contained in the Ten Commandments, but explained the reason why the commandments themselves were given. Ultimately, He showed the people His Father's perfection.[5] He referred to God as His Father and explained His ways to the crowds through His teachings. Often the crowds were amazed at His teachings and compared Him to the religious authorities.[6] He also frequently established the truth of His teachings by performing stunning miracles from feeding large crowds of people to raising the dead. Yet, the leaders criticized Jesus for affiliating Himself too closely with God and with a divine mandate.

All this led to a path of confrontation. Leaders feared the loss of their influence to one who spoke and acted as Jesus did. Jesus claimed to be anointed by God to rule over the Kingdom of Heaven, distinguishing the Kingdom of Heaven from the secular authority of Rome. Inevitably, Jesus' adherence to His Father's decrees was greater than any fear of conflict, persecution, or death.

The early apostles continued in Jesus' path, taking up the same message for which Jesus was crucified. Peter's message on the day of Pentecost was to establish whether or not Jesus was the promised King, according to King David's prophetic declarations. He offered both the text of Scripture and eyewitness testimony regarding the criteria for the determination of the King— that Jesus was indeed the promised one. Peter and the other apostles continued to preach this message and to authenticate it with dramatic and miraculous signs.[7]

Similarly, the people of the early church dedicated themselves to this truth. They carefully applied the prophetic Scripture to their experiences:

> *And when they heard this, they lifted their voices to God with one accord and said, "O Lord, it is You who made the heaven and the earth and the sea, and all that is in them, who by the Holy Spirit, through the mouth of our father David your servant, said, 'Why did the Gentiles rage, and the peoples devise futile things? The kings of the earth took their stand, and the rulers were gathered together against the Lord and against His Christ.' "For truly in this city there were gathered together against Your holy servant Jesus, whom You anointed, both Herod and Pontius Pilate, along with the Gentiles and the peoples of Israel, to do whatever Your hand and Your purpose predestined to occur. And now, Lord, take note of their threats, and grant that Your bond-servants may speak Your word with all confidence, while You extend Your hand to heal, and signs and wonders take place through the name of Your holy servant Jesus." And when they had prayed, the place where they had gathered together was shaken, and they were all filled with the Holy Spirit and began to speak the word of God with boldness.*
> Acts 4:24-31 NASB

The early followers of Christ rooted their lives in the truth that God was in Christ reconciling mankind to Himself.[8] Even though their lives were likely to be endangered, their belief that Jesus was the true and authentic fulfillment of Scripture, naming Him as the King, was greater to them than even the threat of death. Like Jesus, their regard for the truth was greater than their fear even of persecution and death. This regard for the truth of God's governance is the manifestation of the spirit of the Fear of the Lord. Continuing Jesus' work on the earth, the sons of God are called to represent the Father's decrees, which will lead inevitably to conflict and worse. However, dedication to the truth of who Christ is, represented in the Fear of the Lord, functions to release all sons of God from the threat of death so that they, like Jesus, were free to obey God in every matter.

---

[1]Hebrews 1:3 NASB. [2]See, e.g., John 5:30 NASB. [3]See, e.g., John 1:14 NASB. [4]See Matthew 5 NASB. [5]Matthew 5:48 NASB. [6]Matthew 7:28-29 NASB. [7]Acts 3 NASB. [8]2 Corinthians 5:19 NASB.

The Fear of the Lord, the Foundation of Rule

Jesus came into the world carrying the seven Spirits of God, but He still required training and discipline before God presented Him to the earth as His "beloved Son."[1] Jesus went through a period of eighteen years of extreme discipline and training. During this time, "Jesus kept increasing in wisdom and stature, and in favor with God and men."[2] And, Scripture notes that "He learned obedience from the things which He suffered."[3] Scripture makes clear, with Jesus as the prime example, that every son of God is meant to grow in maturity through training that is made up of great suffering and discipline.

This training serves God's purposes for each of His sons. Broadly, one must be mature in order to know God, to be like Him, and therefore, represent Him accurately. This compendium of attributes required to represent God accurately also includes being able to rule according to His righteousness, and the Fear of the Lord. Training teaches restraint. This was inherent in Jesus' mandate in which He did only what He saw the Father doing. In the garden of Gethsemane, He gave voice to this restraint. When He was conflicted about His imminent fate, He prayed, "My Father, if it is possible, let this cup pass from Me; yet not as I will, but as You will."[4] He fully restrained His own will in favor of God the Father's.

This restraint is the hallmark of the spirit of the Fear of the Lord. The emotion "fear" and the characteristic of God known as the Fear of the Lord are not the same. Fear is an emotional motivation, and it is the opposite of Love. The Fear of the Lord is an anointing of rule. By trying to equate these two concepts, some have taught that we should fear God, complying with His wishes under the threat of reprisals or the removal of His beneficence. This type of teaching attempts to import something most people are familiar with, the emotions of fear, into something they do not fully understand. It is fundamentally incorrect because it misunderstands the purpose of the seven Spirits of God.

The Fear of the Lord is an anointing, originally carried by Jesus Christ, and one now that attends His corporate Body. At no time was Jesus motivated by anything other than love for His Father, displayed by unwavering trust. He understood His Father's nature and saw that everything God the Father did demonstrated His love for humanity. Consequently, He gave in to the nature of His Father's love and was Himself perfected in love. He knew that this would involve His own death but understood the necessity of so great a sacrifice within the context of God's love for humanity. Jesus never feared God, or any threat from God. This was not once His motivation.

The Fear of the Lord produces righteous rule within the Body of Christ. As Jesus demonstrated, love exists at the core of His rule. He even issued a final, overarching commandment based on love: "A new commandment I give to you, that you love one another, even as I have loved you, that you also love one another."[5] The restraint of love is the most powerful influence upon human behavior. It does not simply happen. A son of God must be rigorously trained to prefer the nature of God over his own interests. This training results in the love of God becoming the inspiration for the choices of maturing sons. This is the essence of this character of God.

The Fear of the Lord is the restraint upon the rule of God's sons. Rule that comes from the Kingdom of Heaven is supported by the power of heaven's throne. Sons of God must learn the restraints upon power that are exercised by love before they are given access to that economy. The point of every person's rule is to represent God by bringing the order of heaven into earth. The evidence of this rule is righteousness, peace and joy—not the demonstration of power.[6] The standard of love defines the nature of God and love governs the use of power.

A ruler in God's kingdom is wise and mature if he fears the Lord. When God gives someone rule within His house, it is because He has judged that person competent to display His character. The fully mature sons of God who are sent as dispensations of His House are sons that act with restraint toward their own will and who have learned instead to offer themselves as living sacrifices.[7]

---

[1]Matthew 3:17 NASB. [2]Luke 2:52 NASB. [3]Hebrews 5:8 NASB. [4]Matthew 26:39 NASB; Mark 14:36 NASB. [5]John 13:34 NASB. [6]See Romans 14:17 NASB. [7]See Soleyn, *The Elementary Doctrines*, The Elementary Doctrines and the Maturing Son.

The Fear of the Lord, and the Rule of Mature Sons

A simplified contrast between the mature son of God and one whose capacity to rule is still in training: The mature son follows the decrees of the Lord; the young son learns to obey by the things he suffers. This difference is at the heart of what comes from the anointing of the Fear of the Lord.

Understanding the Fear of the Lord for someone who is already assembled to the Body of Christ, comes through Jesus, the pattern Son. He displayed reverence and awe for God's love and voluntarily dedicated His life to the destiny God assigned to Him. The Fear of the Lord anchored in the will of God prevented His soul from being swayed by opportunity or temptations designed to shake His commitment to God.

> *Therefore, since Christ has suffered in the flesh, arm yourselves also with the same purpose, because He who has suffered in the flesh has ceased from sin, so as to live the rest of the time in the flesh no longer for the lusts of men, but for the will of God.* 1 Peter 4:1-2 NASB

Jesus Christ is the template for rule in the Kingdom. If God chose to subject Him to the discipline of obedience in order to establish the Fear of the Lord as the anchoring of the way that all sons rule, then it is to be understood that every mature son to whom rule is committed has been trained to respond in every situation out of the restraint of the nature of God, with which they have become intimately familiar. Whoever God establishes to rule in the Kingdom of Heaven rules under the authority established by Christ.[1] Everyone who has been given authority in the Kingdom of Heaven is a vassal of Christ, since He is the sovereign King. The only authority that exists in the Kingdom is that which comes directly from Christ. Such delegated authority is specific in its purpose. Every sphere of rule in the Kingdom is meant to reflect Christ's rule. His rule is to obey the Father's decrees.

This arrangement is important, because it puts the power of the Spirit under and subject to love. The Word of God is His power. Jesus was the Word made flesh, and Christ is the Spirit that contains the same glory as the Word while assembling human spirits to Him. But, Christ rules by following the Father's decrees, as prophecied by David and demonstrated by Jesus' rule on the earth. This puts the love that defines the nature and character of God the Father above, as a govern to, God's power and authority, embodied in Christ. One who has been trained in the Fear of the Lord views the love of God the Father as an absolute restraint upon every nuance of the person's administration.

As with Jesus, this restraint produces a vision of God that is accurate and reliable.

---

[1] Matthew 28:18 NASB.

The Fear of the Lord, the Beginning of Wisdom

The fear of the Lord is the beginning of knowledge; Fools despise wisdom and instruction. Proverbs 1:7 NASB

Whoever is wise acknowledges the Lord as the final authority in which all things come to rest. Every government must be able to resolve conflict with finality. Human governments can only impose finality over things that they may control based on their constitutions of authority, usually property, liberty, and sometimes the lives of their citizens. These resolutions do not result in rest or finality, only in rewards, punishments, or concepts of equity, leaving the underlying conflict in doubt. Matters resolved consistent with God's nature are anchored in divine grace.

Peace is the result of God's government. His government comprises citizens who choose to subject themselves to Christ, the head. When all citizens voluntarily dedicate their lives to the order of the King, then the King may enact change within the citizens themselves. Concepts of competition, fairness, and equity are moot when each person has a place that suits them perfectly and the King is dedicated to bringing them to maturity in that role. This is rule that establishes peace.

Rule flowing out of reverence and awe of the Lord God the Almighty is the epitome of wisdom. It produces righteousness and peace as the social dwelling place of those who benefit from being under such rule. In the Fear of the Lord, rulers are restrained from profiting from their rule and instead ruling for the benefit of those subject to their rule. By the same spirit, those subject to rule are trained to honor the rules as emissaries of God and submit to the rule of Christ as presented through them. They avail themselves of the benefits of God's government over all spheres of their lives, and they themselves experience a change in culture from that of the world to the Kingdom. This environment supports their maturity and growth as they themselves become mature sons of God capable of operating in the wisdom of God.

PART Three

God is Love

The one who does not love does not know God, for God is love.
1 John 4:8 NASB

You cannot represent God if you do not know Him. God's personhood is incomprehensible to the human mind, the human eyes, and all other senses designed to interact with the natural world. The seven Spirits of God discuss the translation of God's character into creation through Christ and His Body. They are visible as they accompany the sons of God through various stages of representation and maturity. The seven Spirits are like puzzle pieces that when assembled in the corporate Body—it's people, it's function, and the effect ultimately it will have on earth—provide the most complete picture of God in creation that is visible to those who are not led by the Spirit. Merely seeing these aspects of His character does not open the mystery of who God is. That knowledge is the intimate domain of the Father-Son relationship that God seeks with all people but is only granted to those whom Christ has assembled in Him.

The difference between seeing God and knowing God is the difference between being an observer limited to the experience of God made visible in His people and being a participant who chooses to exist as an extension of the Kingdom of Heaven in the earth. The participant is called to show pieces of God's character through actions. These participants are sons of God who are given the opportunity to be like God in the deepest parts of their beings. Their perceptions and motivations, though invisible to the observer, represent the Father.

To be like God, they must know God. His personhood is well established but rarely understood. God is love. He defines love. He is not defined by human perceptions of love. The human experience is one small glimpse, most often blurred by emotion. God's love is only accessible via the same realm and mode of His existence that is spirit.

God is the Father of our spirits. Knowledge of Him is accessible to those who are led by the Spirit. Scripture makes clear that those who lack this access cannot understand spiritual things:

> *See how great a love the Father has bestowed on us, that we would be called children of God; and such we are. For this reason, the world does not know us, because it did not know Him.* 1 John 3:1 NASB

God's love is something hidden in Him and only accessible to His children. Every bit of heaven made visible in the earth serves God's love:

> *If I speak with the tongues of men and of angels, but do not have love, I have become a noisy gong or a clanging cymbal. If I have the gift of prophecy, and know all mysteries and all knowledge, and if I have all faith so as to remove mountains, but do not have love, I am nothing. And if I give all my possessions to feed the poor, and if I surrender my body to be burned, but do not have love it profits me nothing.* 1 Corinthians 13:1-3 NASB

His mighty power which serves Christ and His Body serves His love. The motivation governing every visible or experiential aspect of

PART THREE

God's being is love. The inheritance of man is to be a partaker of the divine nature of God. The essence of that nature is love.

To represent God, you must know God; to know God, you must know His love and as a result you must also love as He does. The commandment Christ gave to His Body that subsumes all other commandments sets a standard for love that is the same for people as it is for God.

> *A new commandment I give to you, that you love one another, even as I have loved you, that you also love one another.* John 13:34 NASB

God intentionally designed sonship to be an exact reflection of the way in which God Himself loves.

One cannot fully know God's love without the direct communion with the Spirit that is part of being assembled to the Body of Christ. However, we can aide the transition a person makes from an observer to partaker of His divine nature by furthering our understanding of what love is and what it is not. Scripture begins this examination for us by providing multiple facets by which we can increase that understanding. These characteristics, or facets, are meant to be a touchstone for maturing sons of God to help ground their development with an accurate picture of God's love. For them to serve this purpose, we must examine them with the clarity of the Spirit, dispel certain misinformation, and place them within the larger picture of God as love.

The Characteristics of Love

> *Love is patient, love is kind and is not jealous; love does not brag and is not arrogant, does not act unbecomingly; it does not seek its own, is not provoked, does not take into account*

> *a wrong suffered, does not rejoice in unrighteousness, but rejoices with the truth; bears all thing, believes all things, hopes all things, endures all things. Love never fails; but if there are gifts of prophecy, they will be done away; if there are tongues, they will cease; if there is knowledge, it will be done away.* 1 Corinthians 13:4-8 NASB

Understanding love is an exploration of a divine standard that characterizes God's nature. His nature defines the concept of love for purposes of representing Him. The first exploration is that this divine standard comes from the realm of spirit. This origin removes the limitations of time and space, physical considerations, mental attributes, and anything else that roots human nature in creation. Love originates from a divine perspective that is mostly inaccessible to the human capacities for thought and action.

The human emotion of love that we are familiar with plays a role in this understanding. It is a shadow of God's love, and it helps those who experience it in its many forms—that of a parent for a child or that of a husband and wife, or simply of one human being for another—to begin to understand God's love. The human capacity for altruism alone is not equal to the divine standard of love.

Christ will supply people from His own Body to enable them with the ability to love every person who chooses to follow Him. But every human being is distracted to some degree by the urgencies of time and the imperatives of survival either personally, or in the lives of those around them. These distractions and personal biases may prevent some people from receiving those sent to love them. Such obstacles are issues related to the believer's maturity and the distractions of their souls and must be remedied. No one, however, is without the opportunity to experience human love as a starting point for the experience and understanding of God's love. Therefore, this examination of love's characteristics will focus on the divine standards while also drawing from human examples of each characteristic.

Love Is Patient

God waits patiently for every person to return to Him. This is not patience measured in time. God's patience is based upon His intent for all creation and for mankind. "[T]he patience of God kept waiting in the days of Noah, during the construction of the ark in which a few, that is eight persons, were brought safely through the water."[1] When all earth's other inhabitants strayed from God, He waited to save eight. He waited because by preserving these eight people, His purpose for creating sons in the earth and His covenant to reconcile them to Himself would continue. Concerning the original intent for humankind, all that must be accomplished will be done. Time is irrelevant.

Before man was created, God knew and understood that by giving him the privilege and responsibility of choice, he would choose to reject God and depart from His intent for man's creation. Knowing that, God planned to redeem him by coming into time in the form of a man to bear the responsibility for all his transgressions as the price for reconciling him both to his relationship to God as a son as well as the restoration of his divine purpose. The love of God pursued this course patiently, for sixty-two generations—from Adam to Christ.

> *God, desiring even more to show to the heirs of the promise the unchangeableness of His purpose, interposed with an oath, so that by two unchangeable things in which it is impossible for God to lie, we who have taken refuge would have strong encouragement to take hold of the hope set before us. This hope we have as an anchor of the soul, a hope both sure and*

> *steadfast and one which enters within the veil[.]* Hebrews 6:17-19 NASB

God's promises are certain. God's timing—the moments in which He brings about His intent on earth—is called *kairos*.² Kairos is a concept of time describing the opportune moment or season for something to occur—it's due time as opposed to a sufficient passage of time. The patience of God's love is also measured according to the *kairos* timing of things, not the passage of time.

God acts and restrains from acting with patience. In seasons or epochs of time upon the earth, God's patience is to act consistent with things that already exist in the eternal. For example, Scripture says that the Lamb was slain from the foundations of the world. This act of redemption was in place before Adam sinned because God knows the end from the beginning. The actual timing of that event occurred four thousand years after Adam sinned because that was when God had finished laying all the groundwork necessary to restore mankind, not just in Christ's death and resurrection but for the duration of human existence. Today we still reference much of that groundwork as we continue to receive revelation and progress along the path of God's original intent.

God's patient love encompasses everybody's life both in the decision to enter into a relationship with God in Christ and in growth as a son of God. "The Lord is not slow about His promise, as some count slowness, but is patient toward you, not wishing for any to perish but for all to come to repentance."³ A person's choice to be reconciled to God as a son is available at any moment during that person's lifetime. No prior thought or action forecloses God's acceptance of one who chooses Him.

> *Therefore we have been buried with Him through baptism into death, so that as Christ was raised from the dead through the*

> *glory of the Father, so we too might walk in newness of life....*
> *Even so consider yourselves to be dead to sin, but alive to God*
> *in Christ Jesus.* Romans 6:4, 11 NASB

This is why a person will first experience a death and resurrection, a rebirth, when he makes that choice. The patience of God is such that no one is prohibited from choosing Him during the person's natural life.

Every believer also experiences this patient love as we mature in Christ. This is particularly true in areas that require the discipline of our souls. As our Father, God accepts the task of disciplining every believer so that everyone has the opportunity to reach the greatest outpouring of his or her individual destiny. Not everyone reaches his full potential. People, even believers, do not always submit their lives to this process at least to the degree required of a mature son of God.[4] There are many reasons for this shortfall. We have discussed at length the effect of an orphan culture that originated in and with Adam's fall, which is the greatest antagonistic influence on the intended relationship between God and people. Regardless of one's reasons for struggling with the process of maturing as a son of God, God's patience is that He gives each believer every available chance to submit and mature in his destiny. Beyond our natural lives, God has promised to finish this work for all those who chose Him but did not reach their full maturity during their natural lives.[5]

Patience is long-suffering—being patient in bearing the offenses and injuries of others.[6] While God patiently waits, at times He suffers the wanton and reckless disregard of His people for Him.[7] God foregoes the option of summarily destroying or even abandoning humanity even though "the intent of man's heart is evil from his youth."[8] Love suffers while the ones who are loved continue in their patterns of rejection of the ways of God.

Jesus showed us how to exhibit God's long-suffering love in relationship to each other. His prophecy of Jerusalem's rejection of God disquieted Him. "Jerusalem, Jerusalem, who kills the prophets and stones those who are sent to her! How often I wanted to gather your children together, the way a hen gathers her chicks under her wings, and you were unwilling."[9] Yet, Jesus' desire for His people, in the face of certain rejection, was that the people be reconciled to God.

Our nature, unlike God's, is impatient with a visceral aversion to suffering, especially when the suffering benefits others but not ourselves. God's patience exposes Him to suffering while He waits to introduce the unfolding of His plan for the appropriate *kairos*. Likewise, we are called, like Jesus, to patience and suffering that will benefit others, giving them every chance for repentance and maturity.

---

[1] 1 Peter 3:20 NASB. [2] See Strong's G2405. [3] 2 Peter 3:9 NASB. [4] See Soleyn, Supra, *The Elementary Doctrines*, Stages of Sonship. [5] Revelation 20:4-5 NASB. [6] See, e.g., 1 Corinthians 13:4 NKJV; see also Strong's G3114, makrothymeō. [7] Isaiah 1 NASB. [8] Genesis 8:21 NASB. [9] Matthew 23:37 NASB.

Love Is Kind

> *But I say to you, love your enemies and pray for those who persecute you, so that you may be sons of your Father who is in heaven; for He causes His sun to rise on the evil and the good, and sends rain on the righteous and the unrighteous. For if you love those who love you, what reward do you have? Do not even the tax collectors do the same? If you greet only your brothers, what more are you doing than others? Do not even the Gentiles do the same? Therefore you are to be perfect, as your heavenly Father is perfect.* Matthew 5:44-48 NASB

Jesus translated God's love into tangible human circumstances and showed the kindness of God in practical expressions such as praying for those who speak evil, blessing those who curse others, and offering more than required from those who would exploit others. Other practical examples include lending to our enemies without expecting to be repaid. It is through kindness that Jesus taught we should love our enemies.

> *But love your enemies, and do good, and lend, expecting nothing in return; and your reward will be great, and you will be sons of the Most High; for He Himself is kind to ungrateful and evil men.* Luke 6:35 NASB

The impediment to kindness is self-preservation. Jesus taught about loving others without expectation of reciprocity. He showed us that some of the greatest expressions of love come through showing kindness when doing so makes you vulnerable to the unkindness of others.

The nature of a son of God as a spirit being is exalted through kindness. Our spirits do not die. They are not perishable or imperfect. They do not depend upon any created thing for sustenance. Our spirits, informed by the Spirit of God, are not vulnerable to harm. They are never uncomfortably self-conscious, and they do not act according to the limited span of a natural lifetime. It is by relying on our spiritual nature that a normal human being can love another to the point of extreme vulnerability. Kindness that shows a love "as Christ has loved us" is perhaps the greatest visible expression of God's love that the individual person is capable of showing.

Kindness represents the standard of God's values. He values spirit over the created or material things. The more mature a son of God the more capable that person becomes of also placing their value on eternal things.

PART THREE

> *Do not store up for yourselves treasures on earth, where moth and rust destroy and where thieves break in and steal. But store up for yourselves treasures in heaven, where neither moth nor rust destroys and where thieves do not break in or steal; for where your treasure is, there your heart will be also.*
> Matthew 6:19-21 NASB

In the case of kindness and demonstrating God's love, the eternal value is placed upon God's desire to show Himself through His Son, the Body of Christ. When we love as God loves, we participate with Christ in making God visible on the earth. By assigning value to heavenly standards, the son of God can love even his enemies in tangible ways. Kindness so contrasts society's prevailing attitudes that it stands out like a light in the darkness. Kindness incites curiosity. True kindness transforms others even as it displays the goodness of God.

Love Does Not Envy, It Does Not Boast, It Is Not Proud

The humility of God is seen radiantly in His willingness to commit the representation of His person to another, namely a son, and to be known as the son presents Him. The display of the grandeur of God is inhibited in its showing by the restricted competence of the immature son. The son reveals the true glory of the Father in an authentic and complete way when the son becomes one in whom the Father is "well pleased."[1] God waits for the son to mature with long-suffering patience. He delights in the son's maturity revealed in Christ as he increases in his grace to represent God the Father accurately.

God does not compete with the Son. God chooses to be seen only through the corporate Son, meaning His entire purpose for creation comes not by His great power, but it comes through His investiture in humans and His dedication to mature them in the role of representing Him. This relationship is the antithesis of competition.

PART THREE

Competition erodes any relationship. Between the Father and the Son, competition would see the Father guarding against potential misrepresentation by His sons. It would also see the son seeking equality with the Father. Instead, Jesus, "although He existed in the form of God, did not regard equality with God a thing to be grasped."[2] As a result, God highly exalted Him so that every tongue will confess that Jesus Christ is Lord to the glory of God the Father.[3] The Father allowed His glory to be seen through Christ Jesus.

Every person in a relationship puts themselves there for some internal motivation. Duty, financial reward, and pleasure all are motivations that seek some individual gain, and all are rooted in competition. Only a relationship that is rooted in love—in which all sides are made vulnerable by their preference of others over their own desires—shows the unrestrained character of each person. You cannot fully invest your person in any other kind of relationship.

So it is between God the Father and the Son. Beyond demonstrating the archetype for personal relationship to God, the relationship between the Father and the Son informs the nature of the relationships that exist within the corporate Son which is the assembling of sons into a corporate whole—the Body of Christ. Specifically, the Body is meant to function harmoniously and without competition.

> *For even as the body is one and yet has many members, and all the members of the body, though they are many, are one body, so also is Christ. For by one Spirit we were all baptized into one body, whether Jews or Greeks, whether slaves or free, and we were all made to drink of one Spirit. For the body is not one member, but many. If the foot says, "Because I am not a hand, I am not a part of the body," it is not for this reason any the less a part of the body. And if the ear says, "Because I am not an eye, I am not a part of the body," it is not for this reason any the less a part of the body. If the whole body were an eye, where*

> *would the hearing be? If the whole were hearing, where would the sense of smell be? But now God has placed the members, each one of them, in the body, just as He desired. If they were all one member, where would the body be? But now there are many members, but one body.* 1 Corinthians 12:12-20 NASB

Each part was designed to fit within the whole and to function optimally from its proper placement within the whole. The relevance of the individual part, though important to the whole, depends upon the existence and functioning of the whole. An eye or a hand, severed from its joining to the body, becomes little more than a curiosity. It is the life of the whole that both empowers and gives relevance to the part. Competition among the parts is patently absurd. It is a culture that is foreign to that of the corporate Son and completely incompatible with the Spirit of God.

> *But if you have bitter jealousy and selfish ambition in your heart, do not be arrogant and so lie against the truth. This wisdom is not that which comes down from above, but is earthly, natural, demonic. For where jealousy and selfish ambition exist, there is disorder and every evil thing. But the wisdom from above is first pure, then peaceable, gentle, reasonable, full of mercy and good fruits, unwavering, without hypocrisy. And the seed whose fruit is righteousness is sown in peace by those who make peace. What is the source of quarrels and conflicts among you? Is not the source your pleasures that wage war in your members? You lust and do not have; so you commit murder. You are envious and cannot obtain; so you fight and quarrel. You do not have because you do not ask.* James 3:14-4:2 NASB

Pleasure, lusts, and envy infect human relationships. These motivations are rooted in the deceptive concept of competition for self-sufficiency common to the culture of the orphan, the fix for which is the restoration of sonship and reconciliation to the Father.

All the parts of the human body may function perfectly, but their optimum expressions transcend even the cooperative result of all the parts working together. The ability to paint a picture, create a thought, or express an emotion is a greater result than may be accounted for by the parts working in perfect harmony. The ability to conceive an idea is something that comes out of the human as a spirit that may be expressed through the cooperative function of the parts. We can begin to understand both the nature and the result of love without envy through this harmony.

Love, like the concept of harmony, is a state of being. To love as God loves, the source of one's state must be His being. The human spirit communes with God's Spirit. Only one led by the Spirit can hope to love as God loves. This is a state of being reserved only for the sons of God in Christ. From the wisdom of the Spirit, every member of the Son reveres every other member's role and all may be in awe of the potential for the corporate whole. To live a life described here, you must begin with reverence for God's nature, which has created this composite structure that gives life and meaning to every assembled part.

---

[1]See, e.g., 2 Peter 1:17 NASB; but see 1 Corinthians 10:5 NASB. [2]Philippians 2:6-7 NASB. [3]Philippians 2:9-11 NASB.

Love Does Not Dishonor Others

The principle of honor is a key component of love. Honor recognizes the manner in which God appears in another. Our behavior toward one in whom God comes to us shows how we submit to God. Everyone was created to put the glory of God on display in the earth. In the mandate to "see no one any longer according to the flesh" God regards everyone as designed to carry His glory in specific manifestations whether or not their present circumstances are aligned to a divine mandate or even that they choose to retain God in their knowledge. Like God, our love for others cannot depend upon who they appear to be at the present. As God's representatives, our interactions with others should demonstrate the seven Spirits of God and be motivated by who that person is created to be. We fail in love when our interactions with others are merely in reaction to their present states of being.

This manner of engaging the world is far beyond showing goodness, kindness, generosity, and other positive traits of which any human being is capable. Our manner is to honor the Spirit of God in others—to recognize that their spirits are capable of responding to God just as we, being awakened from our condition of spiritual death, now live openly for the glory of God. Honoring one who lives apart from Christ is discerning the way Christ would appear if that person surrendered to His rule over his life. Honoring them in their capacities of calling and functioning is the manner in which we would actually honor the appearing of Christ Himself. This is a way to engage the rest of the world that is accessible only to the sons of God.

Giving honor when we disagree or have been injured by others, whether believers or unbelievers, involves following particular protocols of redress. When we are disappointed or offended, it is natural to default to a response of dishonor as a means of showing our displeasure in another. Private or subtle harm may leave the believer to feel justified in simply engaging in a pattern of avoidance and even marginalization of the one who has offended us in this manner. These are responses out of our selfishness and the desire for equitable treatment or even self-preservation. However, these are not the typical responses of the Spirit, and Scripture highlights certain protocols to follow to properly honor those who do harm. The manner of our review is different if the offense is given by a believer or an unbeliever. If the offense is given by a believer, the process of review is meant to "win your brother."[1] The process discloses God's divine intent for the sons of God to prefer one another as an expression of love.[2]

Love for another who is not a believer in the event of harm or scorn is one of the most potent representations of the Father's love.

> *Do not resist an evil person; but whoever slaps you on your right cheek, turn the other to him also. If anyone wants to sue you and take your shirt, let him have your coat also. Whoever forces you to go one mile, go with him two. Give to him who asks of you, and do not turn away from him who wants to borrow from you...I say to you, love your enemies and pray for those who persecute you, so that you may be sons of your Father who is in heaven.* Matthew 5:39-45 NASB[3]

The reason for this behavior is the honoring of the potential for the endowment of grace in the unbeliever. That grace is something that only the Spirit of God can recognize and, thus, this honor for another is strictly the domain of God's sons in Christ.

Honor is one of the easily witnessed out-workings of love. It exists in all human interactions, whether pleasant or adversarial. Honor always preserves the believer's integrity as the character of God is put on display, regardless of the nature or the result of the interaction.

---

[1] Matthew 18:15-17 NASB. [2] See, e.g., Romans 12:10 NASB; Ephesians 4:31-32 NASB. [3] See also Romans 12:17-21 NASB; 1 Peter 4:14 NASB; 1 Peter 3:9; 1 Thessalonians 5:15 NASB.

PART THREE

Love Is Not Self-Seeking

The House of God is the corporate setting in which love is perfected. Apart from this context love remains limited to natural circumstances and experiences and functions apart from the mandate to display the nature of God.

The limits of love among unbelievers are the point at which one's wellbeing is threatened. Although humans may occasionally give up their lives for a friend or a cause, it is the exception rather than the mature expression of human culture in general. However, the laying down of one's life as part of the honoring of Christ in the other is the goal of the culture of believers. It is not a strange or unfamiliar thought to the mature believer:

> *For while we were still helpless, at the right time Christ died for the ungodly. For one will hardly die for a righteous man; though perhaps for the good man someone would dare even to die. But God demonstrates His own love toward us, in that while we were yet sinners, Christ died for us.* Romans 5:6-8 NASB

The mature believer recognizes the value of each part of the whole Body of Christ. The more mature one becomes the more commonplace the response of recognizing and honoring the value of each part placed within the Body consistent with God's design.

Christ gives the apostles, the prophets, the evangelists, the pastors and the teachers to equip His people for works of service, so that the Body of Christ may be built up until we all reach unity in the faith and in the knowledge of the Son of God. We will grow to become in every respect the mature Body of Him who is the head, that is Christ. From Him the whole body, joined and held together by every supporting ligament, grows and builds itself up in love as each part does its work.[1] The Body of Christ is not an adjunct of Christ, doing good works on His behalf. It is, in fact, the host of His person and in a mature expression Christ reveals Himself as He actually is.

Those parts of the body that seem to be weaker are indispensable, and the parts that seem less honorable require special honor. And the parts that are unpresentable are treated with special modesty, while our presentable parts need no special treatment. God has put the body together, giving greater honor to the parts that lacked it, so that there should be no division in the body. Its parts should have equal concern for each other. If one part suffers, every part suffers with it; if one part is honored, every part rejoices with it.[2]

In light of this reality, it would be unseemly for one member to dishonor another or to promote itself separately and apart from the rest of the body. Love, therefore, is not merely an expression of social graces and good manners in referring to another. It is instead the recognition of a divine assemblage, the purpose of which is to present the nature of Christ in all of His fullness and to recognize that each member is designed to function as a valuable part of the whole. Be devoted to one another in love. Honor one another above yourselves.[3]

---

[1]Ephesians 4:11-16 NASB. [2]1Corinthians 12:22-26 NASB. [3]Romans 12:10 NASB.

Love Is Not Easily Angered

It is possible to be angry and still love. But the state of love is not easily angered nor petty in its righteous anger. To be easily angered is to be "irritated, provoked, exasperated and aroused to anger."[1] The condition of being easily angered contrasts starkly with the patience and kindness of love, which bears ill treatment from others and has a nature that is reserved.

Explosive anger commonly results from the feeling of the loss of control and evidences the absence of self-control, which is a fruit of the Spirit.[2] Self-control is not the discipline associated with the soul's ability to behave itself in all circumstances. Instead, it is a fruit of the Spirit. It results from the control of the human soul by the spirit.

When a believer is mature, his soul will have been returned to the control of his spirit and submits to its rule. The spirit has been restored to fellowship with the Holy Spirit and its perception of all things will have been returned to a heavenly vision. A changed perspective from a natural view to an eternal one is essential for the restraint of the soul. The sudden outburst of anger, rooted in frustration, is definitively indicative of the continuation of the soul's rule. It commonly results in the thought that one is not being accorded the appropriate honor and regard and responds angrily, as a means of retaking control over others as well as the situation at hand. Self-control is the return of the soul to the control of the spirit.

When persons in authority respond in anger to those in subordinate positions, they are not acting on the basis of the accurate representation of the nature of God but are showing a deficiency of love. In highlighting this occurrence, the intent is to show that some who have been exposed to the angry and irrational behavior of leaders misconstrue the nature of God by associating this form of the abuse of authority with the character of God.[3]

Anger has the effect of manipulating the emotions of others to forcibly conform to the standard while denying the standard itself. Anger also indicates one's distance from the truth that he or she proposes as the standard. The standard, properly applied, would produce peace. Anger removes peace from the situation and puts everyone in a defensive posture. It is also a means by which persons are able to make unrighteous demands of others and subvert both truth and righteousness in the process.

PART THREE

Every believer carries within himself or herself the standard of Christ which is the template to be applied in all situations. As such, believers are rulers who demonstrate that standard wherever they are placed in the world. Whenever there is a dispute or controversy the believer's representation of God is the sufficient standard to apply to the situation.

Anger may be justified when truth and righteousness are continuously and willfully ignored and when evil is presented as the truth. Jesus cleansed the temple of the money changers by overturning their tables and driving them out with a whip made of cords. As He was doing so, His convictions in the matter were patently obvious. "He made a scourge of cords, and drove them all out of the temple, with the sheep and the oxen; and He poured out the coins of the money changers and overturned their tables; and to those who were selling the doves He said, 'Take these things away; stop making My Father's house a place of business.'"[4] On the other hand, He submitted to great personal injustice "as a sheep to the slaughter." The distinction is that when, in the defense of the truth, one is called to oppose error, anger may be justified.

When one is personally set upon for his stance with the truth, one should not defend oneself. The truth defends itself because it is an accurate representation of the nature and character of God Himself. Truth is a person. One should earnestly and even strenuously advocate the truth and stand firmly in one's conviction. The restraint of love would demand that the righteous refrain from pointing out the obvious faults and flaws in the character of the accuser.

Under no circumstances is it permissible to use anger to manipulate others and to gain a position of dominance over another, resulting in the furtherance of one's interests. To do so would be inconsistent with the spirit of truth. Because love is both patient and enduring, to severely censure those of offensive conduct is inconsistent with

PART THREE

the mature representation of God. The goodness of God would be replaced with an appearance of impatience and rejection of the other as well as the display of prejudicial behavior that shows a character unbalanced by hubris.

---

[1] Kenneth S. Wuest, New Testament: An Expanded Translation p. 407 (Erdman, MO.) [2] Galatians 5:22-23 NASB. [3] 2 Timothy 2:24-25 NASB. [4] John 2:15-16 NASB.

Love Keeps No Record of Wrongs

Forgiveness from an eternal perspective expunges a person's record of transgressions and separates him from them entirely. Because God keeps no record of wrongs, anyone can change and those who love as God does must credit Him with the change. God's forgiveness of our trespasses allows us to mature beyond our base natures into those who represent Him in the earth, crediting us with new aspects of grace along the way. Part of God's glory is His capacity for forgiveness.

> Moses said, "I pray You, show me Your glory!" And He said, "I Myself will make all My goodness pass before you, and will proclaim the name of the LORD before you; and I will be gracious to whom I will be gracious, and will show compassion on whom I will show compassion." Exodus 33:18-19 NASB

In God's own description, His goodness is His glory, and one of the characteristics of His glory is His forgiveness.

God is the standard; Jesus showed how forgiveness works. Peter asked, "Lord, how often shall my brother sin against me and I forgive him? Up to seven times?" And Jesus answered, "I do not say to you, up to seven times, but up to seventy times seven." He then went on to show that how we forgive others reflects, and must be as deep as, God's forgiveness of our own sins.

For this reason, the kingdom of heaven may be compared to a king who wished to settle accounts with his slaves. When he had begun to settle them, one who owed him ten thousand talents was brought to him. But since he did not have the means to repay, his lord commanded him to be sold, along with his wife and children and all that he had, and repayment to be made. So the slave fell to the ground and prostrated himself before him saying, "Have patience with me and I will repay you everything." And the lord of that slave felt compassion and released him and forgave him the debt.

But that slave went out and found one of his fellow slaves who owed him a hundred denarii; and he seized him and began to choke him, saying, "Pay back what you owe." So his fellow slave fell to the ground and began to plead with him, saying, "Have patience with me and I will repay you." But he was unwilling and went and threw him in prison until he should pay back what was owed.

So when his fellow slaves saw what had happened, they were deeply grieved and came and reported to their lord all that had happened. Then summoning him, his lord said to him, "You wicked slave, I forgave you all that debt because you pleaded with me. Should you not also have had mercy on your fellow slave, in the same way that I had mercy on you?" And his lord, moved with anger, handed him over to the torturers until he should repay all that was owed him.

My heavenly Father will also do the same to you, if each of you does not forgive his brother from your heart. Matthew 18:21-35 NASB

Jesus' point in both His direct response to Peter's question and the illuminating story is that God keeps no record of our wrongs and has forgiven our sins so completely it is as if they never existed. Our obligation to love as God loves requires that we offer the same bottomless well of forgiveness to others. God not only forgives our sins, but He then calls us to represent Him to others. There can be no more complete forgiveness than to not only expunge the record of a person's transgressions but to also support and motivate one to a higher standard than that which created the wrong in the first place. This act of love frees us from the weight of the transgression and provides the greatest opportunity for the redemption or reconciliation.

Because forgiveness is a direct demonstration of God's love, Christ named this act when He released the Holy Spirit to continue His work on the earth.

> *So Jesus said to them again, "Peace be with you; as the Father has sent Me, I also send you." And when He had said this, He breathed on them and said to them, "Receive the Holy Spirit. If you forgive the sins of any, their sins have been forgiven them; if you retain the sins of any, they have been retained."* John 20:21-23 NASB

Note that this act of forgiveness resonates in the eternal realms such that their sins have been previously forgiven—as if the sin never occurred. The amplified Wuest translation puts it thus: "If the sins of any certain individuals you forgive, they have been previously forgiven them, *with the present result that they are in a state of forgiveness.*"[1]

The forgiveness of others is not merely a discretionary act that may be engaged sporadically. God views it as essential to the representation of His nature. A basic principle of the Kingdom of God is that unbelievers are meant to encounter the reality of the King. Christ substituted us into His place and charged us with representing Him on the same mission to represent the Father and bring the Kingdom of Heaven to the earth. The Great Commission, as described in John 20, describes in part Christ's "mission for which [He still is] responsible" and on which He also sent those who make up His Body in the earth.[2]

In the matter of forgiveness of sins and the expunging of the record, Christ has delegated to us a function by which His Body represents the Father and His desire for a relationship with every person. Few opportunities for the representation of the nature of the Father are as complete as the commission to forgive the sins of others.

In forgiving others and releasing them from the transcript of their misdeeds, we are afforded the opportunity to participate joyfully in the redemption of others from the sinful nature. This shows us, in an unqualified fashion, to be partakers of the divine nature. As is the case in all of the other facets of love, the ones who exercise or display these conditions are as benefitted from the results as the objects of their kindness and generosity are themselves benefitted.

Shakespeare wrote keen insight into mercy and forgiveness in "The Merchant of Venice."[3]

---

[1] Wuest, *supra* (emphasis added). [2] See Wuest, *supra*. [3] The Merchant of Venice, Act 4 Scene 1:
> The quality of mercy is not strain'd,
> It droppeth as the gentle rain from Heaven
> Upon the place beneath. It is twice blest:
> It blesseth him that gives and him that takes.
> 'T is mightiest in the mightiest: it becomes
> The throned monarch better than his crown;
> His sceptre shows the force of temporal power,
> The attribute to awe and majesty,
> Wherein doth sit the dread and fear of kings;
> But mercy is above this sceptred sway,
> It is enthroned in the hearts of kings,
> It is an attribute to God himself;
> And earthly power doth then show likest God's,
> When mercy seasons justice. Therefore,
> Though justice be thy plea, consider this,

That in the course of justice none of us
Should see salvation: we do pray for mercy;
And that same prayer doth teach us all to render
The deeds of mercy.

Love Rejoices in the Truth

This quality of love has two sides and is described as something that "does not rejoice in unrighteousness but rejoices with the truth." Truth is a person— "I am the way, and the truth, and the life; no one comes to the Father but through Me."[1] Truth was meant to display the person of God in human form. Therefore, truth, unlike facts, is consistent with the Spirit of the person Jesus Christ.

People confuse facts and truth. They recite facts as if they are truth, but truth also requires an underlying purpose. Pure facts serve only the motive of the one presenting them. The distinction between facts and truth is whether the motive served is that of the individual or of the Spirit of Christ in him. The skill of artfully turning a phrase to avoid controversy has become evidence of a brilliant mind and a clever wit. Though neither quality is disfavored in the Kingdom, brilliance is wasted when it serves to obscure the truth. One who speaks truth must say what is factually true and speak sufficiently to disabuse his audience from arriving at an erroneous conclusion based on what was said.

Jesus never spoke untruth or even obscured the truth. But He reserved the truth about certain mysteries for those who also have the Spirit to both hear and understand what He was teaching. He spoke in parables when His audience had no interest in the truth. In doing so, He adhered to the Spirit of truth in Himself. No follower of Christ should delight in the subversion of the truth. Regarding the condition of people's hearts, the mature believer should speak truth that is informed by the Spirits of Knowledge, Wisdom and Understanding.

Never confuse cunning speech that masks a lie as truth with the wisdom of God. The truth is never the companion of deceit, no more than light and darkness are in fellowship with one another. There is no harmony of "Christ with Belial."[2]

---

[1] John 14:6 NASB. [2] 2 Corinthians 6:15 NASB.

Love and Tolerance

All truth is related to the living God. This is a fundamental principle for every believer in Christ. God's incarnation in the person of Jesus Christ put a visible standard of truth in the earth. Jesus' claim to truth, life and access to the Father is exclusive, allowing no other claims to be sources for truth, life in the Spirit, or the ability to know God as "Father."[1] Versions of God that do not include the person of Christ and propose varied ways of access to God or eternal life are belief systems to be distinguished from those who follow Christ. Every believer must be unmitigated in this foundation.

If truth is a person, there is a way of life that exists within all present circumstances that operates from a perspective informed by eternal truths. Jesus' life showed this. By doing so, He disclosed the nature of God, who exists in the eternal realm, to the natural realm and thereby allowing truth to be observed from a multidimensional perspective. This state of truth, or perspective, is accessible only to those whose spirits are in communion with the Spirit of God.

> *For to us God revealed [His wisdom] through the Spirit; for the Spirit searches all things, even the depths of God. For who among men knows the thoughts of a man except the spirit of the man which is in him? Even so the thoughts of God no one knows except the Spirit of God. Now we have received, not the*

PART THREE

> *spirit of the world, but the Spirit who is from God, so that we may know the things freely given to us by God, ...But a natural man does not accept the things of the Spirit of God, for they are foolishness to him; and he cannot understand them, because they are spiritually appraised.* 1 Corinthians 2:10-12,14 NASB [comment added]

The natural mind, limited to observable reality, cannot access this perspective. It can only grasp at understanding it with metaphorical reference to things that are familiar.

These vastly different perspectives present a problem for modern believers. Most of us exist in societies that value the innate altruism of which we are all capable. The outward expression of this value is the desire to be inclusive to all members of society, regardless of race, gender, socioeconomic status, or lifestyle. The practical result is the trend toward equal access to all governmental benefits and protections. This, in general, is a good thing. However, human governments are not based on the immutable principles of heaven's Kingdom. They must change as the make-up of their societies change. Believers are in a position that must oppose certain choices as contrary to the governing of their spiritual outlook while existing within a society in which human rules regulate most of their natural circumstances.

The modern believer must understand that there is not incongruity between one's natural and spiritual self—either in how one represents the eternal God or in how one treats others. For that to be true, the believer must always be motivated by love. The Kingdom of God is greater than any human government and is not subject to a government's rules. Government agencies and society tend to change what is acceptable or allowable which has the potential to pressure the church into altering the standards God has established. Just because the government says something is legal does not trump biblical truth. Whenever governmental policies flagrantly oppose the true meaning of Scripture and introduce a different standard than was established by Christ, particularly in the case of the biblical standard of love and the social standard of tolerance, a genuine conflict between the Kingdom of God and human governments naturally exists. Those who seek to reveal the Kingdom of Heaven in the earth should find peace that no government can affect this task of holding to God's standard. Whether by implicitly following social trends that oppose eternal truths or by outright condemnation and persecution of its citizens, God's Kingdom can and will continue to operate in the earth unimpeded. Therefore, the modern believer's dealings with human governments should acknowledge that it affects his natural life but should never acquiesce to the idea that any vote cast, piece of legislation, or court ruling meaningfully impedes the Kingdom—they do not.

In dealing with others, love—in the manner that God loves—allows believers to meaningfully engage with any person to whom they are called or required to interact with. The descriptions of patience, kindness, honor, selflessness given above should provide a starting place for them to explore this concept and how it looks in practice. More important is the spiritual perspective that supports them in loving one another, which is something meant to set believers apart from the rest of the world. If you love as God loves, you can both represent Him and be Christ-like in your relationships to believers and non-believers.

Those who cannot understand this harmonious dual nature of a spirit being who exists and operates in the natural world, assail the spiritual perspective with the concept of tolerance. Tolerance is the insistence that the standard of truth be modified to accommodate ideas, thoughts and behaviors that are inconsistent with divine truth. Often, the insistence on tolerance as a condition of love is motivated by the experience of impatience and the lack of kindness on the part of those who enjoy positions of preeminence based upon the favor of society in general.

Persons of influence commonly clothe themselves in the most favored positions of a society and are often the voices that speak the collective wisdom and preference of a particular society. In order to preserve their positions of power and influence, they frequently stir the rest of society against a point of view unfavored by the general population. Those inveighing against the diminishment of their standing in society and the backlash that commonly attends such conflicts find a favorable point of reference in labeling the brutish behavior of their opponents as intolerant. The argument for tolerance then becomes a cry for justice and for a level playing field and becomes a cry to the wider society to move from neutrality to acceptance of their point of view.

Whereas this is a common occurrence played out over many and diverse appeals for a just resolution to societal injustices, its effect over time has been to make it a condition of love. In so doing, it has redefined love in the popular imagination as a feeling of inclusion by changing the standard from a reflection of the nature of God to one that accommodates the vagaries of man's situations.

It has been undeniable that religion, particularly Christian religion, has played a seminal role in the development of much of the world's societies. State churches in particular have played a similar role in every aspect of life within the states they defined. Everything from personal identity to the arc of their histories have been substantially shaped by the influence of church. Consequently, the attitude of church toward dissenting voices has often made the difference in how the society evolved. Unfortunately, the influence of the church has been less a representation of the divine person of Christ and more a presentation of an attitude of impatience with those who were perceived to threaten its position of privilege. It has been often the force behind the suppression of legitimate demands for change within societies.

PART THREE

From the practices of the inquisition to its denial of the legitimate aspirations of racial minorities, the institutional church has chronically sided with the forces of evil. In doing so, it has lost the right to represent the person of the truth in the world. Not only has it had a history of siding with the powerful, but it has as commonly been impatient and unkind and refused to suffer for any length of time the unrighteous demands for societal change. Its connection to the political structure of the society often permitted it to be used knowingly and willingly by ambitious political figures to appeal to the prurient interests of societal majorities thus becoming indistinguishable from tyrants and dictators.

By becoming an earthly force aligned with political structures the church has long abandoned even the recognition that its role is to represent the person of the truth. It now finds itself fully open to the reinterpretation of love as "tolerant." It no longer represents an eternal point of view. It is caught in the shift of society from ecclesiastical moorings to decidedly secular ones. The society has abandoned the influence of the church and is charting a separate course forward. In order to regain any semblance of relevance, the church must now baptize secular and ungodly concepts and welcome them as part of its reinvention of itself.

The church never foresaw a time when society would discard its influence and would choose a new foundation upon which to reconfigure its values. This change largely caught its leadership by surprise, although the signs of this evolution have been more than a century in the making. Bereft of its historic influence and burdened with its history of impatience and unkindness to those who disagreed with its policies, the church must refashion itself to appeal to the demands of a godless society in order to regain a modicum of relevance. It finds itself incapable of distinguishing truth from falsehoods. It presents Christ as a sort of modern everyman, an image cobbled together from pieces of societal ideas derived from surveys and polls and clothed in the garb of religious phrases.

Love cannot be tolerant, because it does not rejoice in evil but it rejoices in the truth. Love can only be at one with all that is representative of the nature and the character of God. It cannot also be equally at home with a different standard. While love is intolerant of any other standard, it is simultaneously patient with those who disagree, and it is characteristically kind and merciful to those who espouse a different standard. It is not a reaction to the error of another's position but is the setting forth of the nature of God Himself toward those who disagree with Him. In that capacity, it suffers whatever displeasure or hubris is leveled against it for as long as it takes for those who disagree to see the truthfulness of the alternative fully manifested in their way of life.

The purpose of God being patient, kind and long-suffering is not to endlessly endure the assertion of an alternative point of view and an accompanying way of life. The length of time in which God waits in mercy and compassion for those who resist Him is for as long as is required to fully set forth the nature of the alternative in all of its completeness. That being so, those who disagree have wantonly positioned themselves in a prolonged fashion against the truth for a length of time more than sufficient to show a knowing and complete rejection of the standard of truth. This condition is always accompanied by outcomes that evince the judgment of God.

All choices lead inexorably to consequences. Just as a life that deliberately conforms to eternal standards inevitably results in peace and good order together with a sense of profound satisfaction and contentment, one lived in continuous disregard of divine standards inevitably leads to chaos, disorder, and at the end, a sense of emptiness as if one has missed the mark. It is not so much that God ordains horrific consequences to personally attend those whose lives oppose the standards of His nature, as much as it is that a life lived apart from God will certainly yield the fruit of emptiness, since it may be abundant with temporal accomplishments but devoid of eternal significance.

At times, however, the judgment of God is unmistakably otherworldly and is designed to arrest the drift toward wickedness, rebellion, and sin.[2] Love cannot simultaneously delight in the truth while harmonizing with evil. God is not the author of confusion and does not simultaneously embrace conflicting standards. Righteousness is all that is consistent with the nature of God, and evil is everything else.

Love does not rejoice even when justice comes to the unbeliever, and he suffers harm as the direct and proximate consequence to his misdeeds. Always, for the believer, mercy tempers judgment. The true consequence of man's rebellion against God should be death.[3] But God's love balances the requirements of justice with the extension of mercy. When mankind could not carry the requirements of justice, God came to bear the weight Himself.[4] At some point, God's mercy becomes ineffective and leaves someone with nothing but exposure, by such mercy, to eternal standards and a requirement for God's justice. No believer should rejoice when harsh consequences befall the wicked, even though the behavior of the wicked justifies the consequences. The response of the righteous is tempered with His mercy.

---

[1]John 14:9, 17, 19 NASB. [2]Exodus 34:6-7 NASB. [3]Romans 3:23 NASB. [4]John 3:16 NASB.

Love Always Protects, Always Trusts, Always Hopes, Always Perseveres

Love cannot remain as an unexpressed emotion. If the nature of one is to love, then the mere existence of that nature compels

> *the one possessing it to put it on display. Because God is love, it was always inevitable that He would eventually express His love; and because His love is perfect, His expression of it would also define the nature of love perfectly. That expression would, therefore, involve a creation designed to give expression to the nature of God Himself. The facets of the love of God come together and are seen through the Son. All who individually represent different aspects of the love of God as parts of the body of the Son are destined to be presented together as one corporate entity—the Body of Christ.* Soleyn, Supra, *My Father! My Father!*, p. 47.

The "love always..." characteristics provide specific insight into how eternal love functions in human relationships. These are the architectural aspects that help give applicative shape to patience, kindness, not envying, honor, selflessness, not being easily angered and keeping no record of wrongs. As discussed in the distinction between patience and tolerance, different people can interpret concepts like patience and kindness according to their own experiences and world views. These terms are inadequate to convey the full eternal standards behind them. Adding context to the meaning of love, the "love always...." characteristics winnow its meaning, helping to separate the chaff that is interpreted through purely human experience from the more precise eternal truth of God's being.

Love Always Protects

As we have discussed, love requires action. It is an outward expression of God's person and necessarily involves at least two parties. The quality of love described as "love always protects" requires us to consider who protects whom and under what circumstances.

This is a question of order. The Kingdom of God is based upon an order that mirrors the character of Christ as King and Bridegroom. He is the authority in relationship to those subject to His rule as citizens of His kingdom which is called the Bride in Scripture as well. He is the one in authority, and those who choose to be are under His rule. A primary characteristic of this kingdom is that the subjects are not meant to worry over their own provision and protection.

> *For this reason I say to you, do not worry about your life, as to what you will eat; not for your body, as to what you will put on. .....For all these things the nations of the world eagerly seek; but your Father knows that you need these things. But seek His kingdom, and these things will be added to you. Do not be afraid, little flock, for your Father has chosen gladly to give you the kingdom.* Luke 12:22, 30-32 NASB

Human kingdoms have mostly muddled this principle. When the rulers are preoccupied with personal provision and protection, those who rule will often seek privilege over their subjects. In the Kingdom of Heaven, the King first laid down His life so that those subject to His rule may be first reconciled to God.[1] This principle is a reference point for all relationships in the Kingdom in which a person is granted authority over others.

For example, in the husband-and-wife relationship, the beginning point of rule is the willingness of the husband, the one in authority, to do everything required to protect and secure the one subject to his rule, up to and including laying down his life.[2] Love always protects is the principle that those who are given authority in the Kingdom of Heaven are meant to put the well-being of all those under that authority ahead of their own lives. This is how husbands can love their wives in a manner that allows the wives to submit to righteous authority just as the church is meant to submit to Christ.

PART THREE

One who lays down his life does not rule for personal gain. Trust is built out of this order. Those subject to the rule must trust the one in authority. But trust is not based in an untested assertion of good intentions. It rests on the unshakable foundation Christ laid by laying down His own life. Whoever is entrusted with authority is expected to live out the same mandate as the most basic characteristic of his rule.

This principle, while consistent with the character of Christ's rule, contrasts with the manner of rule of His predecessor, Adam. Although Adam was present at the temptation of Eve, he refused to countermand the enemy's deception and joined her in the disobedient act. "When the woman saw that the tree was good for food, and that it was a delight to the eyes and that the tree was desirable to make one wise, she took from its fruit and ate; and she gave also to her husband with her, and he ate."[3] Adam failed to protect Eve. His role was clear. He was to safeguard Eve from the deceptive enticement of the enemy and to preserve their relationship to God as their Father at all costs. He dishonorably attempted to justify his failure to protect her by blaming his decision to depart from God on Eve and on God Himself.[4]

Christ, on the other hand, gave up His life to reconcile mankind to God by His inclusion of us into a Spiritual person. Both relationships demonstrated expressions of love. Adam's was based in the natural. Christ's was evidence of love perfected. The distinction between the two is obvious. Perfect love "always protects."

Those subject to authority are never intended to be mere cannon fodder to be consumed for the preservation of those in authority. The responsibility to protect lies with those who are in authority and relates to the portrayal of sovereignty in the form of the preservation of those subject to rule. In the Kingdom of God, love always protects.

---

[1]See also John 15:13 NASB. [2]Ephesians 5:25-30 NASB. [3]Genesis 3:6 NASB. [4]See Genesis 3:12-13, 17 NASB.

PART THREE

Love Always Trusts

The fall of mankind precipitated in the garden was a fundamental change in the relationship between humans and God—from what God intended to what the enemy hoped for as a result of his deception. Adam substituted an existence as God's son to one that sought equality with God, seeing God as the antagonist and, ultimately, for his progeny forgetting God in human knowledge and removing the obstacle to mankind's own perceived godhood. Because of this drastic change, anyone seeking the reconciliation of the original relationship to God must learn it anew— in the same way newborns learn about their relationships to their parents—through stages and maturity. God's intent is to reconcile all whom He has received as sons to these eternal standards. One of those standards is trust.

People will balk at certain qualities of love such as "love always trusts" because love's standards expose their bulwarks of self-reliance and the illusion of control. As with every aspect of love, this standard has a context rooted in God's nature. As Son, God did not require Himself to trust any source other than His own unchangeable nature as Father. This existing relationship, God with God, provided a foundation for trust that the Son, Jesus, at His most vulnerable state could rely on. The standard "love always trusts" also refers to an existing relationship— one in which those in authority based their rule entirely on the model God provided in Himself. This relationship begins with the preceding standard for love that requires that the one in authority be willing to lay down their life for the protection of those under their rule.

This unassailable foundation, to love as God loves, requires trust in a heavenly order that places every person under authority. One must trust that this order is for their benefit, even when hardships undermine their confidence in it. The only guarantee that it works for anyone's good is that it is undergirded by the reality of the living God who established it. This order exists to show the divine intention of God toward man. It should permeate every relationship in which authority exists in some form. Scripture uses certain traditional set pieces to show what this order looks like. Some of the most easily discussed are the relationships between husbands and wives, parents and children, and employers and employees. Each of these contexts have elements of authority and submission to that authority. For believers this means that there is the structure for divine order and the opportunity to show the nature of God and demonstrate His love.

The qualities of love are not mere universal principles to be applied selectively and to be attachments to human society to be reminders of a higher form of living. Instead, they display the context in which God moves man to greater and greater maturity, so that one may understand God as God is, and choose to adopt God's ways and His divine nature as the pattern for his own existence. In the process, one consciously and deliberately depends upon the certainty that God will vindicate the choices of those who live to present Him to others in this world. The vindication would be measurable in terms of righteousness, peace, and joy. This result would be unmistakably distinct in its result from all other pursuits of life.

The one under authority benefits the most when he or she trusts the one in authority within this defined configuration. Apart from this context, the potential for abuse is nearly limitless. The responsibility of the one under authority is to pray for the one in authority over them so they may have peace. In addition to trusting the one in authority and praying for them, if the one in authority acts in a manner that endangers his charge, the right of appeal is available, so that the conduct of the one in authority may be reviewed by the authority over him.

The decision to trust another within this context of the showing of God's order depends for the outcome on God's interest in preserving those who obey His divine order as it touches them. Such obedience will produce a closer walk with God in many ways. Sometimes the one in authority may rule for their benefit consistently, but the broken condition of the one under authority is given to mistrust or apprehension, and they are likely to respond to the requirement of trust with skepticism and doubt as to whether or not anyone is trustworthy. Even if they fitfully engage this condition of love, what measure of peace they are able to walk in depends upon the state of their relationship to God. Whereas, if they are more settled, that is also descriptive of how real God is to them. As they see and observe the work of God in changing the ones in authority, they themselves are changed to a greater trust of God resulting in a greater trust of those in authority.

The majority of believers come from very broken and disappointing human circumstances. Coming into a relationship to God is designed to rescue them from a life of self-reliance and to integrate them into the greater corporate expression of Christ. Submission to a greater authority promotes a transition to functioning in the spirit. This change often creates an emotional sense of loss of the familiar before the sense of gain is realized. This transition proves often to be extremely difficult, and the believer is apt to frequently default to the familiar practices related to the soul and to their former life. This behavior is justified in their minds by the thought process that supports the feeling of being diminished from their prior accomplishments. It makes trusting the authority that leads them forward a very difficult undertaking. Most religious circumstances do not require this transition, but simply utilize the soul's competence in the scope of the work of their ministries. Eventually, those utilized for their soul's competence feel used and burned out.

On the other hand, authority that challenges the believer to transition from the soul to the spirit, though resisted initially, will eventually prove to be of indisputable value to the maturing of the believer. The difficulty associated with the unfamiliar path of transitioning from soul to spirit produces an abundance of opportunity to mistrust the motive of those in authority. This is an exact parallel to the way God matures His sons. Jesus had to learn obedience by the things He suffered before He could become the beloved Son in whom God was well pleased.

God disciplines every son whom He receives, through Christ, so that they might become mature enough to display the glory of God in the full measure of their destiny. Believers who are still children in Christ are subject to "guardians and managers."[1] Trust is the necessary requirement to hold the maturing believer in place long enough for the work of maturing to be completed. The process is normally strenuous and will test the relationship thoroughly. However, if the one under authority trusts the Lord in the one in authority, the breakthrough will come at the appropriate time. When it does, the results will justify the requirement of trust.

The one in authority must trust God to faithfully bring about a result eventually. Otherwise, it is possible to become frustrated and to even resort to unrighteous means, such as manipulation, to obtain the desired results. The one in authority must have a clear sense of the gifts and calling of the one under authority and should seek God regularly to understand how the transformation is progressing through the respective stages. The Spirit of Knowledge and of Understanding will assist the one in authority to appropriately interpret the indices of growth and maturity in the ones under their care. Both the one in authority and the one under authority, then, must trust God to control the evolution of the relationship.

---

[1] Galatians 4:1-5 NASB.

PART THREE

Loves Always Hopes

> *Therefore, having been justified by faith, we have peace with God through our Lord Jesus Christ, through whom also we have obtained our introduction by faith into this grace in which we stand; and we exult in hope of the glory of God and not only this, but we also exult in our tribulations, knowing that tribulation brings about perseverance; and perseverance, proven character; and proven character, hope; and hope does not disappoint, because the love of God has been poured out within our hearts through the Holy Spirit who was given to us.*
> Romans 5:1-5 NASB.[1]

The foundation of all of our acts that profess the love of God is anchored in God's promises, guaranteed by the integrity of His person. Even before the creation of the world, He bound Himself through the process of an oath signifying a promise pursuant to which He initiated all of the visible creation.[2] God designed the world around His promises, not on the basis of a whim.[3] Consistent with His promises, God has offered evidence to allow us to rely on His unchanging nature.

Through Christ, He disclosed by word and action the trustworthy nature of His love. Jesus not only interpreted the appearing of God through creation, but in His own person, He established the nature of the love of God with unbreakable certainty. His resurrection and ascension to the right hand of God defy the encroachments of doubt and positions Jesus as the Truth incarnate of the certainty of the love of God. No one who puts his hope in God could possibly be made ashamed when all is redeemed.

One of the characteristics of our love for God is our response in placing our hope in the certainty of the representations of His love. A companion aspect to our love for God is our willingness to represent to others the reliability of His character and His representations. To the mature believer, the coinage of faith in God is a stalwart trust in the promises of God, and beyond the promises, trust in God Himself. A true ambassador of Christ is one who puts his own reputation and life at stake as he reveals the nature of God to others.[4] He invites people irrespective of the desperation of their present circumstances to respond to the invitation of Jesus, to abandon loyalty to the kingdom of darkness and to apply for citizenship in the Kingdom of God.

Ambassadors of Christ represent the hope of a way of life that changes in all of its facets from the present time and place and progresses throughout the course of the rest of their lives. They further offer the status of being the sons of God and invite them to be reconciled to God by being placed in Christ, the corporate Son. To those willing to accept this invitation, they demonstrate the first act of the kindness of Jesus by declaring their liberty from an identity that enslaves them in the kingdom of darkness. That pronouncement takes the form of the declaration that their sins are forgiven.[5]

Currently, hope is confused with wish, and the believer is encouraged to become a consumer of whatever they desire that God should do for them personally. This pattern of thought is usually accompanied by the practice of attaching Scripture to their desires in an attempt to induce a response from God unattached to any other consideration, except a passage of Scripture agreed upon by both the one desiring the result and the one promising that result to him or to her. This is an illegitimate representation of hope. On the other hand, an accurate matching of the promise of God to where the believer is in his or her progress toward maturity, produces an accurate picture of hope, which always manifests itself in the due season of God.

The administration of love, with regard to hope, begins with a clear and firm trust in the unwavering nature of God and the representations that accurately flow out of His nature. It is followed by a qualified ambassador, whose qualification is his or her own experiences with God, interpreting and offering the promises of God, together with His nature, to those trapped in the distress of the kingdom of darkness. Throughout the stages of their growth toward maturity, they are further encouraged to have even greater reliance upon the nature of God.[6] The strength and glory of the House of God is inseparable from the hope of a son of God in the nature of the Father.

---

[1]See also Galatians 5:5 NASB; Ephesians 1:7-8 NASB; Hebrews 10:23 NASB; Hebrews 6:19 NASB. [2]Hebrews 6:18-19 NASB. [3]See e.g., Rev 13:7-8 NASB. [4]2 Corinthians 5:15-16 NASB. [5]John 20:23 NASB. [6]Hebrews 11:6 NASB.

Love Always Perseveres

Paul, in his first letter to the church in Corinth, gave the people a vision for the pilgrimage as followers of Christ.

> *Yet we do speak wisdom among those who are mature; a wisdom, however, not of this age nor of the rulers of this age, who are passing away; but we speak God's wisdom in a mystery, the hidden wisdom which God predestined before the ages to our glory...* 1 Corinthians 2:6-7 NASB

> *For if you were to have countless tutors in Christ, yet you would not have many fathers, for in Christ Jesus I became your father through the gospel. Therefore, I exhort you, be imitators of me. For this reason I have sent to you Timothy, who is my beloved and faithful child in the Lord, and he will remind you of my ways which are in Christ, just as I teach everywhere in every church.* 1 Corinthians 4:15-17 NASB

This same letter describes love's qualities, among them perseverance.[1]

Perseverance, also translated as endurance, implies both a goal and obstacles that prevent attaining the goal. The connotation of love's perseverance is that one should strive to know God, but many obstacles lie in the way of doing so. About love, John wrote:

> *Beloved, let us love one another, for love is of God; and everyone who loves is born of God and knows God. The one who does not love does not know God, for God is love. By this the love of God was manifested in us, that God has sent His only begotten Son into the world so that we might live through Him.*
> 1 John 4:7-9 NASB

He set loving and knowing God as intertwined goals. In this way love, like knowing God, comes in greater degrees with maturity. Ultimately, the individual is supposed to mature to a place where their way of life provides an accurate representation of some aspect of God. The substance of that representation is how the person loves. Corporately, the Body of Christ when fully matured will reveal God to the point of His exact representation on the earth.

How we persevere toward these goals charts our path. One of the main differences between those who are mature and those who are still young in Christ is that those who are mature have persevered through the baptism of fire that leads to maturity.[2]

Every person who pursues their destiny in Christ chooses a certain measure of adversity and suffering. The change into a person who represents God in every aspect of their life requires it. The full metamorphosis represents a complete change from the person they were before, born into Adam's legacy with the eyes of their soul wide open, to a fully mature son of God capable of exact representation. Among other changes, suffering helps the person abandon self-reliance and trust God. The scope of this change is impossible without suffering that is comparable to the death of one's prior self.

Self-reliance is the illusion that peace is possible when you are in control of your circumstances. A self-reliant person sees control as the result of having acquired the necessary skills and resources to retain their position regardless of the forces that inveigh against them. Overcoming this entire mindset is painful because it requires a complete loss of control. Yet, whenever one elects to pursue God, he or she encounters the reality of this change. Since the change itself is from a view of life based entirely in the natural order of things to a spiritual view of all things, the energy and drive that sustain self-reliance suddenly seem misdirected and futile, inasmuch as they support a view that is being discarded. One person cannot harbor a natural view of life and an eternal one harmoniously.[3]

The transition from one view to another involves conflict between a person's soul and spirit, replacing the innate prerogatives of being with a new perspective determined by the Spirit, who "guides you into all the truth."[4] This process—one that saves your soul—is likened to a forge's fire:

> *In this you greatly rejoice, even though now for a little while, if necessary, you have been distressed by various trials, so that the proof of your faith, being more precious than gold which is perishable, even though tested by fire, may be found to result in praise and glory and honor at the revelation of Jesus Christ; and though you* have *not seen Him, you love Him, and though you do not see Him now, but believe in Him, you greatly rejoice with joy inexpressible and full of glory, obtaining as the outcome of your faith the salvation of your souls.* 1 Peter 1:6-9 NASB

This is the common path to all who seek God.

During this process the believer will become discouraged—not just once, but many times throughout the journey. Perseverance is required to navigate this difficult path. In itself perseverance speaks of the attraction of one's changing values. Eventually, it is the decisions to prize eternal realities far above natural goals that keeps drawing the believer forward into greater and greater conformity with the nature and character of God.

"Love perseveres" is the quality that comes from loving God, desiring to know Him and be like Him. It is the quality that motivates to greater and greater levels of maturity, when each level gained comes through hardship, adversity, and even strife—often questioning God Himself before seeing His purpose. But eventually, you learn to cherish the state of being in which your fellowship with God is constant. This is the only way that a person can live in the earth like Christ did, representing the Father in everything they do. Humans default to self-serving motivations in just about everything we pursue with diligence. "But you did not learn Christ in this way."[5] Love for God—the desire to know Him and be like Him—perseveres in the pursuit of righteousness.

---

[1]1 Corinthians 13:7 NIV. [2]Hebrews 5:7-9 NASB; See also, *The Elementary Doctrines*, The Baptism of Fire. [3]Luke 16:13 NASB. [4]John 16:13 NASB. [5]Ephesians 4:20 NASB.

Love Never Fails

God's being exceeds definition through spatial and temporal based comparisons. But His influence permeates all aspects of the created world. As Spirit, God fills everything in every way. And He endows the existences of countless other human spirits. His being is a personhood without references in the familiar experiences of form and visibility. His knowledge, wisdom and understanding similarly come from a place beyond time or experience. They ARE. They are not learned.

PART THREE

We are left trying to define God by what references we can understand. This forms a basis for the deeper understanding of His person that comes from communion with His Spirit. We know that God is love and every other facet of His being reflects this central truth. But understanding love, as God defines it, has required a multi-leveled discussion of certain characteristics of love, all stemming from the heart of the matter, the nature of love.

Paul discussed this essential nature of God—by reference to these qualities of love—while trying to elevate those under his care from a state of childishness to a state of collective maturity. In succeeding chapters, he instructs the Corinthians about the collective Body,[1] then proceeds to instruct them about love,[2] finishing with an admonition to mature:

> *When I was a child, I used to speak like a child, think like a child, reason like a child; when I became a man, I did away with childish things. For now we see in a mirror dimly, but then face to face; now I know in part, but then I will know fully just as I also have been fully known.* 1 Corinthians 13:11-12 NASB

In his care, he hoped that the invisible God, who appeared in the person of Jesus Christ would appear among them collectively as the Body of Christ, and that strangers and unbelievers would accurately understand the nature of the invisible God through them.

Each of the characteristics of love is related to the functioning of the Body of Christ, its collective maturity, and the revelation of God's person in the earth. No aspect of love is a mere behavioral guideline. Paul understood the proper context for love. His teaching is the beginning of a way of life that Jesus demanded of His Body: "Love one another, just as I have loved you."[3] All seven Spirits of God that Jesus exhibited as characteristics of God's personhood are outpourings of the Spirit that serve the greater purpose of love. Without love, the seven Spirits of God are things you can grasp at but never take hold of.

In love, the spirits of Lordship, Wisdom, Understanding, Counsel, Power, Knowledge, and the Fear of the Lord, reveal God through a way of life that was first demonstrated by the Lord Jesus Christ. In Him, the corporate Christ, exists an order that comes directly from God's own nature, based on love, and fulfilling His promise to reconcile humankind to Himself.

Paul understood that because of God's unshakable nature, the triumph of the love of God is inevitable. Therefore, he concluded his elucidation of love with "Love never fails."[4]

---

[1] 1 Corinthians 12:20 NASB. [2] 1 Corinthians 13:1-8 NASB. [3] John 15:12 NASB. [4] 1 Corinthians 13:8a NASB.

PART THREE

PART Four

The Economy of the Spirit

Everything we have discussed so far has focused on accessing a state of being that produces a way of life that reflects God's person. We describe this as a state of being in which the Spirit dominates your being, and your own spirit's communion with the Spirit of God restores you to a relationship with Him as a son to a father which allows you to fulfill the purpose for which He created you.

The purpose of sonship is greater than anyone's individual destiny in Christ. The Body of Christ's role is to reveal the full nature of God in the function of His kingdom on the earth. To achieve this ultimate goal, the Body and its many parts are like conduits through which the entire Kingdom of Heaven may enter into our reality.

The order of the Kingdom cannot thrive without support. In the eternal realm, God's being supports His absolute authority. On earth the grace that supports the Kingdom of Heaven is carried by Jesus Christ and by extension all those who are assembled to Christ and have the capacity to carry His grace as well. We call this manner of supporting the Kingdom of Heaven in the earth the economy of the Spirit.

PART FOUR

The Incarnation

For since the creation of the world His invisible attributes, His eternal power and divine nature have been clearly seen, being understood through what has been made so that they are without excuse. Romans 1:20 NASB

God intended to reveal heaven in the visible creation for the purpose of establishing His perfection in all realms. His nature is love but love cannot be known to exist without expression. Because He chose people as heirs some angels rebelled, calling into question God's nature as the perfector of love. Prior to creation He knew that Adam would be tempted to sin and that mankind would lose the benefit of His presence. He planned to reestablish His presence with mankind by coming Himself in the lowly human form as Jesus, the Son. Even though the enemy killed Jesus, this seeming defeat was God's triumph because death could not hold Him. When God resurrected the Spirit of Christ, He placed in the earth all the grace that was the Son's in heaven.[1] Christ's advent into the world revealed the unseen eternal realm. This included reconciling and assembling our spirits in Himself while we are on the earth,[2] expunging the taint of sin, and removing the sting of death.[3] Heaven is His throne, but the earth is His footstool where all God's enemies are put under His feet.[4]

Everything God made helps reveal Him through His sons.[5] The seven Spirits of God are observable aspects of His person, seen first in Jesus and subsequently through the acts of God's sons.[6] From the beginning God planned to show His presence both indirectly through creation as well as directly through Christ.

In Jesus Christ, God became incarnate. Jesus restored the knowledge of God at the threshold above the veiled references in creation. Now every person has a choice.

> *If I had not come and spoken to them, they would not have sin, but now they have no excuse for their sin. He who hates Me hates My Father also. If I had not done among them the works which no one else did, they would not have sin; but now they have both seen and hated Me and My Father as well.* John 15:22-25

If a person chooses God, then his view of God is restored, and he may know God as He is. In contrast, a person who rejects Christ is subject to the consequence of human culture further separating himself from God and, ultimately, devolving into the worship of the physical creation in lieu of God.

> *Professing to be wise, they become fools, and exchanged the glory of the incorruptible God for an image in the form of corruptible man and of birds and four-footed animals and crawling creatures. Therefore, God gave them over in the lusts of their hearts to impurity, so that their bodies would be dishonored among them.* Romans 1:22-24 NASB

God incarnate provides a living standard by which every human being has an opportunity to see Him and choose how to live their lives.

It was in the man Jesus that the fullness of God could be observed completely. Creation contains aspects of "His invisible attributes."[7] Angels are analogized to the physical creation and are compared to elements of creation such as wind and fire.[8] But the Son exists as "the radiance of [God's] glory and the exact representation of His nature."[9] The Son incarnated not just God's power and the seven Spirits of His character, but He was the only being that could translate God's love also into the earth.

Every son of God—meaning each part of the Body of Christ—can provide some piece of the incarnation of God. This can be seen through the combination of visible aspects of His character and His love presented in one person. Each of these individual parts are unique but not complete unless serving the greater purpose. The complete Body of Christ, the corporate Son, is the only presence in creation that can provide the complete incarnation of God, revealing Him and His glory. This is a human form, made of many people, held together by the order of the Kingdom of Heaven and supported by the Spirit of God that animates it. It is also through this incarnation that the economy of the Spirit is given access into creation.

---

[1]Acts 2:22-36 NASB. [2]See 1 Peter 1:3 NASB; 1 Peter 3:21-22 NASB. [3]1 Corinthians 15:16-18 NASB; 1 Corinthians 15:20-22 NASB. [4]See, e.g., Isaiah 66 NASB; Psalms 110 NASB. [5]Psalm 24:1 NASB. [6]Isaiah 11:2-3 NASB. [7]Romans 1:20 NASB. [8]Hebrews 1:7 NASB; Psalm 104:4 NASB. [9]Hebrews 1:3 NASB.

Incarnation Through Reconciliation

God endowed mankind with a gift of His Spirit by imparting it out of His person and releasing it to become a separate being. The separate being may choose to live apart from God. God's desire to become incarnate in humans requires willing consent. His Spirit within man is not animated until the person is born again, that is, makes a conscious decision to give his or her life to God. When you give your life to God, you're actually giving Him your spirit, making it available, in order for God to establish your identity and purpose and empowerment. This is what makes each person a "living being" according to Scripture.[1]

The owner of the Spirit from God must elect to give the gift back to God. God promised that whoever would return to Him He would never reject. When someone freely gives their spirit back to God, they are assembled into one spiritual Man, the Body of Christ. He places them where He needs them into the whole of who Christ is. The desired response is that of hope, trust and submission.

> *God.... reconciled us to Himself through Christ and gave us the ministry of reconciliation, namely, that God was in Christ reconciling the world to Himself, not counting their trespasses against them, and He has committed to us the word of reconciliation.* 2 Corinthians 5:18-19 NASB

The corporate Son both supports particular aspects of the revelation of God through the individual and provides the vehicle through which the complete nature of God will be seen in the world. Reconciliation to God through the voluntary return of man's spirit, assembled into the corporate whole of the Body of Christ permits the incarnation of God in Christ to be completely accomplished.

---

[1] Genesis 2:7 NASB.

Incarnation, Predestination, and Rest

Since God's underlying intent for the creation of man was to establish for Himself a dwelling place on earth, each person was created to host the presence of God in a particular and predetermined fashion with the intent that the individual beings would, through reconciliation, be precisely assembled as the corporate Body of Christ.[1] In Christ, God simultaneously rescues them from a self-directed view of life and the resulting activities that put this way of being on display and returns them to a state of usefulness to host the presence of God in a predetermined fashion. Everyone was created with the possibility of engaging a form of life that puts the nature of God on display through him or her with particularity.

This display of the presence of God in each one is unique and not subject to duplication in any other.[2] The manner in which God incarnates Himself in each person is precise and specific, showing His deliberate intent to appear at a particular time in a precise manner among mankind in a predetermined location.[3] Sometimes God chooses specific human families and endows them with a specific destiny that relates to His eternal purpose in a central fashion.

The unfolding of this central purpose will often require multiple generations to accomplish. When God chooses to work in this fashion, He installs a culture within this human format upon which He builds an expectation of the fulfillment of His purpose among the members of that family. Although all mankind descended from Adam, the original son of God, God chose Abraham, a Chaldean, as the one through whose family Jesus Christ would be born to redeem all of mankind. At the point of this choosing, Abraham's family was not considered to be of royal lineage. The kingly line was deeply submerged and had become obscured.

This family housed a promise for the redemption of man through "the seed of Abraham." Before the advent of Christ, however, it was necessary to restore the appropriate culture in which for Him to come. Among the matters to be restored were the centrality of God to a people, disclosures of the nature of God through commandments and ordinances, the hearing of God through prophetic utterances, the arrangement of a people to point to the structure of the Kingdom of God, and raising up a kingly line to rule righteously over God's heritage. From this line, Jesus Himself would be born as both a human and the Son of God, King of all Kings. His destiny, therefore, encompassed the specific facts of the time in which He would be born and the people among whom He would be born.

The culture in which He would be born was prepared for forty-two generations since the promise. His advent did not occur in a void, but as the product of deliberate and careful orchestration by God Himself. The manner in which God meant to live in Him and show Himself through Him was by no means coincidental. He was predestined for all that God foreordained to come to pass through Him.

Even among human families of the righteous in the earth, God intentionally creates and nurtures a culture through which He intends to appear exponentially in the second and third generations. God is also establishing spiritual families with the same intent. As greater darkness appears in the earth, the light and glory of God will appear with unprecedented brilliance in the spiritual families, particularly among those whose natural families conserved the culture of heaven for two or three generations.

The works that God foreordains for each person to walk in contemplates both the unfolding of the plan of God for mankind and how He has prepared the individuals to carry out specific aspects of this plan. Sometimes the preparation of a particular person would have begun many generations prior to his or her birth. The manner in which God would live in such ones would be notable and outstanding. It is apparent that the choices of God among mankind for particular destinies may seem obscure. However, He is careful and deliberate in the way He prepares those whom He chooses.

Biblical predestination comprises two understandings. The first is works prepared in advance of our births for us to walk in. The second definition is that we are "predestined to become conformed to the image of His Son."[4] We are continually changed until Christ is formed in us and appears through us.

It is always true, that "from everyone who has been given much, much will be required; and to whom they entrusted much, of him they will ask all the more."[5] The sufferings of some may seem extraordinary by comparison to others. Yet, from a divine perspective the preparation for one's destiny follows an arc of suffering and training that is designed to fully prepare the ones chosen for extraordinary purposes to be able to successfully complete their destinies. In the end, the manifestation of God in any person is the result of the choice that God Himself made. Therefore, even the least conspicuous participation in the corporate destiny is vital to the success of the whole.

God did not choose a form for His appearing that He considered to be unimportant. Equality is not a concept that is relevant to how God chooses or how He acts. The economy of God is dedicated to bringing about the complete result of His presence in the earth. Anything short of that outcome is of no value to either God or man.

In an environment of competition, it is difficult to accept the specific endowment of the presence of God meant to be put on display in each person. In the absence of the understanding that God intends to become incarnate in a fashion He predetermined before He created a person, it is common, even for believers, to relate to God on the basis of things they desire to do with their lives that may or may not be consistent with the works God prepared in advance for them to walk in.

Consequently, the manner in which believers commonly relate to God is to separate their lives into two compartments: Things they wish to do with their lives as humans and things they wish to do in an effort to please God. This common bifurcation does not reflect an understanding that it is God who wills and does what pleases Him. Also, that the manner of His appearing in a person is supported by a specific endowment of His economy. When one lives in this bifurcation, occasionally he will permit God to do through him that which is consistent with His eternal purpose. At that time, the economy of God will support him in the doing of an act or in the following of a particular direction consistent with what he was created for. In those moments, he will experience supernatural support evincing the economy of God functioning on his behalf. This will happen whether or not he is aware of it. Because this is more accidental than by deliberate design, he will divert to the pattern of this bifurcation and will work by the sweat of his brow in furtherance of his own choices. At such times, the results will be unsatisfying inasmuch as his direction is inconsistent with the presence of God in him and the economy that supports him results from his own doing. Sometimes he will pray for the support of God for the exercise of his own will and will experience a denial of divine support.

This typically results in confusion because he lacks understanding as to when the economy of God works on his behalf. Until believers understand that divine economy comes with the presence of God and functions to support what God Himself is doing when He functions through the ones in whom He lives, there will be no opportunity to rest in the reliable nature of God's economy. His economy is present when He is present and will always support what He is doing when He chooses to act from His place of rest in us. In order to rely upon the certainty of the economy of God for our support, believers must increasingly forgo their own plans for their lives and yield themselves to the demands of His presence within us. This is the great struggle.

It is primarily an internal struggle of the human spirit over his soul. The return of the spirit to its primacy over the soul results in the reconnection of the mind of the human spirit to the Spirit of God. At that point, he will cease and desist from every activity in his person that is inconsistent with the will of God that he has been shown. When he does that, he immediately enters into rest and ceases from his independent labors and does the work that God prepared in advance of his birth for him to walk in.[6]

---

[1]See 1 Corinthians 6:19-20 NASB. [2]Ephesians 2:10 NASB; Romans 9:21-23 NASB. [3]Acts 17:26-28 NASB. [4]Romans 8:29 NASB. [5]Luke 12:48 NASB. [6]Hebrews 3:7 to 4:11.

PART FOUR

The Economy of God's Presence

The economy of the Kingdom of Heaven is God's presence—His Spirit. In the heavenly realms, His Spirit is all engrossing. His power and authority that supports His throne exist by the simple fact of His presence. In the natural world God has chosen to be present through the representation of the corporate Son and all those in Him to whom He delegates aspects of this grace. All power and authority is given to and delegated by Christ for as long as His work continues in the earth.[1]

The presence of God in creation constitutes an entire economy which may be thought of as the dispensations of grace out of His being that support every need of His House on earth. God's House is His family. It is organized based on His own model of the Father and the Son as the fundamental relationship between Him and humankind.[2] The book *My Father! My Father!* addresses the details of this order. It can be thought of in broad terms as the order or organization of all God's sons assembled within Christ, the corporate Son.

His presence can be the environment that surrounds anyone, in any place, at any time. When His presence is carried in a son, the eternal realm begins to affect the physical one. Jesus began to show that God's presence is never separate from people. He demonstrated the unity between the Father and the Son, and He made the same unity available to all mankind:

> ...that they may all be one: even as You, Father, are in Me and I in You, that they also may be in Us, so that the world may believe that You sent me. The glory which You have given Me I have given to them, that they may be one, just as We are one; I in them and You in Me, that they may be perfected in unity,

so that the world may know that You sent Me, and loved them, even as You have loved Me. John 17:21-23 NASB

God inhabits His sons so that wherever they are, He is also present.

> *...for in Him we live and move and exist, as even some of your own poets have said, "For we also are His children." Being then the children of God, we ought not to think that the Divine Nature is like gold or silver or stone, an image formed by the art and thought of man.* Acts 17:28-29 NASB

Watch out for those that seek to interpose "the art and thought of man" between God and His people. Too many religions have decided that humans cannot be like Christ because the evidence of the past shows that no one operates with the same power or authority that He had. They failed to understand that God does not want to be seen by His power or external acts of supremacy. Rather, God chooses to be known by His love which is visible in His sons. While power and authority support this goal, great acts of power such as those performed by Jesus and the early apostles rarely serve it because they detract from seeing God for who He is rather than for what He can do. Regardless, religions have made excuses for the lack of power by distancing the average person from God. Instead, they purport to invest certain people, items, or traditions with a closeness to God by which people may access a limited measure of His presence. For example, certain religions invest in very few individuals the power to forgive sins. Such power then is exercised on a limited basis for those who follow the proper procedures and are "properly disposed." Christ regularly forgave people their sins and delegated this authority to His Body.[3] The result of this separation is that these organizations have stifled God's presence among His people. Religion that separates people from the routine presence of God condemns their followers to permanent immaturity because God's presence is what allows the people to "move and exist."

PART FOUR

We are made to live consciously in His presence while engaging in all activities related to our purposes for being on the earth. God is present in both heaven and earth and harmonizes the interchange between both realms to meet His goals. When the Lamb was slain in heaven, something happened in the eternal realms but is described as having a permanence that existed before the foundations of the world. Heaven sang a song describing the result of His sacrifice:

> *Worthy are You to take the book and to break its seals; for You were slain and purchased for God with Your blood men from every tribe and tongue and people and nation. You have made them to be a kingdom and priests to our God; and they will reign upon the earth.* Romans 5: 9-10 NASB

The song prophesied the holy nation of God that is meant to exist on the earth. An earthly nation can only fulfill this prophecy if there is an interdependency between it and the Kingdom in heaven. This involves a transfer of things from heaven to the earth. When God initiates the transfer of eternal things to the earth, He prepares the earth to receive it, usually through symbols, types, and shadows of the eternal thing.

The introduction of the realities of God to the earth is staged in such a manner as is required by the very order of earth's construction. God is the arbiter of all eternal matters and is the one who knows the end from the beginning and ordains all the steps by which a reality comes from the mind of God to final execution in both heaven and on earth. Both realms depend upon the reality of God for the uniqueness of their existences as well as to be sustained in the fashion in which they have both been created. Everything required within either realm is supplied by the presence of God and never apart from it.

Man upon the earth, without the knowledge of God, lives in an economy of his own making. A soul, unfettered from the rule of the Spirit loses direct connection to the presence of God and his own destiny. The economy that functions apart from the presence of God is identified by its principal ethic: the toil of man in support of his independence.[4] It is the economy resulting from "the sweat of the brow."

Before He created the earth, God planned to restore man to His economy as part of the restoration of man to Himself. In the continuing history of God's dealing with mankind, He continued to maintain connection to the ultimate outcome in His dealings with both people groups and individuals.

---

[1]See Matt 28:18 NASB; See also 1 Corinthians 15:24-25 NASB. [2]See Soleyn, *My Father! My Father!* for a complete discussion of the order of God's House. [3]John 20:23 NASB. [4]Genesis 3:17 NASB.

A Table in the Wilderness

When God extends Himself into human realms, His Spirit commands all creation to serve His purposes. His presence supplies His purpose. The story of Exodus and the survival of God's people in the wilderness shows this principle in the form of a sustained economy as opposed to instances of supply. This was an intentional foreshadowing of God's presence among the holy nation prophecies in the Book of Revelation.[1]

God supplied Israel's daily sustenance for forty years in the harsh Sinai desert.[2] This was a nation meant to carry God's promise of kings and it could not simultaneously be a nation of slaves. Their culture and economy had to be replaced from one in which they survived by "the sweat of their brow" with one focused on the stewardship of God's promise to Abraham. God chose the desert to show His commitment to His promise.

Humans are relatively frail creatures. The lack of food and water, exposure to the elements, or the lack of protection should have caused the entire nation to perish. Moses, however, led them as God directed him into an environment in which they could not have survived on their own. The presence of God alone altered the environment, allowing the nation to survive. His presence also guided them. Failure to move when guided by His presence would return them to the economy of their environment.

God supplied food from heaven every morning, six days out of seven.

> ...Jesus then said to them, "Truly, truly, I say to you, it is not Moses who has given you the bread out of heaven, but it is My Father who gives you the true bread out of heaven. For the bread of God is that which comes down out of heaven and gives life to the world." Then they said to Him, "Lord, always give us this bread." ....Jesus said to them, "I am the bread of life; he who comes to Me will not hunger, and he who believes in Me will never thirst. I am the bread of life. Your fathers ate the manna in the wilderness, and they died. This is the bread which comes down out of heaven, so that one may eat of it and not die. I am the living bread that came down out of heaven; if anyone eats of this bread, he will live forever; and the bread also which I will give for the life of the world is my flesh." John 6:32-35, 48-51 NASB

Physical food was the spiritual antecedent to the person of Jesus, coming from the Father. The table of show bread symbolized God's intent to feed the spirit of man with His presence.

As with each aspect of God's care for Israel in the desert, the food from heaven and the table of show bread were veiled references to a greater truth. Jesus was the amalgamation of both symbols. He was the bread of life from heaven and the person of the Word.[3] Feasting upon Him would sustain the human spirit in a relationship with God and we could be supplied both physically and spiritually by His economy.

God also supplied water to the Israelites.

> *"Take the rod; and you and your brother Aaron assemble the congregation and speak to the rock before their eyes, that it may yield its water. You shall thus bring forth water for them out of the rock and let the congregation and their beasts drink."* Numbers 20:10-11 NASB

Those were the waters of Meribah, because the sons of Israel contended with the Lord, and He proved Himself holy among them.

The rock, like the bread, symbolized Christ:

> *For I do not want you to be unaware, brethren, that our fathers were all under the cloud and all passed through the sea; and all were baptized into Moses in the cloud and in the sea; and all ate the same spiritual food; and all drank the same spiritual drink, for they were drinking from a spiritual rock which followed them; and the rock was Christ.* 1 Corinthians 10:1-4 NASB[4]

This supply further emphasizes His superintending presence.

Despite the Lord's supply, the nation of Israel suffered in the desert, and with their suffering came much questioning and complaint.[5] Their grousing exasperated Moses who was known for his humility. He was supposed to entreat the person of the rock inasmuch as it symbolized Christ. God used a rock to show the implausibility of water springing forth as a natural occurrence in the desert. Instead, Moses struck the rock:

> *Moses and Aaron gathered the assembly before the rock. And he said to them, "Listen now, you rebels; shall we bring forth water for you out of this rock?" Then Moses lifted up his hand and struck the rock twice with his rod; and water came forth*

> *abundantly, and the congregation and their beasts drank.*
> Numbers 20:10-11 NASB

Because the rock symbolized Christ and the presence of God, and Moses did not treat it as holy, God prevented him from leading the people into the land God had prepared for them.[6]

God told Israel that His purpose in taking them into the wilderness was to humble, test, and teach them.

> *You shall remember all the way which the LORD your God has led you in the wilderness these forty years, that He might humble you, testing you, to know what was in your heart, whether you would keep His commandments or not. He humbled you and let you be hungry, and fed you with manna which you did not know, nor did your fathers know, that He might make you understand that man does not live by bread alone, but man lives by everything that proceeds out of the mouth of the LORD.* Deuteronomy 8:2-3 NASB

In this economy, they would be supplied with food from heaven and water from the presence of God. Each element revealed the nature of God in supplying things their physical environment could not provide for them.

God also provided clothing. He did so by converting the garb of their slavery, in which they left Egypt, to the robes of favor by the showing that their garments did not wear out.[7] What started out as shameful and beggarly was transformed into the very symbol of favor associated with the promise. The undeniable evidence of their slavery was transformed into the enduring symbols of their blessing. The story of the returning son provides greater clarity of this principle.

PART FOUR

> *So he got up and came to his father. But while he was still a long way off, his father saw him and felt compassion for him, and ran and embraced him and kissed him. And the son said to him, "Father, I have sinned against heaven and in your sight; I am no longer worthy to be called your son." But the father said to his slaves, "Quickly bring out the best robe and put it on him and put a ring on his hand and sandals on his feet; and bring the fattened calf, kill it, and let us eat and celebrate; for this son of mine was dead and has come to life again; he was lost and has been found." And they began to celebrate.* Luke 15:20-24 NASB

His father's first act was to command a stripping away of all of the filth and indignity of the son's impoverishing choices and to restore his identity. In the command, "bring forth the best robe" the father chose to clothe him again with the status of a son. The son's act of repentance was obvious by his decision to return to his father's house. No long period of penance and proving was required to restore his status even though during the time of his departure and rebellion he was still a son.

Clothing symbolizes the most basic element of protection for the shell that is the physical human body. Adam's first act when he began to see himself as a physical being rather than a spiritual one was to clothe himself.[8] Adam's response to the new awareness of his physical state immediately informed God as to what had happened.[9] Prior to the fall, they were naked, but felt no shame because their perspective was that of being spirit beings, housed within flesh.[10]

Clothing became a symbol of man's condition in relationship both to himself and to God. Jacob showed his preference for his son Joseph over all his children by making him a coat of many colors. The promise of the redeemer of mankind was framed in the language of clothing, both in His death and in His triumph:

> *...He washes his garments in wine, And his robes in the blood of grapes.* Genesis 49:11 NASB

> *On His robe and on His thigh He has a name written, "KING OF KINGS, AND LORD OF LORDS."* Revelation 19:16 NASB

Jesus included the need for clothing, along with basic sustenance, as things that distract from the presence of God:

> *For this reason I say to you, do not be worried about your life, as to what you will eat or what you will drink; nor for your body, as to what you will put on. Is not life more than food and the body more than clothing? ...And why are you so worried about clothing? Observe how the lilies of the field grow; they do not toil nor do they spin, yet I say to you that not even Solomon in all his glory clothed himself like one of these. But if God so clothes the grass of the field, which is alive today and tomorrow is thrown into the furnace, will He not much more clothe you? You of little faith! Do not worry then, saying, "What will we eat?" or "What will we drink?" or "What will we wear for clothing?" For the Gentiles eagerly seek all these things; for your heavenly Father knows that you need all these things. But seek first His kingdom and His righteousness, and all these things will be added to you.* Matthew 6:25, 28-33 NASB

The readiness of the bride to be presented to Christ, the husband, is also described in terms of clothing.

> *Let us rejoice and be glad and give the glory to Him, for the marriage of the Lamb has come and His bride has made herself ready. It was given to her to clothe herself in fine linen, bright and clean; for the fine linen is the righteous acts of the saints.* Revelation 19:7-8 NASB

The picture of man's righteousness is presented through the motif of clothing.[11] The symbolic search for clothing relates to fear and shame resulting from separation from God, requiring the assertion of separateness and individuality as the basis of a personal identity. The return to innocence, though described in the language of clothing, references a state of being that evinces the incarnation of God clothed in human flesh. The fine clothing of the readied bride is in fact her righteous acts.

For the Israelites, the time of the wandering in the wilderness was to change the mind-set in order to restore the promise made to their father, Abraham. That their clothing did not wear out during this time was one of the undeniable signs of the lifting of their status from slaves to the favored generation of promise. All of the elements of their need corresponded to a spiritual antecedent and both the manner of their supply and the supply itself pointed them to God and were designed to lift their view from the natural to the spiritual. Jesus was the rock who supplied water, and the water itself referenced eternal life.[12] Jesus is the source from which eternal life flows into the realm of mankind. Eternal life is not merely life after death, but it is life that may be entered into in the present. It flows from God and is sustained by the presence of God. Although it is common to think of eternal life as life after death, properly understood, it is an alternative source of existence supported entirely by the presence of God and may be entered into by belief in Jesus as the sole and exclusive access to this life that is in the Father:

> He said, "Father, the hour has come; glorify Your Son, that the Son may glorify You, even as You gave Him authority over all flesh, that to all whom You have given Him, He may give eternal life. This is eternal life, that they may know You, the only true God, and Jesus Christ whom You have sent." John 17:1-3 NASB

PART FOUR

This life is a relationship to God as Father, inasmuch as the definition of father embodies the concept of the source from which one's life comes. Indeed, it is the reconciliation of the human spirit to God as Spirit that connects this source of life to the earth. The means by which this connection is both understood and entered into is embodied in the relationship of father and son, the available prototype of which was put on the earth in the person of Jesus who related to God as Father and gives us access into the same relationship. Therefore, this life is only available through Christ Jesus.

---

[1]Revelation 5:9-10 NASB. [2]Deuteronomy 8:15 NASB. [3]John 1:1-12 NASB. [4]See e.g., Matthew 7:25 NASB, Matthew 16:18 NASB, Habakkuk 1:12 NASB, Daniel 2:34-35 NASB, Psalm 94:22 NASB, Deuteronomy 32:4-18 NASB (highlighting the symbol of Christ as the rock). [5]Numbers 20:3-5 NASB. [6]Numbers 20:12 NASB. [7]Deuteronomy 8:4 NASB. [8]Genesis 3:7 NASB. [9]Genesis 3:11 NASB. [10]See Genesis 2:25 NASB. [11]Revelation 3:18 NASB; John19:23-24 NASB. [12]John 4:13-14 NASB.

The Brazen Serpent

> *The people spoke against God and Moses, "Why have you brought us up out of Egypt to die in the wilderness? For there is not food and no water, and we loathe this miserable food." The Lord sent fiery serpents among the people, and they bit the people so that many people of Israel died. So, the people came to Moses and said, "We have sinned, because we have spoken against the Lord and you; intercede with the Lord, that He may remove the serpents from us." And Moses interceded for the people. Then the Lord said to Moses, "Make a fiery serpent and set it on a standard; and it shall come about that everyone who is bitten, when he looks at it, he will live." And Moses made a bronze serpent and set it on the standard; and it came about, that if a serpent bit any man, when he looked to the bronze serpent, he lived.* Numbers 21:5-9 NASB[1]

PART FOUR

The enduring symbol of Satan, mankind's enemy since the garden of Eden, was the serpent.[2] He comes by God's permission to disclose the hidden conditions of human hearts. All enmity between mankind and God and between man and man stems from the spirit of animosity and alienation sown by the enemy.

In their grumbling against the sufficiency of God's care for them, the Israelites showed that they harbored resentments in their hearts toward God, because His supply was different in form from their expectations as former slaves. This was due in large measure from the fact that they did not understand the necessity of the experience in the desert. Although it was indispensable to their mental transformation from slaves to sons of the promise, they assumed that simply because they were set free from Egypt they were ready to take up their inheritances in the promised land. They had no way of assigning value to the experience that was designed to undergird their existence with the presence of God Himself and the requirement that they would live and make their decisions upon a fundamental trust in the goodness and faithfulness of God.

Mentally, they were no different from the Egyptians, from whose enslavement they were freed. It is why they easily defaulted to Egypt as the place of their sustenance. When they complained against the supply of God, they readily expressed a preference for the return to Egypt. They ignored both the denial of their destiny as a people and the harshness of their enforced toil and focused only upon the certainty of their daily diet as slaves. They equated the predictability of their supply with their toil. They showed how completely entrapped in the economy of the sweat of their brow they had become, and they were no different from their great ancestor, Adam, who listened to the serpent.

God meant to show them this source of their dissatisfaction with Him through a visual representation. He permitted that animosity together with its source to take the form of poisonous snakes whose affliction of them resulted in physical death in the same manner in which Satan's craft in alienating man from God also results in spiritual separation, a condition referred to in the Scriptures as death.

In order to reconcile man to God, it was necessary for Christ to come and die upon a cross. The symbolic connection between the brazen serpent on the pole and Jesus on the cross is directly connected in Scripture:

> *As Moses lifted up the serpent in the wilderness, even so must the Son of Man be lifted up; so that whoever believes will in Him have eternal life.* John 3:14-15 NASB

Yet, the connection does not seem to be of the same kind because the serpent of bronze was the cause of their deaths and Jesus is the cause of life.

The death of Jesus upon the cross is meant to be viewed both from earth and from heaven. From the earth, Christ is offered as the only sinless man. He came into the earth to satisfy the justice of God in paying the price for the transgressions of all men. He who had no sin represents all who have sinned. Viewed from heaven, His substitution is acceptable to God. In the same instance, He is the total innocent and the most culpable. In His own capacity, He is the total innocent. In His representation, He bears the sins of all completely.[3]

The justice of God demands that the sinner pays the price for his sins. Jesus, therefore, becomes the consummate representation of all who have sinned and pays the price for the transgressions of all mankind as He hangs upon the cross. The requirements of justice are fully satisfied, and He is able to say, "It is finished." In His representational capacity, as the one who becomes sin personified, He embodied all that wickedness and sin spawned in the earth from the activities of the serpent in the garden. For all intents and purposes, everything that the serpent engendered in the earth is fully paid for. Nothing remains outstanding in the indebtedness of mankind to the standards of God's justice. However, the nature of God prefers mercy.

When one arises from the earth who satisfies the demands of God's justice but does so from a position of personal innocence, he has accomplished the perfect sacrifice. It elicits the deepest expression of the mercy of God, and He decrees that the way is open for man to return to the presence of God but only as part of the One whose sacrifice has been accepted by God. Mankind, then, may advance to the presence of God if he comes in the recognizable form of the corporate Christ. In this arrangement, all the works of the devil have been destroyed.[4]

The Israelites were healed from the snake bites when they looked upon the brazen serpent. It seemed an improbable cure and even less likely correlation to Jesus on the cross, reconciling man to God by negating the work of Satan. But, when viewed as the undoing of the work of the devil by taking on fully the weight of his role in the separation of man from God, it is, in fact, the perfect metaphor. God designed it to simultaneously annul the effects of sin and reopen the avenue of reconciliation to Himself.[5]

When Adam hid from God, he took on the mindset of Satan and viewed God as his enemy. He shared a common mindset with Satan and viewed everything in his world, including God, from that viewpoint. This mindset informed his culture from this point forward and was imparted to his generations. Cain interpreted his interaction with his brother Abel through this understanding. It was why he could view him without brotherly affection.

The devil does not typically approach man in a symbolic form. The entire notion of man viewing his fellow man as both his enemy and his opportunity is an underlying perception which is demonically informed, although the interactions are lived out in familiar human circumstances. The economy of the presence of God offers protections from all forms of endangerment resulting from the activities of Satan, and even death may be swallowed up in victory through the resurrection of the dead:

> *But when this perishable will have put on the imperishable, and this mortal will have put on immortality, then will come about the saying that is written, "Death is swallowed up in victory." "O Death, where is your victory? O death, where is your sting?" The sting of death is sin, and the power of sin is the law; but thanks be to God, who gives us the victory through our Lord Jesus Christ.* 1 Corinthians 15:54-57 NASB

One should understand the connection which is expressed in God's address to Eve and to the serpent at the time of the fall: "And I will put enmity between you and the woman, and between your seed and her seed; He shall bruise you on the head, and you shall bruise him on the heel."[6]

---

[1]See also 2 Kings 18:4 NASB. [2]Revelation 12:9 NASB. [3]2 Corinthians 5:21 NASB. [4]1John 3:8 NASB. [5]2 Corinthians 5:14-15 NASB. [6]Genesis 3:15 NASB.

Contrasting Economies

Although God showed the nation of Israel that His presence addressed all their physical needs, they failed to enter into His rest. God judged that an entire generation was unprepared to enter the promised land which symbolized His promise to Abraham. He had provided the opportunity to elevate their culture from being slaves to being sons of God.[1]

PART FOUR

This was necessary to fulfill its destiny as the nation from which the Redeemer would come. They carried the seed of this promise and had to be ready to receive Him when the promise was fulfilled. For them to transition into this new culture, they had to be able to enter into God's rest.

> *For if Joshua had given them rest, He would not have spoken of another day after that. So there remains a sabbath rest for the people of God. For the one who has entered His rest has himself also rested from his works, as God did from His.* Hebrews 4:8-10 NASB

But Israel continued to resort to the default culture of all humanity.

The spiritual economy's hallmark is displayed in the Son's ability to rest in God's presence. Adam shifted from rest to agitation in God's presence as the first consequence of sin. Jesus, however, showed how one can be at rest while vulnerable.[2] Because of Jesus' unfailing accordance with the Father's will, all the resources of heaven were at His command. Creation itself would meet His call. He understood His calling and lived in full obedience to its demands. The Father's presence supported His every step.[3] Christ's rest was only broken at the end, just before His Spirit left His body, when for the sake of all people He died and was separated from the presence of the Father. "My God, My God, why have You forsaken me?"[4]

Jesus' disciples experienced the economy by which He lived:

> *When evening came, His disciples went down to the lake, where they got into a boat and set off across the lake for Capernaum. By now it was dark, and Jesus had not yet joined them. A strong wind was blowing, and the waters grew rough. When they had rowed about three or four miles, they saw Jesus approaching the boat, walking on the water; and they were frightened. But He said to them, "It is I; don't be afraid." Then they were willing*

> *to take Him into the boat, and immediately the boat reached the shore where they were heading.* John 6:16-21 NIV

Jesus' approach did not fit the environment, which frightened the disciples. Jesus was proceeding in the economy of God's presence. Neither the water, waves, nor wind had any effect upon His progress. The disciples were focused on their environment, propelling themselves by their own efforts and fighting the elements. Juxtaposed are the divine economy with the sweat of their brow.

The wind represents the Spirit of God.[5] In the story of Jesus walking on the water, the wind represented opportunity in the economy of the Spirit but opposition for the disciples struggling in the boat. When people do not anticipate God's presence, they try to reach their destinations through their own strength and resources. Locked into this mindset, they cannot simultaneously rely on the presence of God. If you are unprepared to rest in God's presence, you cannot intentionally benefit from it. The mature son of God expects God's presence and is at rest while it changes the surrounding environment to fit the son's purpose in Christ.

Others see the presence of God with uncomprehending awe or fear, just as the disciples did in the boat. The economy of the Spirit does not serve this mindset:

> *[Jesus] said, "Come!" And Peter got out of the boat and walked on the water and came toward Jesus. But seeing the wind, he became frightened, and beginning to sink he cried out, "Lord, save me!"* Matthew 14:28-30 NASB

Those who cannot rest in God's presence cannot stand fully upon the economy of the Spirit.

Jesus was in the economy of heaven and His disciples were in the default human economy. Both economies were one step away from each other in the same environment. When Jesus stepped into the boat, the Spiritual economy was superimposed upon the disciples' struggle.

When they occupied the same space in time, one person walking in the economy of the presence of God transported all others to the intended destination. The Spiritual economy is always greater than human efforts. When the Spiritual economy enters into a place of human efforts—in the form of a son of God—even those who are not at rest in God's presence may witness and benefit from His grace. The Spiritual economy always serves God's purpose for His sons, and that purpose usually results in the sons of God showing His goodness to others through their own persons.

---

[1]Deuteronomy 8:2-5 NASB. [2]Matthew 26:52-53 NASB. [3]Matthew 6:25-26, 33 NASB. [4]Matthew 27:46 NASB. [5]See John 3:8 NIV.

Truth and the Divine Economy

When the Spirit of God entered the natural realm, "the Word became flesh" bringing the divine economy with Him. Jesus was "full of grace and truth."[1] He brought with Him everything necessary to sustain the spiritual lives of humans and support their divine purpose. Grace comprises the dispensations of the Spiritual economy with divine supply. Truth accompanies grace because the divine economy only supports God's purposes. It is the standard that determines the focus of the supply.

Because grace and truth go together the relationship between God and the Son is important. Grace only supports truth and truth exists in God. Therefore, the Body of Christ must have access to the

Spirit of God in order to be the vehicle for divine grace to enter the natural world.

Jesus the Son is the source of this relationship and the access to the Spirit of God. He is "the way, and the truth and the life" and the exclusive access to the Father.[2] He modeled the relationship with the Father for everyone assembled to the corporate Son. Through Jesus, we know that as we grow in maturity, we attain a oneness with God through our spirits.

> *Sanctify them in the truth; Your word is truth. As You sent Me into the world, I also have sent them into the world. For their sakes I sanctify Myself, that they themselves also may be sanctified in truth...that they may all be one: even as you, Father, are in Me and I in You, that they also may be in Us, so that the world may believe that You sent Me. The glory which you have given Me I have given to them, that they may be one, just as We are one; I in them and You in Me, that they may be perfected in unity, so that the world may know that You sent Me, and loved them, even as You have loved Me.* John 17:17-19, 21-23 NASB

The goal of this oneness is for our thoughts and actions to be exactly consistent with God's intent while remaining the product of our independent choice because we are sons, not slaves.

> *Truly, truly I say to you, the Son can do nothing of Himself, unless it is something He sees the Father doing; for whatever the Father does, these things the Son also does in like manner. For the Father loves the Son and shows Him all things that He Himself is doing; and the Father will show Him greater works than these so that you will marvel.* John 5:19-20 NASB

All those who are included in the corporate Son are meant to be brought into the reality of the love of the Father. But the son must obey and trust the Father before he may wield the Spiritual economy as Jesus did.

Truth is the key to the application of the economy of grace and it is through a relationship to God as Father that makes one available for the incarnation of God. Through this relationship God's love is put on display. The grace of God does not exist to supply anything other than the economy of a son. Every other purported form of access to God falls short of this model, not one of which acknowledges the possibility of sonship.

The requirement of truth is a prerequisite for determining who or what among human belief systems might enjoy the benefit of support of the economy of God's presence. Although it is common for religious practice to cite Scriptural texts as the basis of belief, unless the practice of doing so leads to the substantive result of a relationship to God as Father and son, the economy of His presence is unavailable for the support of those assertions.

---

¹John 1:14 NASB; see John 1:17 NASB. ²John 14:6 NASB.

The Fullness of Grace

> *As each one has received a special gift, employ it in serving one another as good stewards of the manifold grace of God. Whoever speaks, is to do so as one who is speaking the utterances of God; whoever serves is to do so as one who is serving by the strength which God supplies; so that in all things God may be glorified through Jesus Christ, to whom belongs the glory and dominion forever and ever. Amen.* 1 Peter 4:10-11 NASB

Grace in the spiritual economy is in God's strength and in His words that accompany one's journey of sonship—from a newborn believer to a son who accurately represents God in everything they do. Sonship is a progression. No one is born again and can immediately claim, "If you have seen me, you have seen the Father."[1]

To become sons of God, one must die to that state of being born into Adam's legacy and be reborn of the Spirit.[2] "You have died, and your life is hidden with Christ in God."[3] Your life is no longer your own; you are a living sacrifice dedicated to revealing God's glory. "When Christ, who is our life, is revealed, then you also will be revealed with Him in glory."[4] Christ ensures that one will leave behind their prior self.

> *Consider the members of your earthly body as dead to immorality, impurity, passion, evil desire, and greed, which amounts to idolatry, ...and in them you also once walked, when you were living in them. But now you also, put them all aside: anger, wrath, malice, slander, and abusive speech from your mouth.* Colossians 3:5,7-8 NASB

The process of this renewal involves learning who God is, both His character and His personhood.

> *You laid aside the old self with its evil practices, and have put on the new self who is being renewed to a true knowledge according to the image of the One who created him--...So, as those who have been chosen of God, holy and beloved, put on a heart of compassion, kindness, humility, gentleness and patience; bearing with one another, and forgiving each other, whoever has a complaint against anyone; just as the Lord forgave you, so also should you. Beyond all these things put on love which is the perfect bond of unity.* Colossians 3:9-10, 12-14 NASB

PART FOUR

From rebirth to one's complete destiny, each son of God is meant to undergo a progression that changes their personhood until everything that person does and says reflects Christ.

> *Let the peace of Christ rule in your hearts, to which indeed you were called in one body; and be thankful. Let the word of Christ richly dwell within you, ...Whatever you do in word or deed, do all in the name of the Lord Jesus, giving thanks through Him to God the Father.* Colossians 3:15-17 NASB

We are assembled to Christ so that He may take stewardship of our lives as sons.

> *Therefore, prepare your minds for action, keep sober in spirit, fix your hope completely on the grace to be brought to you at the revelation of Jesus Christ. As obedient children, do not be conformed to the former lusts which were yours in your ignorance, but like the Holy One who called you, be holy yourselves also in all your behavior; because it is written, "YOU SHALL BE HOLY, FOR I AM HOLY."* 1 Peter 1:3,6-7, 9 NASB

There are five archetypal graces, each of which signals a different phase of one's progression and comes with all that any son of God needs to complete their calling within that stage of their journey. The endowment of grace increases as one increases in maturity so that they may represent the Father in a higher, or more complete, form.[5]

The five stages of sonship are: 1) the grace of salvation, (2) the grace of reconciliation, (3) the grace of conformation, (4) the grace of maturation, and (5) the grace of exact representation.[6] The sequence of these five graces shows the path one follows from the legacy of Adam to a carrier of God's presence as a part of the Body of Christ. This represents a complete metamorphosis—from seeing oneself as merely flesh, through processes of renewal and ultimately to seeing oneself as a spirit being and a son of God.

These graces are what comprise the makeup of Christ's anointing when He came to the earth. Christ was "full of grace and truth."[7] When He was in heaven, He was the Word of God. His glory included all God's creative competence.[8] When He came to earth, He was the Son. His glory on the earth was to demonstrate God's love in the relationship between Him, the Son, and the Father.[9] The goal was to reconcile humankind to God. In His glory on the earth, He displayed all five graces in His life and ministry.

In showing the grace of God to man, He was not only approved of God, but was opposed by both Satan and men under the control of the evil one. Satan challenged the right of His Sonship and the prerogative to do these things on the earth while religious men questioned His authority to speak and act as the Son of God. God fully authenticated Jesus' right to represent Him up to and including His physical resurrection and ascension to the throne of God, leaving no doubt that He portrayed the nature of God fully during His time on the earth. His administration revealed Him as the Son of God.

The same economy of grace remains in the House of God through His Body. This was always God's intent.[10] Each of the five graces contains specific endowments of power that progressively transforms the recipient internally and empowers his external functioning. The person is transformed from a captive in the domain of darkness under the rule of Satan, to a mature believer capable of putting the nature of God on display in his person as well as effectively participating in the functioning of the corporate Son. It must, however, be reiterated that the economy of God exists to support His divine purposes and is neither available to support the choices of man nor is it subject to the control and use of men and institutions for their own will.

The graces are progressively revealed in a specific order since they form the layers of one's progression from salvation to exact representation. However, each endowment of grace is introduced strategically as the believer progresses on his journey. The depth of transformation contained in each grace continues to unfold, even as new graces are introduced. The strength and power of each grace continues to unfold and interlace with that of succeeding graces. In this manner, the believer matures, from glory to glory. As he becomes more familiar with foundational graces, he is made ready for larger endowments of succeeding graces.[11] A pattern of transformation is introduced and sustained throughout the life of a son of God.

These graces cannot be formularized nor applied by rote. They are subject to the administration of the Spirit of God Himself, which determines how the graces operate with the corporate Son.

---

[1]See John 14:7, 9 NASB. [2]John 3:3 NASB. [3]Colossians 3:3 NASB. [4]Colossians 3:4 NASB. [5]See, e.g., Philippians 3:14 NASB; 1 Corinthians 2:1-6, 3:1-3, 13:11 NASB. [6]Soleyn, Supra, *The Elementary Doctrines*, The Elementary Doctrines and the Maturing Son. [7]John 1:14 NASB. [8]John 17:5 NASB. [9]John 17:22 NASB. [10]Ephesians 3:9-13 NASB. [11]2 Corinthians 3:18 NASB.

The Grace of Salvation

The grace of salvation rescues one from the kingdom of darkness and places them in the Kingdom of God under the rule of Christ as king. One changes kingdoms and kings.

> *For by grace you have been saved through faith; and that not of yourselves, it is the gift of God; not as a result of works, so that no one may boast.* Ephesians 2:8-9 NASB

Salvation begins with a new life and is brought with faith and fire.

PART FOUR

> *Blessed be the God and Father of our Lord Jesus Christ, who according to His great mercy has caused us to be born again to a living hope through the resurrection of Jesus Christ from the dead... In this you greatly rejoice, even though now for a little while, if necessary, you have been distressed by various trials so that the proof of your faith being more precious than gold which is perishable, even though tested by fire, may be found to result in praise and glory and honor at the revelation of Jesus Christ; ...obtaining as the outcome of your faith the salvation of your souls.* 1 Peter 3, 6-7, 9 NASB

Christ awakens the human spirit that is assembled to Him and stewards the process that puts the soul under the Spirit's rule over the person's thoughts and actions. Everything you need for this saving of the soul is imparted as "the grace to be brought to you at the revelation of Jesus Christ."[1]

The purpose for being born again is that the new creation is born of the Spirit, which is of God rather than the flesh which carries Adam's legacy. This is a change of both perspective and the nature of being. When you are born again you are choosing to recognize the spirit in you that cries out to God as Father as the source of your perspective. The physical body remains the same, but a person who is led by the Spirit can see themselves as a spirit-being merely clothed in flesh. The source of your existence then is what happens in the spirit. Previously, the source of your existence was only what the physical body could experience. Once you begin this change of perspective, or renewing of the mind, the spirit is restored to the place of primacy, and God begins to communicate with you directly. As a spirit, you are a son of God and the salvation of your soul is assured because He will not forsake His sons.[2]

The process of the saving of the soul becomes a work to be undertaken throughout the remaining lifetime of the believer. It is a process that parallels the stages of sonship. From the point of being received as a son, he is transferred from the domain of darkness into the Kingdom of Heaven. When he dies, his position changes from being in the Kingdom of Heaven while on the earth, to being in the Kingdom of Heaven in heaven itself. However, it is not the end of the journey since Christ will return to earth, bringing with Him all those who are in heaven.[3]

The process begins with the forgiveness of sins. Jesus' death on the cross was judged by God to be a sufficient price for the sins of all mankind.[4] When our sins are forgiven, the enemy no longer has a legal claim over us, nor is he able to assert his rule over our minds or persons. We become dead to the kingdom of darkness.[5] We can no longer be defined by the fallen nature.[6]

The forgiveness of sins comes with the declaration of the mercy of God toward mankind. This has the effect of overthrowing the legal claim of the enemy to keep man captive under his influence and in the culture of his dark domain. Simultaneously, one is both rescued from the control of the evil one and set into the Kingdom of Heaven as a citizen under the authority and rule of Christ. It is nearly inconceivable to grasp the quantum of power and authority exerted in this grace. In one instance, all of the activities of Satan by which man was separated from God and enslaved in a condition of opposition to God and alienation from His purpose is undone. The authority that established disorder in creation is destroyed. The captive is set free and returned to his original position.

Whereas man is the beneficiary of this outcome, he typically remains unfamiliar with the scope of his freedom from the control of Satan. It is this lack of familiarity with the extent of what has been accomplished on his behalf that permits the enemy to continue to be effective in continuing to bring man under his influence by means of this deception. If the believer truly understood, the enemy's attempts to define him by reference to the familiar would become completely ineffective.

When Jesus was sending out his disciples, He informed them that they were substituted in His place and commissioned them to function in exactly the same manner in which He functioned and to exercise the same authority that He was given.[7] Some religious groups lay claim to this power as the justification for their existence. It is significant to note that Jesus gave this authority to His disciples, since He was sending them out into the world as his ambassadors.[8]

The message of the grace of salvation must include the authority to declare that sin no longer separates man from God because Jesus has paid the price and God is no longer counting man's sins against him. An ambassador of the Kingdom is authorized to make this declaration and to introduce them to the reality of the Kingdom of Heaven as the place of their new citizenship and to the authority of Jesus, the king over this Kingdom, by whose authority they were released from the devil's control. An ambassador is further empowered to extend to them citizenship in the Kingdom of Heaven and the accompanying status of sons of God. This officially starts them on the journey of being fully restored to God and functional for the original purposes for which God created man.

---

[1] 1 Peter 1:13 NASB. [2] Hebrews 13:5 NASB. [3] 1 Thessalonians 4:14 NASB. [4] 2 Corinthians 5:18-19 NASB; Colossians 2:13-14 NASB. [5] Ephesians 2:1-5 NASB; Colossians 1:13 NASB. [6] Romans 8:1 NASB. [7] John 20:21-23 NASB. [8] 2 Corinthians 5:20 NASB.

The Power of the Grace of Salvation

The beneficiary of the grace of salvation receives the power of his new status in the form of both a changed identity as well as his status as a citizen of the Kingdom of Heaven. Being restored to the identity of a son of God, the authority of the accuser to hold him captive to his former way of life and to restrict and imprison him in that identity is destroyed. The enemy's ability to define one's personhood is the greatest source of his control over mankind. As long as one is subject to an identity controlled through accusation and guilt, the scope of one's progress toward God may be indefinitely frustrated. Humans may be made to function predictably in the pursuit of mere survival. Breaking free by the ever-increasing power of this grace from this orbit of predictable control allows the believer to benefit from being under the authority and administration of a new king as a citizen of the Kingdom of Heaven. It is not just the opportunity for new surroundings but for a genuinely new life as a new person.[1]

Amazingly, the truth of a new identity and the courage to assert that truth causes a dramatic shift in one's perception of oneself and of the world around him. Like the turning on of a light in a dark room, the darkness immediately disappears because it is powerless to control the effects of the light. The battle that continues is essentially a conflict that stems from the familiar identity of the past. The enemy hopes to negate the effects of the power of salvation by an appeal to the old identity. This appeal is to the soul, which he knows is still functional although its authority over the person is a diminishing one.

The value of a spiritual father and membership in a functioning spiritual household is inestimable in keeping the soul from arising to a place of dominance and re-empowering the false, but familiar, identity of the past. The exhortation and encouragement of a spiritual father and other members of the spiritual family together with the willingness of the new believer to accept the reality of a new identity is more than sufficient to destroy the hold of the enemy upon the mind of the soul.

God permits these battles to occur in order to train the believer in the exercise of the authority inherent in his new estate as a son of God.

PART FOUR

As authority is exercised consistently in this area, the results become increasingly clear that a son of God possesses the power to eliminate all of the vestiges of the works of Satan in his or her life. Fortified with the truth of this experience the believer may proceed to eliminate the works of the devil from all the spheres of authority over which he or she has been set.

Typically, the eviction of the influence of the enemy in one's life begins internally, within the soul, but moves externally into the spheres of authority that include natural family members who are submitted to the authority of Christ as well as members of a spiritual household in whose lives one has been given authority to act. It further progresses into the spheres of business and beyond. It must be noted, however, that in every case the destruction of the works of Satan by the believer depends upon whether or not the believer actually has or has been given legitimate authority to act within these lives and spheres.

Ordinarily, it is normal and customary for believers to think about possessing power to act at will, purely on the basis of the assumption that being born again entitles them to be victorious over Satan. They are unfamiliar with the different forms of grace together with the accompanying power that has been restored to man in and through Christ and how these graces empower the believer to a triumphant life. This unfamiliarity with both the nature of the power inherent in the grace and the accompanying administration is one of the greatest hinderances to a triumphant life.

The scope of the power invested in the grace of salvation is virtually unimaginable since it is able to cancel and rescind all of the mindsets to which men have become enslaved in their departure from God. It is able to eliminate all of the divisions that have grown up between mankind—from global issues such as racism and genocide to deeply personal issues of shame and depression. It would bring into being the entire governance of the Kingdom of Heaven and offer a model of life that contrasts starkly with the present existing order.

The transformation from an identity based in the soul and subject to captivity by Satan to one based in the Spirit and subject to the rule of Christ would produce a shift in the very essence of how the human being is defined—soul to spirit. Mankind would be reconciled to God and to one another. The scope of this power is so vast and sweeping that the enemy devotes much of his time and effort to the perfecting of the deception that blocks the view of men from seeing such hope. For those who have escaped the pull of this deception and are moving toward a clearer view of their authority as sons of God, this deception is rapidly disappearing.

---

[1] 2 Corinthians 5:17 NASB; Revelation 21:5 NASB.

The Principle of the Resurrection

The principle of the resurrection is the power of God that underlies the grace of salvation.

> *I am the resurrection and the life; he who believes in Me will live even if he dies, and everyone who lives and believes in Me will never die. Do you believe this?* John 11:25-26 NASB

Within our bodies of flesh is a seed from God. This seed is a spirit and God is the Father of our spirits. Every aspect of God's personhood is derived from His nature as Spirit. Every human spirit is capable of representing God because it is part of Him. Our spirits are what make humans like God, in His image and likeness.

Like every seed in nature, our spirits are given their full expression through resurrection. Christ's death and resurrection was the full demonstration of this spiritual principle. Within the man Jesus, was the Spirit called Christ. He was given to the earth through a perishable, physical existence. But when the shell died, the imperishable Spirit of Christ remained and was resurrected. The Spirit of Christ remained in the earth and continued to be the open door between heaven and earth. Christ went from showing the relationship between the Father and the Son as a man to assembling human spirits to Him as the means of reconciling God and people.

By the resurrection of the Spirit of Christ, people can be assembled to Him as part of the corporate Son. The corporate Son, or the Body of Christ, is made up of the entire church of His followers united under the headship of Christ. This is only possible because we are all spirit beings. Part of the translation into the Body of Christ requires our own resurrection as spirits. While we remain on the earth, our resurrection involves a symbolic death to our old selves, but a very real awakening as a new creation when we are born again.

The grace of resurrection is that which awakens our spirits to our sonship in Christ. We have been given a calling, or destiny, and everything needed to accomplish it. The principle of resurrection facilitates the change of one's being from natural to spiritual and the greater destiny that comes with that change. By the power of resurrection, the mind of one's spirit experiences a rebirth, thereby reestablishing communication between the human spirit and the Spirit of God. As spirit, one is capable of transcending carnal limitations that block active fellowship with the Spirit of God.

The most important change that occurs through resurrection, is establishing one's sonship. As a son and representative of God, the purpose of living is given expression through representing Him within circumstances that require the power and authority of His throne. This transition would be deemed resurrection and would result in "the newness of life."

PART FOUR

The Power of the Resurrection

> *I count all things to be loss in view of the surpassing value of knowing Christ Jesus my Lord, ...that I may know Him and the power of His resurrection and the fellowship of His sufferings, being conformed to His death; in order that I may attain to the resurrection from the dead. Not that I have already obtained it or have already become perfect, but I press on so that I may lay hold of that for which also I was laid hold of by Christ Jesus. Brethren, I do not regard myself as having laid hold of it yet; but one thing I do: forgetting what lies behind and reaching forward to what lies ahead, I press on toward the goal for the prize of the upward call of God in Christ Jesus. Let us therefore, as many as are perfect, have this attitude; and if in anything you have a different attitude, God will reveal that also to you; however, let us keep living by that same standard to which we have attained.* Philippians 3:8, 10-16 NASB

Paul understood that the transformational power of the resurrection effectively positioned him to see all things from a heavenly point of view. Already willing to uncerimoniously discard as worthless his laudable accomplishments from a religious point of view, he expressed his strong preference for a view obtained from the throne of God. His efforts were dedicated to reaching the goal for which God called him heavenward. He considered that the prize was to see all things including himself from God's point of view and thought that the maturity of a believer was inseparable from having reached the point of a heavenly view. This, he considered to be the transcendent power of the resurrection.

The inherent power of the resurrection is its triumph over the limitation upon human perspectives that the fear of death exerts. Anyone who sees his life ending upon his death is conditioned to the urgency of accomplishing their life's purpose before they expire.

Resurrection is inseparable from an identity as a spirit being who is made alive and triumphs over death. Such a person lives forever in the corporate Christ.[1]

This vastly extended view of life overcomes the limitations of death by introducing the believer to the power of life sustained from the realm of the eternal and frees the believer from the constraints of expiration to both live beyond the fear of death and empower subsequent generations by their way of life.[2]

> *All these died in faith, without receiving the promises, but having seen them and having welcomed them from a distance and having confessed that they were strangers and exiles on the earth. ...And all these having gained approval through their faith, did not receive what was promised, because God had provided something better for us, so that apart from us they would not be made perfect.* Hebrews 11:13, 39-40 NASB

One of the most significant manifestations of the power of resurrection comes in the form of an impartation of faith to see what is not yet in existence but is certain to come in due course. It is what is meant by "living in the spirit," and it is to have the same understanding and point of view as God Himself. Such a mindset cannot vest in a person who still sees himself as a stranger to the ways of God. It can only be embraced by someone governed by the mind of the Spirit, who identifies God as his Father, and has come to see his role in the earth as that of putting on display the nature of his Father.

Once the life within a seed breaks free of the outer casing and is drawn upward to the surface by the light and warmth of the sun, it begins to put on display the nature of the source from which it originally came. Although it is a distinctly different plant from the one that bore it as a seed, its resemblance to the source of its origin is unique and compelling—so much so that if the source of its origin were not available

PART FOUR

to be viewed and observed it would serve fully to accurately portray the source from which it came.

The believer carries the power of resurrection and possesses the authority to demonstrate the nature of God in any circumstance or relationship in which God chooses to manifest Himself through one in whom He lives. As with the grace of salvation, all five graces represent administrations of God's power and authority presented in the earth, first through Jesus and now through the corporate Christ. Both by His words and acts Jesus explained and demonstrated that He was the incarnation of the authority and power of God to present an exact picture of the invisible God to the natural world.

The enemy desires to obscure the nature of God from human view. The love of God naturally draws man to God. "Men will repent when they see the goodness of God in the face of Jesus Christ."

> *The god of this world has blinded the minds of the unbelieving so that they might not see the light of the gospel of the glory of Christ, who is the image of God. For we do not preach ourselves but Christ Jesus as Lord, and ourselves as your bond-servants for Jesus' sake. For God, who said, "Light shall shine out of darkness," is the One who has shone in our hearts to give the Light of the knowledge of the glory of God in the face of Christ.*
> 2 Corinthians 4:4-6 NASB

The power of the replication of the nature of God is present in the grace of resurrection. In whatever manner this grace would be effectively substantiated in the present world, the demonstrations of proof are available. It must be noted that before Jesus raised the dead, He was the resurrection and the life.

The proof of a thing is never the thing itself, but the evidence that substantiates the claim. The more telling proof today of the existence of the grace of resurrection may not be in the demonstration of raising the dead, but in a pristine showing of the nature of God against the background of duplicity and self-promotion.

The grace of resurrection moves beyond overcoming the works of the devil to the restoration of a picture of God shown in the earth. It is a message that speaks of the restoration of the original purpose for which God placed man whom He had made as a son in the earth.

---

[1]John 11:25-26 NASB. [2]Hebrews 2:15 NASB.

The Grace of Reconciliation

> *Now all these things are from God, who reconciled us to Himself through Christ and gave us the ministry of reconciliation, namely, that God was in Christ reconciling the world to Himself, not counting their trespasses against them, and He has committed to us the word of reconciliation. Therefore, we are ambassadors for Christ, as though God were making an appeal through us; we beg you on behalf of Christ, be reconciled to God. He made Him who knew no sin to be sin on our behalf, so that we might become the righteousness of God in Him.* 2 Corinthians 5:18-21 NASB

Reconciliation refers to a prior existing reality to which one returns. Every human spirit carries the seed of a destiny that determines who that person is when they are led by the Spirit. "Before I formed you in the womb I knew you, and before you were born I consecrated you; I have appointed you a prophet to the nations."[1] Without a sense of calling and the traits that make up an individual's character— one's gifts or talents, interests— unique competences serve only the imperative to survive. They are not given their full intended expression. The grace of reconciliation is the way that God restores people to their greater purpose.

The Spirit that God placed in man as a gift carried the ability to be reconciled to God. In each endowment, God specifically placed a likeness of Himself within that Spirit in anticipation of becoming incarnate in that person's form. However, because He gave a gift, He could not continue to lay claim to an inherent right to possess the endowment once the gift had fully vested and had resulted in a separate and distinct new being. Every gift requires the intent of the donor to make the gift. A gift is not a gift without a voluntary intent on the part of the one who possesses the thing in the beginning. It cannot be coerced nor is it a gift if released in satisfaction of an existing obligation. God gave endowments of Spirit out of His person, which He intended to result in beings who were "in His image and likeness."

In order for them to fulfill His purpose in their creation, they had to be separate and distinct from Himself. He not only had to intend to make this gift of Spirit, but He also specifically conveyed the gift. This delivery of Spirit took place when He breathed into formed clay that which He intended. By forming the receptacle and imparting the endowment, the gift was not only imparted but received, and the result was the establishment of a new being.

Once the intended gift has been delivered and received, the giver has lost all rights to the thing so conveyed. The recipient becomes the true owner of the thing conveyed. The source of the origin of the gift is prevented from exerting a superior right against the claim of the recipient. Once God gave man a gift of Spirit out of Himself, and man became a new life in being, God would no longer assert claim over the spirit found within man even though He is the source from which the spirit of man originated.

PART FOUR

With the fall of man, his spirit became subject to the rule of his soul and God was denied fellowship with the human spirit. Man not only lost his identity as defined by the presence of God, but also lost his connection to the gifts and calling within him that were endemic to his being as having originated out of the person of God.

In order to retake this identity, he must reverse the gifting process and offer his spirit back to God to be reintegrated into the person of God and to experience the reactivation of both his identity and his purpose. Man had no way of offering himself again to God. God had to send the proper reconnection in order for man to be afforded the means by which to become reconnected to God.

That means was contained in the person of Jesus and is called the Spirit of Christ. It is the sole and exclusive means by which access to God is afforded. God intended to become visible in Christ. To the extent that the living God could become visible and understood in creation, He designed the Body of Christ to accommodate the fullness of this expression. The Spirit of Christ is inherently given to accommodate a corporate expression of God, since the plentitude of God cannot be adequately expressed apart from a corporate form.

Each individual possesses a spirit capable of a particular expression of God which is a limited view of the divine Spirit from which it originated. His original design was to enable particular facets of Himself to be on display in the earth. That perfect display through an individual remains a singular facet of the beauty and complexity of God's total being. The presentation of an accurate picture of God in the earth requires that the individual spirit be restored to its original mandate and function while it is reintegrated into the corporate whole of the Body of Christ.

---

[1] Jeremiah 1:5 NASB.

PART FOUR

The Grace of Conformation

The sufficiency of the power of God includes the power to conform us to the standard of existence God envisioned for our earthly existence before we were placed in our mothers' wombs. "The gifts and the calling of God are irrevocable."[1]

Before a human being's first contact with the natural world, that being his mother's womb, God encodes in his spirit the particular form in which he or she is designed to put the nature of God on display in the earth. The advent of every new person in the earth is designed with great specificity. Not only is each one designed to put a particular aspect of the invisible God on display through gifts and callings, but even their moment in history is specifically ordained.

> *He made from one man every nation of mankind to live on all the face of the earth, having determined their appointed times and the boundaries of their habitation, that they would seek God, if perhaps they might grope for Him and find Him, though He is not far from each one of us.* Acts 17:26-27 NIV[2]

God appoints even the times in which everyone is destined to live and the places and families among whom they are to grow up.

The destiny of everyone is foreordained, and the only choice that each one has is whether they would elect this destiny or design their own. When one is saved, he or she is saved from the destiny of their own creation and made to conform to the plan God originally designed for him or her. One is not free to modify God's foreordained plan. One is only free to be conformed to it or to reject it altogether.

One's destiny in the earth is to accurately present the nature of God within the context of one's appointed circumstance. Since everyone has been endowed with gifts and a calling, the representation of God in a particular epoch of time is diverse. However, the design for the representation of God is not merely individualized but collected up into a corporate form that gives the maximum display of the nature of God in a particular moment in time.

The administration of the Holy Spirit is to divest the glory of God into the Body of Christ and to show this glory in its many forms through the dispensing of gifts and callings in every historical epoch. The diversity of gifts serves to represent the glory of the administration of Christ through both governmental forms as well as practical functioning. The operation of a corporate form inherently requires that a coherent picture of the invisible God may be brought forth through the functioning of the corporate Man.

Gifts of government ought never to become an end within themselves, since the purpose of all governments is to provide a context of peace and good order in which the display of the nature of God may be shown in its vast array. All gifts of government are for the disciplining and maturity of a son of God.

---

[1] Romans 11:29 NASB. [2] See Galatians 1:15 NASB.

The Grace of Maturation

Apostles, Prophets, Pastors, Evangelists and Teachers are given as special endowments from God to bring order to the functioning of the Body of Christ, and to cause the Body to be accurately aligned to the head for mature functioning.[1]

This order is not engaged by fiat but by impartation so that everyone drinks deeply from this order and experiences a cultural shift from the competitive order of the kosmos out of which they were saved.

PART FOUR

The Kingdom of Heaven does not change those who emerge from the rule of Satan by an oppressive demand that they conform to the dictates of the Kingdom through threats and intimidation leveled at their newly discovered statures as sons of God. Instead, the order of the Kingdom of God works to change their culture. They are placed in households under the care of mature fathers and within a spiritual family comprised of fellow believers who are at various stages of maturity themselves. It is within this environment that they are effectively exposed to the workings of these five endowments, or callings, that are necessary to bring them to maturity.

These endowments are carried in persons and are designed to impart different aspects of the culture of the Kingdom of Heaven. They have both the singular and cumulative effect of shifting the new believer from his or her prior culture to that of the Kingdom of Heaven. This cultural shift does not occur purely as an intellectual awareness of the existence of the Kingdom's culture. It permits an experiential familiarity with the key elements of the culture of the Kingdom of Heaven. The combination of the knowledge and experience of this new culture together with the working environment of a spiritual family, over time results in the transformation of the individual.

The apostolic gift is foundational to the understanding of the Kingdom's existence, its nature, and its function. It introduces the believer to the concept of divine order to one's personal life as well as to the spheres in which one is placed. It permits an understanding of the possession and use of authority. Through this same gift the spirit of the individual is awakened to the reality of the invisible realm and he or she is conditioned to access that realm for wisdom, knowledge, understanding and counsel. Apostles are placed in the Body of Christ as those with the gift to reveal the mysteries of the Kingdom of God.

The mindset of the believer is made to be attuned to the frequencies of the Spirit of God so that even the normal exercise of reading the

PART FOUR

Scriptures imparts an understanding of what is being communicated beyond the limits of human reason. One begins to see all things from the throne of God. This marks the first, and most important, shift in the culture of the new believer.

The impartation from the grace of the prophetic is essentially the understanding that the Spirit of God speaks to the spirit of man and reveals the mind of God continuously to the believer. It is not strange for the mature believer to act in all the circumstances of life from the knowledge and insight that comes from hearing God. Absent the gift of the prophetic, reason will triumph over revelation, and the knowledge that comes directly from God to the human spirit will be supplanted by human reason which is, by definition, devoid of heavenly content. The impartation of the grace of the prophetic opens the believer to the possibility of functioning in the earth in all matters from a position of being seated in Christ upon the throne of God.

The evangelistic gift contains the most concentrated form of the love of God for undeserving mankind. In this gift, God has placed Himself on display in the showing of mercy to all mankind, from the most pleasant of human beings to the most depraved. The evangelist, more than any other gift, is the carrier of the message of the love of God for lost humanity. This gift elevates the vision of someone whose culture was shaped by the kingdom of darkness to be concerned only about their own interests to becoming carriers of the mercy of God for those who represent the worst forms of threats to their self-interests.[2]

Pastors, or shepherds, care for the households of faith, which may include both natural and spiritual family members. For a person who grew up in the culture of an orphan, to be transitioned to a functioning member of a spiritual household and to belong to a family that includes them as beloved members of that family, by choice and not by obligation, serves to expose them to being part of something much greater than themselves. This sense of inclusion and belonging imparts the understanding of functioning as part of the corporate entity, without competition for place or diminishment of relevance.

The grace of a teacher imparts both knowledge of Scripture and the peaceful exercise of communicating profound insight. It equips the new member of the Body of Christ with deeper insights into complex understandings of eternal truths while exposing them to the practice of communicating such insights without striving to prove oneself right. At the same time, the new believer experiences the result of the word of life affecting those who are receptive and working unimaginable change in otherwise impossible circumstances.

Together these five particular endowments equip the believer to function as part of the corporate whole. These grants of authority enable changes in mindsets from the kingdom of darkness to the culture of the Kingdom of Heaven. If the growth in the believer is to be sustained, it must take place within the context of a fundamental change of the underlying culture. Without a cultural shift, it is inconceivable that the believer could become mature.

Culture is the referential framework by which everything a person perceives is interpreted. The kingdom of darkness is equipped with one form of culture and the Kingdom of God with an entirely different one. Without the renewal of one's mind, the old assumptions will invariably migrate into his surroundings and continue to exert the same influence upon the mind of the believer. When one comes into the Kingdom of Heaven, one discovers that God established the governmental order of the Kingdom to reposition the mindset away from the culture of the orphan to that of a son.

The Kingdom of God cannot be understood from the viewpoint of an orphan.

> *Unlike an orphan, a son represents continuity in his generation and carries forward the purposes for which a family exists. The House of God derives its relevance from God Himself. In every successive generation, God reveals Himself more completely until He is fully disclosed. Whereas the purpose of an orphan is always completed within the span of his own lifetime, a son's destiny represents the ongoing disclosure of the purpose of the house to which he belongs. Therefore, the purpose of a son, though unique in its expression, is intimately tied to a predetermined purpose.* Soleyn, Supra, *My Father! My Father!* P. 113.

The operation of the grace of reconciliation requires that a person be able to receive a destiny that comes from sonship and to function from the cultural change of being a son.[3] Accompanying reconciliation are the gifts that enable the believer to function in his calling. These gifts often include such things as healing, the working of miracles, the ability to discern spirits, the impetus to speak in tongues, or the ability to prophesy. They may also include miraculous transfers of wisdom, knowledge, and understanding. All gifts, whether they be gifts of governments or of enablement, are meant to function within the context of the corporate Son.[4]

Being reconciled to God, one is restored to the original intent of God for that person. Being equipped with a new culture, one's view of his purpose in life changes. Endowed with the understanding of a different calling and empowered by gifts of the Spirit, one is capable of living in the present world from an eternal point of view. The manifestation of the power of this grace typically takes the form of superlative understanding and wisdom. The counsel that one may offer as a result of the grace of reconciliation is capable of transforming situations of hopelessness and despair and bringing about healing and life.

As one progresses in engaging a new culture, and in living the life that flows from it, one moves through the stages of being born again and understanding the newness of life in Christ to functioning as a fully mature son of God. As one enters each new stage defined by the progression of grace, the previous stages continue to unfold with greater depth and intensity producing a cumulative effect invariably leading to new levels of growth and maturity.

> *Things which eye has not seen and ear has not heard, and which have not entered the heart of man, all that God has prepared for those who love Him.* 1 Corinthians 2:9 NASB

Because the Gospel has been presented as mankind's need to be saved from its sins in order to go to heaven, and because the goal of one's faith has been identified as being prepared to go to heaven when one dies, almost no attention has been paid to the need to become a mature believer. In fact, in many circles, the thought that a believer might become mature is viewed as a striking lack of humility and dangerously arrogant. It is often thought that being "poor in spirit" implies a condition in which one never assumes he or she is anything more than "a sinner saved by grace."

Although it is commonly recognized that one begins the journey of salvation by being "born again," there is almost no recognition that this concept implies the need of the one newly born to progress naturally through the stages of growth to maturity. This critically important concept is so widely overlooked that even Scriptural passages addressing a state of permanent infancy and exhorting believers to move on toward maturity are misconstrued. For example, it is common for leaders, in a show of feigned humility, to cite Paul's declaration to the Corinthians, stating "For I determined to know nothing among you except Jesus Christ and Him crucified."[5] Within the same context, Paul explains that there is a message of wisdom that is designed for the mature:

> *Yet we do speak wisdom among those who are mature; a wisdom, however, not of this age nor of the rulers of this age, who are passing away; but we speak God's wisdom in a mystery, the hidden wisdom which God predestined before the ages to our glory; the wisdom which none of the rulers of this age has understood; for if they had understood it they would not have crucified the Lord of glory.* 1 Corinthians 2:6-8 NASB

He went on to explain his decision to assume a state of willful ignorance.

> *And I, brethren, could not speak to you as to spiritual men, but as to men of flesh, as to infants in Christ. I gave you milk to drink, not solid food; for you were not yet able to receive it. Indeed, even now you are not yet able, for you are still fleshly. For since there is jealously and strife among you, are you not fleshly, and are you not walking like mere men?* 1 Corinthians 3:1-3 NASB

His express reason was that the behavior of the people—jealousy, envy, strife, and division among themselves—showed they had chosen to remain in a state of carnality. Paul equates this state with being infantile, qualifying them only for the "milk" of the most basic elements of the gospel, not the solid food of wisdom for the mature. He could not impart the message of wisdom to them without first reclaiming this basic truth.

Paul left no doubt that there was a higher order of life available to them, but in his judgment, they were not ready for the impartation of the message of wisdom since their condition was not yet suitable. Instead, he was reduced to speaking a message designed to rekindle the fire of their desire to move on from their present state of immaturity. Although this is the evident meaning of Paul's declaration regarding his choice of message to the Corinthians, many leaders today will relate to this statement of choice as proof of their own humility while ignoring Paul's stated reasons for making such a choice.

The view that humility and the acknowledgement of immaturity are synonymous is quite erroneous. True humility can only be practiced from a condition of maturity. The proper definition of humility is the conscious and voluntary yielding of the totality of one's person to the service and use of another. It inherently implies a knowing and deliberate choice on the part of one who elects to humble himself. Such a choice cannot be made by the immature since immaturity is made evident through self-preservation.

---

[1]Ephesians 4:11-12 NASB. [2]See 1 Corinthians 6:9-11 NASB. [3]Romans 8:14-17 NASB. [4]See 1 Corinthians 12:7-11 NASB; Ephesians 4:11-13 NASB. [5]1 Corinthians 2:2 NASB.

Wisdom for the Mature

Among the seven characteristics of the Spirit of God, wisdom, knowledge and understanding are meant to be imparted more completely among the mature. One is born again with the intent of being made mature. Paul connects the state of maturity with the impartation of greater measures of these Spirits.

This wisdom does not come from the collection of human experiences over time, nor is it contained in trite expressions known as truisms. Instead, it is characterized as the wisdom of God. As such, it can be viewed as hidden mysteries to which God alone is privy and has existed before even time itself began. For example, Paul wrote to the Ephesians:

> *You can understand my insight into the mystery of Christ, which in other generations was not made known to the sons of men as it has now been revealed to His holy apostles and*

> *prophets in the Spirit; to be specific, that the Gentiles are fellow heirs and fellow members of the body, and fellow partakers of the promise in Christ Jesus through the gospel, of which I was made a minister, according to the gift of God's grace which was given to me according to the working of His power. To me, the very least of all saints, this grace was given to preach to the Gentiles the unfathomable riches of Christ and to bring to light what is the administration of the mystery which for ages has been hidden in God who created all things; so that the manifold wisdom of God might now be made known through the church to the rulers and the authorities in the heavenly places. This was in accordance with the eternal purpose which He carried out in Christ Jesus our Lord, in whom we have boldness and confident access through faith in Him.* Ephesians 3:4-12 NASB

This measure of revelation is inaccessible to the immature believer. Rather, God's wisdom is beyond the conception of the human mind and beyond the vision of the human sight to grasp and apprehend. "Things which eye has not seen and ear has not heard, and which have not entered the heart of man."[1]

It is the Spirit of God alone who is capable of searching all things, even the deep things of God, who is able to take these treasures from the deep places in which they reside in God and bring them forth into human time and reveal them to the minds of men who in turn are themselves led by the Spirit of God. A "natural man does not accept the things of the Spirit of God, for they are foolishness to him; and he cannot understand them because they are spiritually appraised."[2] There is a direct connection between the believer's state of maturity and the characteristics of wisdom, knowledge and understanding in the Spirit of God.

Whereas the value of an eternal perspective is highly prized by the mature, to the immature its value is negligible. Jesus himself cautioned against giving prized treasures to those without the capacity to appreciate their value.[3] It is not the practice of God to entrust the holy things to those who lack the preparedness to appreciate the value of eternal treasures. In order to appreciate these superlative endowments, one must be prepared to view them from an eternal point of view.

Paul claimed to have been given such treasures. One of the most prized was the revelation of the mystery of how God was reconciling the Jew and the Gentile to Himself in the Body of Christ. This was a major fulfillment of a sacred promise to which God had bound Himself by oath and had declared to Abraham that a seed would accomplish. In Christ, the seed of Abraham, God meant to "bless all the nations of the earth." By bringing the Jew and Gentile together, God meant to undo one of the most egregious effects of Satan's rule over humankind. He meant to reunite brother to brother in one functional form in which they would exist together, reconciled to God in the form of the Corpus Christi, the Body of Christ.

To the Jewish people, this great treasure of understanding was of no particular value since they were the direct descendants of Abraham, who had received the promise of this fulfillment. Their interests were consumed with the fact of their natural ancestry and not with the reason that lay at the heart of their existence. The relevance of the nation that descended from Abraham in the flesh was by no means the end within itself. Instead, they were the means to the end.

God's intent was to reconcile the world to Himself and to do that through Christ. The promise that Abraham received from God was that God would facilitate this result through the nation that came out of His person. To separate the nation from the promise of reconciliation is to give greater relevance to the natural than God ever intended. Indeed, God is no respecter of persons, because "in every nation, he who fears God and works righteousness is accepted with Him."[4]

The prophet John the Baptist challenged the Jews to abandon their faith in the trivial and the marginal in favor of the substantive and the eternal. His role was to prepare the Jewish people for the coming of Christ, and he had clear understanding regarding the obstacles in their thinking that would make his task of preparing them for the disclosing of the promised seed difficult to the extreme. He assaulted the state of stasis into which their minds had fallen with an uncompromising appeal:

> *And do not suppose that you can say to yourselves, "We have Abraham for our father"; for I say to you that from these stones God is able to raise up children to Abraham. The axe is already laid at the root of the trees; therefore, every tree that does not bear good fruit is cut down and thrown into the fire. As for me, I baptize you with water for repentance, but He who is coming after me is mightier than I, and I am not fit to remove His sandals; He will baptize you with the Holy Spirit and fire. His winnowing fork is in His hand, and He will thoroughly clear His threshing floor; and He will gather His wheat into the barn, but He will burn up the chaff with unquenchable fire.* Matthew 3:9-12 NASB

He pointed them instead to the true purpose of God's promise to Abraham; the arrival of the precious seed, the Lamb of God who would take away the sins of the world and reconcile man to God through Himself.

Paul understood that he had been given the revelation of the original intent of God in giving the promise to Abraham to restore all mankind to Himself in Christ. Once this mystery was revealed, it brought again into the light the original intent of God for all mankind. It rescued the promise from the darkness of human culture that had obscured both the original intent of God and the methodology by which He would arrive at this intent. It required the Spirits of wisdom, knowledge and understanding to excavate this promise and restore its luster so that mankind may once again come boldly before God through Christ.

All of the value of being children of Abraham in the natural perishes at the point of death. By contrast, all who have been reconciled to God through Jesus have been given eternal life and have overcome death itself. This was part of the good news of the Gospel. John the Baptist understood that the Jewish emphasis on being the natural children of Abraham fell abysmally short of God's eternal purposes for them as well as for all mankind. It is why he challenged them with such force to abandon the lesser position in favor of the greater.

Throughout the Scriptures, those who represent God are constantly faced with the challenge of lifting the vision of others from their addiction to the marginal and the predictable to that of the substantive and the eternal. The immature always value the natural over the spiritual and eternal. In order to have an eternal perspective, one must overcome the soul's affection for the natural and consent to the rule over his being by the Spirit. The most valuable resource to accomplish this transition is suffering in the flesh.

---

[1] 1 Corinthians 2:9 NASB. [2] 1 Corinthians 2:14 NASB. [3] Matthew 7:6 NASB. [4] Acts 10:34-35 KJV.

PART FOUR

Suffering and Maturity

Therefore, since Christ has suffered in the flesh, arm yourselves also with the same purpose, because he who has suffered in the flesh has ceased from sin[.] 1 Peter 4:1 NASB

Since the fall of man, his focus has come to be upon his survival. His every consideration is in furtherance of that end. This emphasis came as a result of the loss of the view of himself as spirit. His soul began to interpret the world around him and to define the purpose for his existence. Prior to his separation from God, he viewed himself as one with God. His future as well as his present purpose was inextricably bound up in the representation of God. He was part of a whole. His role was to be the face of that whole in the visible world. He was sustained and provided for in every way by the corporate reality of God seen only through Adam, his prime actor and in a veiled way, by the physical creation and the systems that maintained it.

Separated from God, Adam is starkly alone. He begins to think and act as an individual unconnected to any reality other than his own. Suddenly, he lives apart from creation and his environment is as much his enemy as the fact that he is a stranger in paradise. From then on, all of his acts evince his mindset. He is afraid. Even his view of his wife changes from his initial reception of her as "... bone of my bones, and flesh of my flesh; She shall be called Woman, because she is taken out of Man," to "the woman you gave me."[1]

Not only did his vision change from the corporate to the singular, but the resulting culture took on the harsh edge of competition. His hiding indicated his perception of God as his enemy. In one generation, competition had fully blossomed into envy and murder, graphically demonstrated when one of his sons murdered the other. The change to the individualized view from the corporate saw competition replace cooperation with an attitude of striving to dominate in order to feel secure.

To this day, the culture of individualism flourishes and is the background against which the activities of God in the believer's life is commonly seen and evaluated. Every effort is made to secure God's commitment to preserving man's view of what he needs. Man continues to reserve the right to order his own steps according to the wisdom of survival. Within this framework, he sees God as either an ally or an enemy depending upon whether or not God acts in support of man's predetermined plans. A state of immaturity persists as long as the believer's view of his purpose is that of mere survival, and as long as he continues to act in furtherance of that goal.

In the effort to mature a believer, God is determined to replace individualism with a corporate identity and survival with the goal of representation. By returning man to a state of representing God as a son and making him secure in the knowledge that all of his Father's actions are for his benefit, God means to transition him again to the view of himself as a spirit clothed in flesh. In order to achieve this transition, God has chosen to disrupt man's settled view of himself as an individual tasked with survival by threatening his very survival. Without disturbing this foundation, man would consume every gesture of God toward him in his bid to survive. Every endowment of authority and power meant to serve the representation of God would be predictably diverted to serve the interests of his own survival. If he had authority and power to put the nature of God on display, he would expend both first to secure himself.

God employs the redemptive power of suffering as His primary focus against the stronghold of the soul. The choice of this ordinance is masterful in that it does no harm to the spirit but is rigorous in its ability to conquer the flesh. Suffering has the ability to prove to the soul that it has no options. Its reliance upon the systems of the world, or the kosmos, is unable to rescue him or her from the dilemmas in which they find themselves. The hope that is vested in the kosmos is that, somehow, in the most serious of circumstances there will be an answer based in what one is able to do or what one may persuade others to do with or for them. Suffering is capable of reducing man to a condition of ineptitude and vulnerability that can cause him to despair. It is this state of feeling both feeble and helpless that a person is likely to turn from his settled view of his purpose and to begin to seek God for answers.

When he turns, he is typically still searching for answers, but because he is motivated to change views and possibly his behaviors, God will meet him in that condition. The answers that God speaks to him at that time will contain the seeds that, if permitted the appropriate soil, will grow up and produce the fruit of wisdom, knowledge and understanding. Over time, and with the help and guidance of a spiritual father and the resources of a spiritual house, this experience will lead to greater and greater understanding of a higher order of maturity.

It is inevitable that one will suffer as a believer.[2] This form of suffering produces the requisite character of maturity that qualifies the believer to carry the glory of God in the earth. Paul said, "...for Christ's sake, I delight in weaknesses, in insults, in hardships, in persecutions, in difficulties. For when I am weak, then I am strong."[3] It indicates that the soul has been brought back under the rule of the spirit and the person is able to hear God clearly and distinctly.

Even when we are in periods of relative peace, we should voluntarily introduce suffering into our lives in order to retain a state of spiritual alertness and not devolve into a form of complacency that allows for the possible reemergence of the soul. The form in which suffering can be introduced in a regular fashion is through fasting and prayer. Fasting has the effect of denying the body's need for food and effectively debases the body and denies it a role of primacy. At the same time, the spirit's awareness is heightened, and the spiritual man consciously communicates with God through prayer. Fasting and prayer work effectively in identifying the activities of evil spirits that utilize their familiarity with persons and their generations to masquerade and conceal their activities. It is common to insist that a person controlled by a familiar spirit should fast and pray before deliverance is attempted. Fasting and prayer in that event has the effect of separating the person's soul from the activities of the evil spirit and permits his own spirit to receive insights from the Spirit of God regarding the schemes of the enemy by which they have been entrapped.

When the spirit of a person can agree with the Holy Spirit, the characteristics of the evil spirit are easily distinguishable. Usually, for the first time, the person is able to see himself or herself in clear contrast from the lie they have believed about themselves. The success of an evil spirit in controlling a person is in projecting their own nature upon the person's view of self, making itself indistinguishable from the person. Fasting and prayer create the appropriate separation that works effectively in enlisting the cooperation of the affected person in the battle against the deception perpetrated by the familiar spirit. This example serves to highlight the importance of suffering in reducing the dominance of the soul over the spirit which results in a less than accurate view of reality.

For this reason, the maturity of the believer does not occur apart from suffering. Jesus modeled this behavior as part of the showing of His fullness of grace.

---

[1] Genesis 2:23; 3:12 NASB. [2] 1 Peter 4:12-13 NASB. [3] 1 Corinthians 12:10 NASB.

PART FOUR

Carrying the Glory of God

Prior to His coming into the world as the manifested Son of God, known to us as Jesus, He was the executive power of God by whom the world was created. All of the glory of His prior existence was laid aside as He took up the role of the representation of the Father.

He became a Son to the Father in order to show the nature and character of the love of God. He started out in His earthly existence as an infant, born to the most modest of human circumstances. He was required to go through the exact stages of growth through which any other human child would matriculate. At the age of thirty, His preparedness to represent the Father was announced by God Himself and was immediately confirmed by His responses to temptation.[1]

From then until His ascension to the right hand of God, He put the character of God on display. For the first time since Adam's fall, the earth saw the glory of God in a human form.

When He returned to heaven, He was clothed again with the glory He had with God before the foundation of the world.[2] However, the glory He was given to represent the Father while He was on the earth, He left as the inheritance for those who are in Him.[3] The display of this glory reveals the corporate Man as the designated carrier of the presence of God and the qualified representative of God to show the world His love.

It is beyond the reach of the immature, since they continue to emphasize their individual needs and individual goals, separate and distinct from the corporate Man. The mature, however, are rescued from this condition and renewed in their understanding regarding the corporate Christ. Paul could not speak to the Corinthians about such a message as this. Yet, it is the representation of God left in the world for the mature Body of Christ. With this understanding as a key, the great mystery of the love of God can be unlocked and revealed..

God put in Adam the entire human race with the command to be fruitful and multiply. Since then, every human has come from the seed of this one man. Initially, God separated the woman from the man by taking her out of him and revealing her separately. In the basic element of this showing, God reveals that both the seed and the womb that carried it to the form of a new life and sustained it until it could function independently, were both part of the same being known as man. Both parts working together could produce an independent likeness of the source of its origin.

Within the person of Adam was also the distinct person of Eve, whose name means "life" or "living." Adam and Eve lived together as one—separate parts of the same whole—working together in harmony and in peace toward a common end, namely the representation of God. They both held dominion and pursued the mandate of God to replenish the earth in distinct and perfect harmony. As such, they presented a prophetic picture of Christ who would come as the last Adam with the intent of including in Himself all those He would redeem. Those would be His bride, carried in His person and presented to the Father through a corporate expression. Inasmuch as He and the Father were one, all those who are in Him would be included in the oneness that the Father had with Him. Their existence would be indistinguishable from His own and the world would see in God's acceptance of them in Christ how much God loved both them as well as the rest of mankind.

This was the message for the mature that Paul could not impart to the Corinthians because they were deeply steeped in the competitive culture of their individualism. This blinded them to the reality of the corporate Christ and made them an easy prey for their enemy. "For this reason many among you are weak and sick, and a number sleep."[4]

PART FOUR

God waited until Jesus had become perfect through suffering to present Him to the world as the Son who represents the Father.[5] His intent is to also bring everyone He receives as a son to maturity through the same process.[6] Jesus Himself modeled the grace of maturing through suffering as a clear and unequivocal example of what is required of every son whom God receives.

> *You have not resisted to the point of shedding blood in your striving against sin; and you have forgotten the exhortation which is addressed to you as sons, "My son, do not regard lightly the discipline of the Lord, nor faint when you are reproved by Him; For those whom the Lord loves He disciplines, And He scourges every son whom He receives." It is for discipline that you endure; God deals with you as with sons; for what son is there whom his father does not discipline?* 1 Peter 4:1 NASB

The qualification for sharing in the glory that Christ left as an inheritance on the earth for those who are in Him requires the refinement that comes through suffering.

There is an abundance of grace available to bring each son to maturity. God Himself intends to perfectly prepare Him for His distinguished role as the beloved Son in whom He was well pleased, so also, He arranges the circumstances by which each one whom He receives as a son is brought to maturity.

The arrangement of circumstances by which a son is disciplined is uniquely the role of God Himself. The spiritual father's role is to help the son interpret God's intention in the adverse situation the son is facing and to help him or her to extract the value God inserts into the trial. We are assured that "all things work together for good to those who love God, to those who are called according to His purpose."[7]

From the time one is received as a son, he enters an economy of grace designed to propel him through the various stages of sonship, resulting in maturity. Throughout the process, he is given incrementally greater and greater endowments of both responsibility and opportunity to reflect the nature of God. When he is brought to maturity, it is the pleasure of God to present him to others as the son who represents His nature and character. A mature son fully understands that the presence of God is carried in a corporate Man and therefore takes his place within that divine order to function fully from within that context. Then, he is most useful in portraying the nature of Christ within him especially in the way his behavior models the respect and honor given to Christ in others through whom Christ also appears in a mature fashion. They work together in harmony and in peace as different but complementary parts of the same Body.

---

[1]Ephesians 3:4-12 NASB. [2]1 Corinthians 2:9 NASB. [3]1 Corinthians 2:14 NASB. [4]Matthew 7:6 NASB. [5]Acts 10:34 KJV. [6]Matthew 3:9-12 NASB. [7]1 Peter 4:12-13 NASB.

The Grace of Exact Representation

> *[The Son] is the radiance of [God's] glory and the exact representation of His nature and upholds all things by the word of His power.* Hebrews 1:3 NASB

God committed the representation of Himself to His Son, the Lord Jesus Christ. The essence of the love of God is presented to creation through the theme of Father and Son.

The role of the husband-and-wife relationship permits mankind to be included in Christ and to be presented to the Father as part of the corporate Son. Access into the Son is provided through the relationship between Christ and the church, expressed as Bridegroom and Bride. In this expression, man is included in Christ and presented exclusively, by this means to the Father as the corporate Son. "No one comes to the Father but by me."

PART FOUR

God, who is Spirit, intended to become visible through an expression of Himself as both Father and Son. Yet, neither role is compromised, but fully and completely expresses the nature of God as Father and also as completely and distinctively as Son. The righteous standards of God would remain clear and exact while the standard of the Son would be the template for obedience and trust. The cross displayed the integrity of God in requiring the rigorous standards of His nature to be fully met while the Son, in His unflinching devotion, drinks the complete cup of suffering.

This form of diversity is nearly unimaginable to man. For God it could not be otherwise since He is perfect in everything, including particularly the display of the nature of love.

When God undertook the showing of His love, He chose the perfect and complete form in which to establish the exactitude of this display. The creation that surrounded man and formed the background of the environment in which he was placed all pulsated with this message of Father and Son. God established all the forms of life in creation to reflect this reality. The whole earth and every ecosystem pulsate with the model of Father and Son.

> *For since the creation of the world His invisible attributes, His eternal power and divine nature, have been clearly seen, being understood through what has been made, so that they are without excuse.* Romans 2:20 NASB

It is only when mankind chooses to not retain God in their knowledge that these ancient truths become obscured or even lost for generations. When God reconciles mankind to His original intent, these truths are inevitably restored. It should not be a surprise that Jesus Christ would be the carrier of the image and likeness of God and His life would be an exact depiction of the source of His origin.

The purpose of showing the nature of God is inseparable from the identity of the Son of God.

> *For in Him all the fullness of Deity dwells in bodily form, and in Him you have been made complete, and He is the head over all rule and authority; and in Him you were also circumcised with a circumcision made without hands, in the removal of the body of the flesh by the circumcision of Christ; having been buried with Him in baptism, in which you were also raised up with Him through faith in the working of God, who raised Him from the dead.* Colossians 2:9-12 NASB

John said, "We saw His glory, glory as of the only begotten from the Father, full of grace and truth."[1] And, it is why Jesus would say, "He who has seen Me has seen the Father."[2] Although man has long strayed from this original divine intent, it remains the purpose of the invisible God to put Himself on display.

When God is accurately portrayed in creation, He draws all men to Himself. Whereas creation itself is a veiled showing of this principle, it is however portrayed unabashedly in mankind and with pristine clarity in Christ Jesus. It is for this showing that all creation groans in anticipation of seeing and longs for. The earth itself cannot be set aright apart from the functional representation of the Father in the corporate Son. God did not just intend to call Jesus His Son. He intended that His Son be the image and likeness of His Father and that the glory of the Father would appear exactly in and through the person of the Son. The Son would simultaneously restore the standard of the Father's nature in creation while being surrounded by the present condition of fallenness to which man had descended. It would juxtapose the light and glory of God with the darkness and depravity of man under the control of the enemy.

---

[1] John 1:14 NASB. [2] John 14:9 NASB.

Conclusion
THE IMAGE AND LIKENESS OF GOD

The End From the Beginning

God speaks with the language of timelessness and sees all matters from the realm of the eternal. He, therefore, knows the end of every matter from the beginning and His point of view is the only complete view of anything. If we are to understand His declarations, we must appreciate His point of view.

He imparted His Spirit in flesh, establishing an image of Himself in the earth—that image being Spirit because God is Spirit. It was His intent that humankind would mature from the seed that was Adam into a complete likeness of God, giving form to the person of God in creation. Adam was the seed leading to the complete representation of God in the earth, which is Christ.

God can only be replicated in character through spirit. The Spirit of Christ is the man that God envisioned in His image and likeness. The Spirit of Christ that was in Jesus of Nazareth receives and assembles all the human spirits to be reconciled to God as a corporate Man with many members in one Body.

This spiritual being is the complete expression of God's intent when he declared, "Let us make man in Our own image, after Our own likeness." This finished result, known from the beginning, was comprised of the spirits of all those who voluntarily chose to submit to the rule of Christ and to be conformed to the standard of the firstborn. This creation God regarded as 'Son'.

The Extent of the Fall

As noted earlier in this book, man's departure from his Father resulted in a fundamental change of all things regarding his life on the earth. Some of the more profound changes to be noted are that man desired a separate identity from his Father and created an understanding of being different from Him when he hid from Him and clothed himself with fig leaves. He was clearly portraying his belief that God was his enemy whose presence threatened his existence. Furthermore, by clothing himself, he displayed a mental state that no longer viewed himself as a spirit being. He no longer viewed himself as being like his Father. Until then, Adam carried the brightness of God's glory in his person and was, therefore, clothed with the glory of God although he was naked.

The glory of God in Adam had been his mantle. When he clothed himself, Adam's cultural mindset shifted from an identity with his Father as spirit to an identity with the creation around him as part of the creation itself. He rejected the role of representing his Father and embraced instead the task of his own survival. So, God declared an acknowledgement that man's economy had come to be one based on his own capabilities and ingenuity and not one of representing his Father and relying upon His goodwill to support him in creation.

Having rejected his Father through the process of reasoning, Adam was no longer connected to the wisdom of the heavens. He then reasoned from the position of fear because his life was no longer understood as an extension of the invisible God. The closing of the eyes of his spirit and the opening of the eyes of his soul established a vision of reality derived in its entirety from the world around him. His soul was fully in charge and his culture began to emerge away from God and toward survival. No other life was considered to be preeminent or have value other than his own.

The Entrapment of the Systems of the Kosmos

Satan's role has been to aggressively entrap humankind in their estrangement from God the Father by developing an earthly economy that keeps them separate from the heavenly one. This economy, known as the kosmos, is made up of systems that induce reliance based on the human soul's desires: the lust of the flesh, the lust of the eyes, and the pride of life.

These systems are mirrors of the reality of the Kingdom of God and have become so thoroughly foundational to human culture that it is virtually impossible to think of culture separate and apart from references to them. The extraction of man from these systems is the process of saving his soul. It requires the closing of the eyes of the soul and the reopening of the eyes of the spirit that man might see things from an eternal point of view.

Suffering That Saves the Soul

Suffering is the methodology by which God rescues the souls of mankind from the control of the systems of the kosmos which lure one into believing there is always an answer or a different way of being.

The strength of the soul lies in its conviction that there is always a way out of the adversity or unpleasantness of the moment. However, suffering disabuses a person of the notion that he or she is self-sufficient and can fashion an escape regardless of how difficult the place one might find oneself in at the time. If the author of our salvation was made perfect through suffering, then we also ought to arm ourselves with the same understanding. Paul understood that in following the Lord, the believer will ultimately be brought to the place in which there are no remaining alternatives. In this place, he learned the marvelous truth that when the soul does not have the ability to function, because the quantum of suffering is 'beyond measure' and the reserves of strength are entirely depleted 'above strength,' the spirit is brought back to its preeminence and heaven opens to the believer once the soul is out of the way. The strength of God floods the human being by the reestablishment of the connection between the human spirit and the Spirit of God. The result is that the soul is saved.

Biblical Predestination: Conformation to the Firstborn

Paul makes it clear in Ephesians that the Biblical definition of predestination is "predestined to be conformed to the likeness of Christ, to the praise of God's glorious grace." It is of critical importance in a time of restoration that the original standard be returned because all restoration, which ultimately leads to reconciliation, is to the prior existing standard. Christ represented the eternal standard brought back in the fullness of time to which all are meant to be conformed if they are to be included in the designation "Son of God."

The image and likeness of the Father presented in the earth in exact representation would come through the spiritual Man, comprised of many members under the rule of Christ who is the head because He is the standard. In this regard, a ruler is not merely one who gives commands, but is in fact the exact standard to which all are meant to be conformed. Biblical predestination is not the question of who is predestined to go to heaven or hell. The glory of God was intended to be modeled in the earth through a corporate Son whose assembly was to the pattern of the firstborn, who is Christ, and whose function would be a mirror of the life and presentation of Him who is the image of the invisible God and whose stated purpose for coming into the world was "to show us the Father."

Entering God's Rest

When a believer is trained through suffering to rely on and offer no resistance to the Spirit of God, to be in God's rest, that state of being conformed to His original intent is made available. In the economy of God lies His mighty strength, epitomized by the follower of Christ being raised up from the condition of being dead while still alive. In this condition the soul is returned to the original position of being subject to the rule of the Spirit—ceasing from one's own labors and expelling the desires of provision and protection and the need to find relevance through one's work. In this state a human being may access the power of God and enter into His rest.

When God created the heavens and the earth in the six days of creation, He was finishing the establishment of the environment in which He intended to put on display all that He had foreknown from the foundation of the world. The precreation covenant was undertaken with an eye toward establishing on the earth that which was ordained from heaven before the earth itself was created. On the sixth day God completed creation, the crowning act being the creation of man in the image and likeness of God. All was done to set in motion that which God already foreknew. Knowing the end of the matter from the beginning, and having reached completion, God entered into His rest and has been in that state of rest since. This state of rest understands that nothing could possibly interrupt the order and flow of what God has established. Since God knows the end of the matter from the beginning, there are no intervening factors that may ordain a different outcome. The only time that God may come out of rest is when, as Jesus did, the persecution of the believers caused Jesus to stand on the right hand of God. Even then, it is not so much a work as it is an acknowledgement of the significance God assigns to the obedience of sons in times of adversity. He is touched by the feelings of our infirmities and arises to address them, but those are temporary, momentary and largely individualized circumstances. In the main, the rest of God is undisturbed because He is certain of the outcome.

The departure of Adam from God as his Father caused his soul to come out of rest. When Jesus came, He restored that rest to us. This rest occurs when the soul comes back under the rule of the spirit and because the spirit has the ability to hear God, the condition that is restored is that of a Father and son. The intent of God where His sons are concerned is that they enter into the prior existing state that God established and that He Himself has remained in since the creation of the world.

The rest of God is supported by His very nature that underlies all of what has been created. It is impossible for the economy of God to fail. This is consistent with the prayer of Jesus that the Kingdom come and the will of God be done on earth as it is in heaven. The economy to support this form of existence was established concurrent with the completion of creation and is the economy in which God Himself rests and into which all those who pursue Him, as sons, are invited to come again and repose with Him. It is fully available within the created world.

CONCLUSION

Corporate Man in the Image and Likeness of God

The vastness of God does not permit Him to be observed from any vantage point outside of Himself, inasmuch as everything is included in His being. Those who are supported by His strength live in Him, move in Him and have their very beings in Him. Nothing is hidden from the Lord. The realms of time and space permit things of the eternal to be displayed when God allows. Time was designed to host the realities of eternal things and becomes allegorical, or at least hosts the allegory, of the eternal. One should always be aware of the fact that everything in time points to something greater.

Types and shadows hold in place the realities of heaven which are destined to come into the earth. The intent of the Lord in establishing the heavens and the earth was to cause a migration of specific things in heaven into the venue of time and space. By these things, the invisible nature of God would be revealed in the earth. All of God to be revealed in the earth was meant to be put on display ultimately, in its perfection, in one spiritual Man. The arrangement of all the systems of the earth and the construction of the creation was meant to be the perfect host to this spiritual Man. Therefore, everything on the earth was created with heaven in mind and in anticipation of hosting the divine presence of God, who had chosen to make Himself known through a spiritual Man comprised of many members, each member being a person whose spirit had been redeemed and returned to God and thus assembled into this spiritual Man known as Christ.

It was God's intention to establish creation in a way that His character and nature, the aspects of His being, could be seen. This was supported by the seven attributes, or Spirits. His essential nature is love and it was His intention to impart fully all the various aspects of love into one visible being: a corporate Man comprised of many peoples of the earth and across the entire spectrum of humanity. He calls the people to Himself and arranges them according to the divine order known as the Kingdom of Heaven. He intends to put Himself, His glory, on display through all those in the earth who are governed by His Spirit and rule themselves by the dictates of heaven, as displayed by Jesus Himself when He lived on the earth. The corporate Man, though comprised of many members, is capable of presenting the intricacies of the divine nature of God in one observable, functional people. Their presence in the earth will be as light in the darkness.

The destiny of this corporate Man is to come forth at a period in time when the darkness is profound. The darkness of mankind, having lost its way and stumbling, lacks hope and direction. All the plans and schemes offered by the kosmos that have appealed to the soul are now being routinely disclosed as useless and failing. Against this background, as a city upon a hill, the light and glory of God in His revealed nature will appear in the form of a holy people comprised of every tribe, tongue, language and nation, drawn from all aspects of human existence, from every walk of life, and from every stratum of society.

Through their suffering and trials, they will have rejected the call and pull of the kosmos and turned away from reliance upon it, turning instead to the economies of grace, undergirded by the very descriptions of the attributes of God, and living in an eternal reality within the framework of time. Among this people, the glory of God will arise and be on display. The corporate Man will exemplify in a mature, functional, and everlasting fashion the immutable characteristics and the changeless nature of the living God. So it shall be upon the earth as it is in heaven.

The light and glory of God will fill the earth with the knowledge of God even as the heavens are full of His glory. God will look with great delight upon the corporate Man who bears His image and likeness in the earth. He will look upon this spiritual Man with the same favor with which He beheld His first appearance in the earth in the person

CONCLUSION

of the Lord Jesus Christ. As He arose from baptism in the river Jordan, the Spirit of God descended on Him in the form of a dove. And God, unable to restrain His enthusiasm, declared in thunder from heaven, "This is my beloved Son."[1] God will look upon the corporate Man with the same favor and declare to all creation, "This is my Son, in My image and in My likeness, Spirit as I am Spirit, and one who loves as I love." Creation was designed in its entirety to host this manifestation of the living God.

---

[1] Matthew 3:17 NASB.

Let There Be Light

From the beginning of the physical creation, the presence of God entering is described as light coming in the darkness. This is meant to be a framework of reference for Christ who, in His prior state as the Word, is the power of God who enters creation as light and from whom all of the natural order of creation comes as a result. In the account of creation, the first declaration of God was, "Let there be light."[1] Although it is common to associate the result of this declaration with the establishment of the sun, moon and stars in the firmament of the heavens, this in fact did not occur until the fourth day. The light that came into creation at that time was the entrance of the characteristics of wisdom, knowledge and understanding from the presence of God.

God knew and understood exactly what He was forming in this creation. The foundations of this order were established according to the wisdom of God.[2] This exact principle is articulated in Paul's writing to the Corinthians: "For God, who said, 'Light shall shine out of darkness,' is the One who has shone in our hearts to give the Light of the knowledge of the glory of God in the face of Christ."[3] Since God knew the end from the beginning, He established creation in support of all that He foreknew and intended to bring into reality in the fullness of time.

The coming of Christ into the world was meant to show the glory of God in very distinct ways. The overriding purpose was to establish a functioning body capable in its propriety to host and display the complete character of the love of God. He also came to confront the advanced structure of evil by which man had become enslaved and which also obscured God's original plan for man. In His confrontation of this system, His intent was to overthrow it and eventually to destroy it altogether.[4]

This task would consume His life utterly. He would be required to forego any choice related to living separately from the destiny assigned to this role from before the worlds were framed. He would not be permitted to order His own steps and even His request for the mercy of His Father would be superseded by the demands of God's righteous justice.[5] If He were not resurrected from the dead, then his existence upon the earth would not have been continued.

It is not inappropriate to refer to Jesus as the 'Light of the World.' It is in His face that the message of light coming into darkness at the creation of the world is reflected in its stunning brilliance. The Son, indeed, is the radiance of God's glory. It is in His face also that the love of God is perfectly reflected. He, indeed, is the Light of the world. All those who have been received by God as sons are assembled by the Holy Spirit into the corporate anointing of Christ. It is in this capacity that we stand before God as sons. The sons within the Son are therefore known as the sons of God.

The same glory that was given to Jesus by the Father remains upon His Body in the earth. There is no separate glory to which a person may individually accede. The primary bequest of the new covenant is that as the heirs of God we are joint heirs with Christ and have been given access into this glory.[6]

In this capacity, Christ continues to appear through us as the light of the world.[7] Previously, Jesus had said, "I am the Light of the world."[8] He supported that declaration by saying, "I am He who testifies about Myself, and the Father who sent Me testifies about Me."[9] It is the appearing of God through the person of Jesus that bears witness that He is the Son of God and, therefore, the Light of the world. In the same way, it is the appearing of Christ in us that testifies that we are the light of the world, because the light that is shown through the person of Jesus was the reality of the Father's presence in Him. His perfect representation of the Father did not obscure in any fashion the reality of the Father. The light was pure and exactly representational.

In the same way a mature son is mature because, through suffering, he has been conformed to the likeness of Christ and therefore, permits the radiance of Christ's nature to be exhibited exactly through him. The Father is as capable of making His abode in a mature son as He did in Jesus. Since a mature son is competent and capable to reflect the glory of the Father in the particular manner in which that son was designed to carry the presence of God, as a mature son he or she is an accurate representation of Christ who, in turn, was an accurate representation of the Father. Just as Jesus was the light of the world, the assembled corporate Son is destined, in its maturity, to be brought to the completeness of the standard of Christ Himself.[10]

Christ is the standard for the maturity of the Body. No reflection of the glory of God is possible without the superintending control of Jesus Christ who is the head. The whole Body derives its order and function from the person of Jesus Christ. All that was in Him on the earth is now being put on display through the Body. The manner in which this glorious representation of God was designed to function as it presented God in the world was through the governmental order in which the assembled Body would function.

---

[1] Genesis 1:3 NASB. [2] See e.g., Job 38 NASB. [3] 2 Corinthians 4:6 NASB. [4] 1 John 3:8 NASB. [5] See Isaiah 53:8 NIV. [6] See Romans 8:17 NASB. [7] Matthew 5:14-16 NASB. [8] John 8:12 NASB. [9] John 8:18 NASB. [10] Ephesians 4:13 NASB.

The Church of the Firstborn

> *But you have come to Mount Zion and to the city of the living God, the heavenly Jerusalem, and to myriads of angels, to the general assembly and church of the firstborn who are enrolled in heaven, and to God, the Judge of all, and to the spirits of the righteous made perfect, and to Jesus, the mediator of a new covenant, and to the sprinkled blood which speaks better than the blood of Abel.* Hebrews 12:22-24 NASB

> *He is the image of the invisible God, the firstborn of all creation. For by Him all things were created, both in the heavens and on earth, visible and invisible, whether thrones or dominions or rulers or authorities—all things have been created through Him and for Him. He is before all things, and in Him all things hold together. He is also head of the body, the church; and He is the beginning, the firstborn from the dead, so that He Himself will come to have first place in everything. For it was the Father's good pleasure for all the fullness to dwell in Him, and through Him to reconcile all things to Himself, having made peace through the blood of His cross; through Him, I say, whether things on earth or things in heaven.* Colossians 1:15-20 NASB

As the image of the invisible God, the Son is the chosen and exclusive means by which the Father elects to appear as Himself. The Father does nothing independent of the Son. He appoints the Son "the firstborn over all creation." The designation "firstborn" implies that He, in the capacity of His role as Son, has been appointed the heir over all creation. "All authority has been given to Me in heaven and on earth."[1]

"Firstborn" is the recognized holder of the double portion. God grants to the firstborn authority and power to fulfill the promises that have been given to a particular family. For example, the tribe of Judah from among the sons of Jacob was chosen to be the recipient of the double portion. Adam, though he was the first in time, was not the firstborn, because Jesus was before Adam. For his part, Adam was given a portion of authority from God his Father. The span of that authority covered the whole earth. As the firstborn Son, however, Jesus was given the double portion, and His authority was established over both heaven and earth.

It is clear that Jesus as the firstborn was not created as some would suggest.[2] His status as the firstborn refers to Him in His position as the Son and not as one whose existence was derived from creation. "He is the head of the body, the church; He is the beginning and the firstborn from among the dead, so that in everything He might have supremacy."[3] When we are assembled into this corporate Son, we are said to be in "the church of the firstborn."[4]

The critical understanding is that the members assembled to this body have been integrated into an existing commonwealth. They do not bring new initiatives and directions to the corporate whole. Instead, they are integrated into the purposes of God that have been ongoing in Christ since before the foundations of the world. It would be unthinkable to suggest that the assembled parts of this spiritual body exert any measure of decision making over the head, or that they might bring some form of power and authority that enables the head to accomplish His purposes.

CONCLUSION

It is common in the present church, in all of its permutations, to consider how it may enable the purposes of Christ. That would be analogous to Jesus instructing the Father in the appropriateness of His actions and in attempting to provide support to the Father for the Father's initiatives. God both wills and does according to His predetermined pleasure. His position works as an effective preemption of any ideas or thought originating in the mind of men.

Assembly to the firstborn is to be integrated into both His preexisting condition and power. We have what He has. We are, collectively, the form through which He executes His intentions. Our economy of grace belongs entirely to Him. The head and the body together are the firstborn. The power of the Body of Christ comes directly from the head. The Body has neither power nor standing distinct from the head. Everything that the Body does, has been predetermined by the head, including the timing, the manner of administration, and the extent to which the head plans to appear in the earth in a particular epoch.

Each member of the Body has been endowed with a particular distribution of grace, or giftings, by which to put the head on display. That grace is focused and directed through a calling that determines the path of the individual's life in Christ. Collectively, all the parts are formed together into one corporate whole and fulfill the destiny of representation in a particular epoch according to the foreknowledge of God for each stage of the revealing of Himself in the earth. The function of the corporate Body in any epoch has been predetermined by God and is specific to that epoch of time. The glory of God that appears through the corporate Man in that time is meant to be both distinctive as well as a steeped increase over previous epochs.

The glory of God's revealing is progressive from glory to glory. Accordingly, the endowments of grace that accompany and support the increased revelation of God's glory is itself an increased economy. The glories of past revelations were both consistent with the intent of

God for those epochs and were as much as God determined the world could see of Himself at that time. Past standards would be inconsistent with the intentions of God for succeeding epochs.

> *But if the ministry of death, in letters engraved on stones, come with glory, so that the sons of Israel could not look intently at the face of Moses because of the glory of his face, fading as it was, how will the ministry of the Spirit fail to be even more with glory? For if the ministry of condemnation has glory, much more does the ministry of righteousness abound in glory. For indeed what had glory, in this case has no glory because of the glory that surpasses it. For if that which fades away was with glory, much more that which remains is in glory ...Now the Lord is the Spirit, and where the Spirit of the Lord is, there is liberty. But we all, with unveiled face, beholding as in a mirror the glory of the Lord, are being transformed into the same image from glory to glory, just as from the Lord, the Spirit.* 2 Corinthians 3:7-11, 17-18 NASB

Since the glory of God is ever increasing and each epoch is meant to show an increased measure of this glory, a greater economy is required to reveal and sustain the glory of God in that epoch. Since the economies of God are given in increasing measures to the maturing corporate Son, the intention of God is that the son matures individually and corporately in greater levels as well. With this increased maturity comes greater weights of glory and more wide-ranging spheres of responsibility leading eventually to the disclosure and functioning of a holy nation among the nations of the earth.[5]

---

[1] Matthew 28:18 NASB. [2] Colossians 1:16-17 NASB. [3] Colossians 1:18 NIV. [4] Hebrews 12:23 NASB. [5] Revelation 5:9-10 NASB.

CONCLUSION

The Government Shall be on His Shoulders

For a child will be born to us, a son will be given to us; And the government will rest on His shoulders; And His name will be called Wonderful Counselor, Mighty God, Eternal Father, Prince of Peace. There will be no end to the increase of His government or of peace, On the throne of David and over his Kingdom, To establish it and to uphold it with justice and righteousness from then on and forevermore. The zeal of the Lord of hosts will accomplish this. Isaiah 9:6-7 NASB

Any corporate act of the parts of the human body that shows a transcendent quality above the capability of individual parts requires a trained response to which all the parts involved in that activity must be disciplined. The concept to be demonstrated originates with the head and from its place of governance it directs the activities of the individual parts.

If the head wished to demonstrate the beauty of dance, it begins with an understanding of what it intends to communicate through movement. The choreography is the pattern of training and repetitive practice required for movements to be perfected. Although each person may engage in a different choreography ordained by their designated role, each one is hearing the same music at the same time. When properly executed, this art form transcends the order of movement of each individual and may become a thing of beauty.

The sounds that come from heaven are the same sounds that every part of the Body of Christ should hear at a moment in time. The response of each part may be different, according to their roles and designs, however, the harmony of their movements enables the showing of the widest possible expression of the nature of God.

If each part claims to be hearing a different sound and is moved to respond according to their own pleasure, then jealousy, envy, and

CONCLUSION

strife will be on predominant display, and every evil thing will flourish. The functional framework in which the parts are disciplined to the choreography of heaven is the authority and order associated with the Kingdom of Heaven.

The grace of exact representation contains the distinctive elements of order and governance. These elements are largely responsible for the result of a harmonious interaction between the parts that comprise the corporate whole. The order that results from the rule of the head over each part of the Body is seen in the qualities of righteousness, peace, and joy.

Apart from this provision of divine order, a corporate functioning is not possible. People will do what is right in their own eyes, and the glory of God will remain hidden. The divine authority of Christ to rule over the Body was initiated with a grant of authority from God to the Lord Jesus Christ. Jesus' obedience to the Father inevitably led Him to the cross. Everyone whom God receives as a son is expected to go through a process of refinement and sacrifice. This should not be viewed as working to the disadvantage of the son. In the case of Jesus, when the task for which He came into the earth had been completely fulfilled, God raised Him from the dead and seated Him at His right hand upon the throne of God. By resurrecting Him, God showed that Jesus was His chosen and faithful representative who would never be abandoned to death.[1]

Although each part of the Body has a relationship with Christ the head, all relationships are established and perfected within the Body. Just as with the human body, all of the parts are connected to the head and to one another. The government of God is designed to establish the order of functioning, and each part is subject to the mandate of Christ's authority. Because Jesus was subject to the authority of His Father, God's glory appeared fully in and through His life. The assembled Body of Christ is subject to the same authority and for the same purpose.

---

[1] Acts 2:27-31 NASB.

Jurisdiction

As the firstborn Son, Jesus inherited the double portion of rule. The first Adam was given rule of the earth. Jesus as the last Adam has dominion over both heaven and earth. This is the sphere of rule entrusted to the corporate Man. It is within these domains that the exact representation of Christ is meant to be shown.

> *[T]he manifold wisdom of God might now be made known through the church to the rulers and the authorities in the heavenly places. This was in accordance with the eternal purpose which He carried out in Christ Jesus our Lord[.]*
> Ephesians 3:10-11 NIV[1]

Although Christ is sovereign over the realms of heaven and earth and His authority has been committed to the corporate Man to go into the natural world as well as the spiritual world, it is common for present day believers to cite a passage of Scripture, which speaks of general jurisdiction, and to assume that it applies to them personally. Often these passages of Scripture are considered the personal mandates for the life and ministry of individuals.

The manner in which anyone is called to represent the Lord is pre-determined by God and constitutes his or her calling. It determines the sphere of authority to which the person has been sent to put the nature of God on display. Whereas, the entire corporate Man has inherited the spheres of rule originally consigned by God to the

CONCLUSION

Lord Jesus Christ Himself, the individual functioning is determined by God and is the subject of one's calling. The gifts of God by which that calling is empowered also reflect the limitations placed upon the individual.

For example, the apostle Paul was set apart even from his mother's womb so that he might preach God among the Gentiles.[2] As he moved around in the Greco-Roman world, his calling was confirmed by the grace that attended him. Doors opened to him by divine favor. He eventually went to Rome and his case was heard before the emperor.

By contrast, among the Jews he was widely hated and despised although he began his career as a favored son. When he became a convert to Christ all the favor he once enjoyed as the champion of Judaism disappeared summarily. He was even stoned and left for dead by the Jews in the city of Lystra. "But Jews came from Antioch and Iconium, and having won over the crowds, they stoned Paul and dragged him out of the city, supposing him to be dead. But while the disciples stood around him, he got up and entered the city. The next day he went away with Barnabas to Derbe."[3]

God predestined each son to be conformed to the image of Jesus Christ, the pattern Son, and assigned callings to them consistent with how He placed them in the earth to function.[4] The biblical concept of predestination centers upon the basic concepts of being conformed to the standard of Christ as well as to participate in works prepared in advance for the son who has been conformed to the image of Christ to walk in.

These twin imperatives define both God's intended purpose as well as the process by which that purpose is attained. The process is designed to produce maturity so that the purpose for which the individual has been created might be brought forth accurately. The goal of maturation is that the host of the presence of God is sufficiently prepared to carry His presence and that nothing remains within the host that offends or objects to the revealing of the person of God in him or her. When Christ is presented in this fashion, there is no distinction between who He is and in whom He appears:

> *For you have died and your life is hidden with Christ in God. When Christ who is our life, is revealed, then you also will be revealed with Him in glory. ...Whatever you do in word or deed, do all in the name of the Lord Jesus, giving thanks through Him to God the Father.* Colossians 3:3-4, 17 NASB

The good works prepared in advance for us to walk in apply both to the individual and to the corporate Man. These good works are the measure of our particular calling. God ordains the times in which everyone is born and establishes the works they are to do within the boundaries of their existences.

Paul's calling was to the Gentiles. Although he may have been frustrated by his lack of reception among the Jews, when he dusted his feet at Lystra following the attempt on his life by the Jews, he emphatically declared that from then on he would go to the Gentiles. He was, in fact, stepping into the fullness of his calling. Even he became impressed with the results of his work among the Gentiles, but attributed it all to the grace of God working through him:

> *For this reason I, Paul, the prisoner of Christ Jesus for the sake of you Gentiles—if indeed you have heard of the stewardship of God's grace which was given to me for you; that by revelation there was made known to me the mystery, as I wrote before in brief. By referring to this, when you read you can understand my insight into the mystery of Christ, which in other generations was not made known to the sons of men, as it has now been revealed to His holy apostles and prophets in the Spirit; to be specific, that the Gentiles are fellow heirs and fellow*

members of the body, and fellow partakers of the promise in Christ Jesus through the Gospel of which I was made a minister, according to the gift of God's grace which was given to me according to the working of His power. Ephesians 3:1-7 NASB

But by the grace of God I am what I am, and His grace toward me did not prove vain; but I labored even more than all of them, yet not I, but the grace of God with me. 1 Corinthians 15:10 NASB

The good works prepared in advance of Paul's birth was to preach the good news to the Gentiles. This was not an afterthought of God, but a conscious fulfillment of His promise to Abraham that "in [his] seed all the nations of the earth [would] be blessed."[5] The time in which Paul would be born and his purpose were foreordained to fulfill this ancient promise. God arranged for the sufferings and trials of Paul to refine him to the point where he could be the instrument by whom this promise would be launched into the earth.

Since God knows every obstacle created by the enemy to impede, frustrate, or delay His purposes in the earth, He prepares the instruments that carry His presence to be able to specifically overcome and even destroy the enemy's works. Whereas God could unilaterally overthrow the enemy and establish His purposes in the earth by the force of His omnipotence, He has chosen instead to raise up man and to train him to receive and carry the presence of God as a mature son positioned in a condition of dependency upon God as his means of overthrowing the enemy and destroying his schemes.

By this approach, God forgoes the use of superior force in dismantling the works of the devil. Should God, by the power of His omnipotence, destroy the devil's works, He would establish only that He is more powerful than Satan and that Satan was not His equal. He would not, however, answer the question of whether or not He was right. And, although the enemy would be removed, the challenge that his existence has articulated would remain unanswered. Indeed, for this challenge to be appropriately addressed, man, the son of God, would have to choose and live the fullness of that choice. It is in man that God overcomes His enemy and establishes the righteousness of His person through His sons' choices.

Whereas the first son was seduced from loyalty and duty to his Father, the last Son put the glory of His Father on display in all fullness. By His righteousness and the power of His "indestructible life" He crushed the head of the enemy and ruined the authority of the enemy's kingdom to enslave men to his will.[6] The righteousness of God was always meant to be vindicated through the choice of His Son, who was positioned "a little lower than the angels" and was, therefore, required to put His trust in the unfailing love of His Father. It is impossible for the Father to abandon the Son to the ravages of His enemy, even as God placed Him positionally inferior to the angels.

This location in the heavens exposes the Son to all of the advantages enjoyed by the angelic, inclusive of Satan and his schemes. The only way in which a son, placed in this condition, could overcome his enemy is to clothe himself with the presence of his Father to whom all angels are subject. When a son clothes himself in this fashion, he has the authority of his Father, and all angels, in turn, are subject to him.

This is particularly true of the corporate Son, and it is also true of the individual son, provided that he observes the jurisdictional boundaries established by his Father, consistent with the limitations upon his calling.

Jesus fully accomplished the overthrow of the seat of the enemy's authority. That source of authority is deception, which works effectively as long as man consents to it. It was unchallenged from the

CONCLUSION

days of Adam, as men worked under the canopy of growing darkness. To restore the light of God's glory, man had to be elevated from the encroaching darkness so he could see again from a heavenly viewpoint.

The standard of sonship had to be reintroduced so that man could once again see how he ought to behave as a son of God in creation. This standard was restored with pristine clarity in the person of the Lord Jesus Christ who illuminated the darkness of man's understanding as the light of the world. Whoever has been assembled to Christ has been translated from the kingdom of darkness. In Christ, he is seated upon the throne of God and has a heavenly point of view.[7] This has the effect of destroying the deception that seeps into the souls of men when they live in the darkness of the enemy's domain. The destruction of the works of the enemy cannot be accomplished while this veil of deception remains upon the minds of men.

In Christ, we function from the throne of God where Christ Himself is seated. This is why we are of the priesthood of Melchizedek and not of the priesthood of Levi. The order of the priesthood of Levi functioned to present the sacrifices of men to God as a way of imparting His mercy to them. By contrast, the order of Melchizedek presents God to men. In this fundamental distinction, the location from which men function is of critical importance. Functioning from the earth inherently implies that man operates from under the cloud of deception and sees God adversarially. He hopes to take advantage of the mercy of God by appealing to Him through sacrifices and bargaining. It is never possible to draw near to God through sacrifices of any kind.

> *For the Law, since it has only a shadow of the good things to come and not the very form of things, can never, by the same sacrifices which they offer continually year by year, make*

perfect those who draw near. For it is impossible for the blood of bulls and goats to take away sins. Hebrews 10:1, 4 NASB[8]

By clothing oneself with the reality of Christ, one is automatically removed from the jurisdiction of the enemy. This was accomplished in Christ; however, the deception lingers because it has been attached to human existence in an enduring fashion through the culture of the orphan. It remains the task of the Body of Christ to rescue mankind from this deception in every generation. Although the work of Jesus on the cross has effectively introduced the standard by which the enemy's power is undone, it remains the task of the corporate Christ to show this triumph to the demonic realm as well as to mankind in every age.

This is the work which the Father gave to Jesus to accomplish, and about which Jesus said on the cross, "It is finished."[9] Jesus worked from this place of representing the Father exactly. God gave Him this assignment and He was clothed with the glory of it as long as He remained in the earth. His resurrection and subsequent ascension to heaven displayed the glory of God in its completeness.

Always, in the earth, the authority to represent the Father as He is has been the defining mandate of the corporate Christ. The grace to accomplish this was bestowed upon Jesus by the Father. He, in turn, designated His Body as the carrier of this same grace.[10] This grace is the birthright of the corporate Christ for all the epochs of time since Jesus bequeathed it to the church through His last will and testament. The specific endowments of this grace to each part are defined by God before one is even put into the earth.

Jesus Himself did not engage His calling until God had fully prepared Him to do so. The years between His appearance in the temple at the age of twelve and His presentation to the world by His Father at His baptism by John were occupied with the discipline and training

CONCLUSION

required to bring Him to the sufficiency of His maturity that was required of Him to take on His calling. It was after the Father had determined His readiness to assume the mantle of His calling that He was presented to the world. He was thirty years old when this occurred. It is noteworthy that Joseph in the Old Testament was released from prison and became ruler of Egypt at the age of thirty, and that David himself emerged from the wilderness of his trials and was crowned king in Hebron over all Israel at the age of thirty. Paul spent fourteen years in obscurity after his encounter with the Lord on the road to Damascus before he emerged as the light to the Gentiles. Between the time of one's calling and the circumstances that prepare one to assume that calling are the events that shape and make one ready to assume the mature representation required by that calling.

No one can be exempt from this process since the purpose of the process is the readying of the person to assume the requirements of his or her calling. The representation of the Father is meant to be an exact representation; a result that can only be accomplished by the Father Himself. Jesus defined this reality in the terms "You are in Me and I am in You."[11] By this He meant that all of His hope and all of His authority came from the Father and that His unshakable trust, by making Himself vulnerable, would allow Him to be most secure. The Father would choose to fully inhabit the Son, so through that, everything that was done or declared through the Son would be the Father's work. Jesus' prayer was that just as He was in the Father and the Father was in Him and that they were one, in the same way, we would be in Christ and the Father would be in us. This is the arrangement by which the grace of exact representation is imparted to the corporate Christ. Each part is endowed with a component of this grace consistent with His calling and also with the level of maturity to which the part has attained. Consequently, everyone is admonished to observe the metes and bounds of His calling.[12]

CONCLUSION

The boundaries of one's sphere as well as the authority to operate within that sphere are determined by one's calling. The application of the grace of exact representation is limited by the demands of one's calling. Even though the corporate Man has general jurisdiction to exactly present Christ in the world, the personal limits on the authority to represent Christ are set by one's calling. The wider the spheres of one's authority the more rigorous one's preparation becomes. One should not desire a greater measure of authority and rule than is determined by their calling, and no one, regardless of the spheres of their authority, may be brought to their places without being thoroughly prepared to function within those callings. The corporate Man was put on the earth to carry and display the presence of God in every epoch. As the time draws near for the display of the fullness of Christ through a holy nation, the grace of exact representation will be deployed in the earth in its complete measure.

At that time the glory of God will appear among the peoples of the earth in the fashion of a city upon a hill. This city, known as Zion, will display the fullness of the rule of Christ in the earth by showing a people drawn from every tribe, tongue, language and culture of humankind and assembled together in tribes, arranged according to spiritual families. Their government will result in good order and peace. They will succeed in eliminating all of the problems relating to human divisions, such as race and class. Their model will not be based upon achieving political ends. Instead, they will corporately show the glory of God who has reconciled all men to Himself in Christ.

The grace of exact representation is even now being poured out into the earth to accomplish this final summation of God's purposes for the creation of man as His son.

---

[1] See Mark 16:15 NASB; Luke 24:46-47 NASB; Matthews 28:18 NASB. [2] Galatians 1:15-16 NASB. [3] Acts 14:19-20 NASB. [4] Romans 8:29-30 NASB; Ephesians 2:10 NASB. [5] Genesis 22:18 NASB; Galatians 3:28-29 NASB. [6] Hebrews 7:16 NASB. [7] Philippians

3:14-15 NIV. [8] See also Hebrews 7:11 et seq. [9] John 19:30 NASB. [10] John 20:21 NASB. [11] John 17:21 NIV. [12] 1 Corinthians 7:20, 24 NIV.

OTHER BOOKS BY SAM SOLEYN

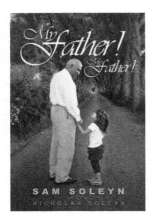

In the Kingdom of God, each person's destiny is the playing out of that person's unique identity as a son of God, regardless of gender, race, or background. To embrace one's identity as a son, one must change his prevailing culture.

In this season, God is building His House in the earth, with the relationship of fathers and sons as its foundation. Effecting cultural changes requires a trans-generational effort, in which a change in the culture is but one of the first steps of a long journey to reestablish, fully, the House of God. This journey is meant to reposition man in the relationship with God as Father, as God intended from the beginning. The purpose of repositioning humankind as sons and heirs to God is to establish the family of God on the earth and to display the love of God, through his sons, to all of creation. Whereas the destiny of each son of God is vitally important, the entire purpose of God can only, ultimately, be accomplished through the corporate form—the House of God.

Those who have willingly accepted being conformed to the will of God through their sufferings are finding themselves becoming deeply transformed, and nothing is remaining the same. They are finding their security and well-being in new insights into the nature of God's character. They are discovering the spiritual reality of an entire existence based upon the reliability of the love of God, the Father. They are themselves becoming visible and accurate representations of the Invisible God. Trials and sufferings are understood to be essential parts of this process of transformation. These adversities are bringing to light the hidden areas that must be brought to accurate alignment with divine standards. A great separation has begun. It is resulting from the stark distinctions between the choices that have been made and the resulting patterns of life that flow from these radically dissimilar choices. The result will come to be clear and unmistakable: "The wicked are wicked still, and the righteous are righteous still."

Two final results of the removal of restraint will ultimately war with each other. One will be that all divine standards are rejected in favor of a view of God that is a product of the popular secular imagination. A god created of the popular demand by the popular imagination and for the popular consumption. The other will be the mature expression of Christ appearing as a "City upon a hill." All humanity will be ultimately of one or the other condition.

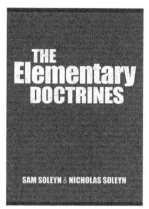

Just as we all begin our natural lives as infants and progress to maturity, so do all believers begin their walks with Christ as infants who are newly born again, but whom God intends to forge into mature representations of His being.

Yet the basic doctrinal Christian message has mostly ignored the need for maturity in individual believers, leaving scores of church members in perpetual infancy and the Church as a whole divided into denominations each focused on their own doctrinal emphases.

Scripture, on the other hand, identifies certain aspects of one's spiritual education that form the foundation of maturity for all believers: "repentance from acts that lead to death, and... faith in God, instructions about baptisms, the laying on of hands, the resurrection of the dead, and eternal judgment" (Hebrews 6:1b-2 NIV). These are known as the *Elementary Doctrines*.

These concepts are not a set of distinctive doctrines relating to group membership. They are cultural imperatives for the path to maturity in the Kingdom of Heaven. Choosing to walk this path may begin with studying the matters presented in this text. The process itself, however, involves the regular observation and daily practice of these *Elementary Doctrines*. This is the process Christ uses, in many different forms, to reshape any willing believer's way of life, so that the individual may progress toward his or her mature representation of God's being in the earth.

AVAILABLE ON
SAM SOLEYN APOSTOLIC MINISTRY APP

(Apple App Store and Google Play)

Made in United States
Orlando, FL
20 May 2023